FIGHTING HAMAS, BDS and ANTI-SEMITISM

Fighting violence, bigotry and hatred

Barry Shaw

Copyright Barry Shaw – 2015.

All rights reserved. No part of this publication may be reproduced, stored in a retrieval system, or transmitted or distributed in any form, without the prior permission in writing of the author.

A catalogue copy of this book is available from the Library of Congress and the British Library.

Cover design by Spotlighting and is copyrighted by them exclusively for use as the book cover for 'Fighting Hamas, BDS and Anti-Semitism.' All rights reserved.

ISBN: 978-1508595533

Copies of **'FIGHTING HAMAS, BDS and ANTI-SEMITISM'** are available from www.barryshawbooks.com or contact israelnarrative@gmail.com

Contents

Page 5. INTRODUCTION.

Page 9. FIGHTING HAMAS.

Page 104. ADDITIONAL INSIGHTS INTO FIGHTING HAMAS.

Page 147. FIGHTING BDS.

Page 200. ADDITIONAL INSIGHTS INTO FIGHTING BDS.

Page 212. FIGHTING ANTI-SEMITISM.

Page 287. ADDITIONAL INSIGHTS INTO FIGHTING ANTI-SEMITISM.

Page 310. RECOMMENDED READING.

Page 311. ACKNOWLEDGEMENTS.

Contents

Page   5.   INTRODUCTION.

Page   9.   FIGHTING HAMAS.

Page 104.   ADDITIONAL INSIGHTS INTO FIGHTING HAMAS.

Page 147.   FIGHTING BDS.

Page 200.   ADDITIONAL INSIGHTS INTO FIGHTING BDS.

Page 212.   FIGHTING ANTI-SEMITISM.

Page 287.   ADDITIONAL INSIGHTS INTO FIGHTING ANTI-SEMITISM.

Page 310.   RECOMMENDED READING.

Page 311.   ACKNOWLEDGEMENTS.

4

INTRODUCTION.

When an anti-Israel obsession is linked to Jew-hatred this inevitably must explode into violence and acts of terrorism.

It appears as if anti-Israel activity is dragging individual acts of anti-Semitism in its wake. This book argues that it is the other way round.

It is anti-Semitism that sparked, and is fueling, the anti-Jewish state movement. It has been that way since the Arab and Muslim world rejected the notion of a Jewish state, and has been perpetrated by the Palestinian Arab leadership, from Haj Amin al-Husseini, the self-appointed Grand Mufti of Jerusalem, who sat at the feet of Adolf Hitler, to the Holocaust denying Mahmoud Abbas and his partner in government the vocally anti-Semitic terror organization, Hamas.

The cudgels of their venom have been taken up by well-organized groups as the Free Gaza and BDS movements that are supported by far left Socialists with a detestation of capitalism and anyone they perceive as representing that system, and by replacement theology church groups and leaders with a history of distain, if not worse, for Jews.

The union of a green-red alliance (Muslim and Far Left) has been joined by a sector of the Cross with an agenda that is more anti-Jewish state than pro-Palestinian. Their noisy demonstrations and activism has given a legitimacy to the rank and file anti-Semite who can now express his bile under the guise of professing moral concerns for the human rights of an oppressed people.

This is not to say that everyone critical of Israeli policies are anti-Semites. Far from it. However, the case presented in this book is that the main engines of the anti-Israel movement are driven by anti-Semitic motives and their numbers increase with the support of groups and individuals who are jaundiced against Jews.

This book offers a compelling portrait of the hybrid links between the pro-Palestinian leadership to global support groups and into local and national politics and the media.

By ignoring Hamas's anti-Semitism, by picking on Israel ii its dispute with the Palestinians, by the use of boycotts and other measures against Israel with no counter punishment for Palestinian transgressions, by the use of legitimate forms of expression to delegitimize Israel but not a terrorist-led, human rights abusing, regime, leads one to suspect deeper motives than an altruistic desire to achieve peace.

I talk of active hate, not criticism. I talk of actively and physically closing down debate from the Israeli side, instead of engaging in open debate. I talk about ignoring facts and replacing them with emotionally charged exaggerations and downright lies. I talk of ignoring historical recorded facts and legal rulings by introducing misinterpretations and wrongly declaring advisories and resolutions as international law. And I talk of victimizing Jews, when Israelis are not readily available for assault and venom. This is hate, violence and lies. This is also anti-Semitism.

For the purpose of this book, Hamas is the figurehead for all of Palestinian, Arab and Muslim Jew-hatred. In Palestinian politics and society, anti-Semitism is not confined to Hamas. This book may be an eye-opener for many.

People may prefer soft nuance on aspects of the Israeli-Arab-Palestinian conflict that has plagued us for far too long. You won't find soft nuance in this book. You will find hard evidence, irrefutable facts and comment by reputable voices.

Pen was put to paper to show the undeniable links between anti-Israel activism and anti-Semitism. Read how anti-Zionism and support for activism in that cause is steeped in Jew-hatred.

For those looking for facts, case histories and anecdotal evidence, this book lays out a convincing narrative that is impossible to ignore.

This book examines the Muslim-Left Wing alliance that erupts in displays of anti-Semitism when linked to a pro-Palestinian, anti-Israel political agenda.

If this book calls for anything it calls for decency when discussing Israel. It calls for pause when placing total blame on Israel and partial blame on Jews. It calls for a reassessment of responsibility and a fairly, more balanced perspective for the failure of an Arab-Israeli peace deal when it comes to the Palestinian issue.

It calls for leaving Jews in peace, where ever they may be. It is a peace that the vast majority of Israelis would grant its neighbors, if only they would rid themselves of the sickness of anti-Semitism and grant Israel the right to call itself the Jewish state with full rights, respect and equality for all its citizens, and for all its neighbors to live in peace and security.

FIGHTING HAMAS.

For the purpose of this book Hamas is a metaphor for all Palestinian terror and anti-Semitism. Palestinian terror is not confined to the murderous acts of the Islamic terror organization that controls Gaza. The Palestinian Authority, formerly the PLO, has blood stained hands through Fatah, the party of Palestinian leader Mahmoud Abbas. Fatah fought alongside Hamas in the 2014 Gaza war against Israel yet Abbas, the Teflon head of the PA, escaped global condemnation for not preventing their terror activities. The PLO affiliated Al-Aksa Martyrs Brigade remain active as Israeli intelligence and security forces work to prevent additional terror attacks by this group.

In a New York court, the Palestinian Authority was found guilty on multiple terrorism charges, a class action law suit brought on behalf of American victims of Palestinian terror. Evidence was given that Palestinian terrorists continue to receive money from the PA as they sat in Israeli jails, convicted of appalling and deadly attacks against innocent Israeli civilians. Evidence showed that the families of dead terrorists, including Palestinian suicide bombers, received *"martyr"* payments from the Palestinian Authority.

The terror links between the PA, PLO, Fatah, and the Al-Aksa Martyrs Brigade are all interconnected and Palestinian terror is not limited to Hamas or Islamic Jihad.

What is Hamas? What does it represent?

President Obama, John Kerry, his Secretary of State, European politicians and diplomats, the media all ignore the mobilizing energy of

Hamas for the destruction of Israel and the hatred of Jews as its major platform above all other considerations.

They ignore the fact that Hamas is the majority preference of Palestinian voters as proven in all their elections and polls and will remain so no matter that concessions are given by Israel.

For Palestinians, as long as the *"enemy Israel"* exists, Hamas exists.

Welcome to the dark world of Hamas!

This book is not about the 2104 Gaza conflict, although there are numerous references to it. This is because the mini-war illustrated the sharp divide that polarized opinion, enhanced by a media fixation on casualty figures and an almost complete lack of context.

The violence was initiated by an obsessive Hamas passion to hurl hatred and damage onto an Israeli population. Was it done to advance Palestinian statehood? Was it done by a Hamas that saw a Palestinian Authority moving to unilateral steps without them? Was it a badly timed rush of psychotic anti-Semitism, fevered by the enthusiasm of having achieved a share hold on the reins of Palestinian power? Was it done out of desperation by an isolated bankrupt leadership that decided to strike out in the name of a wider Islamic cause thereby drawing attention to themselves? Perhaps it was a mixture of all or some of these ingredients. Whichever it was, they succeeded in grabbing world attention and a not inconsiderate amount of sympathy and support. The global effect had little to do with the Palestinian cause. It had more to do with the problem and fear of global jihad, and it exposed a raw nerve of deep anti-Israel bias that shocked many by the overt anti-Semitic rhetoric that came with it.

Understand this. When you see massed demonstrators noisily marching on the streets of Europe, America and South Africa screaming, *"We are Hamas!"* and *"We are Jihad!"* they mean it. They are marching to announce that Hamas, Jihad and everything this represents, is now rooted in your country. That includes anti-Semitism.

Don't fool yourself that these people are simply expressing their concerns for poor Palestinians. They were not. You see the roots of jihad on your streets, in your towns. You are witnessing the infiltration of jihad into your society. Listen out for the slogans. Look out for the signs, the green and black flags, and know that the enemy is within.

What they were telling you is jihad is in your land. They have raised their voice and their flag. Today it's jihad to remove Israel for the Palestinians. Tomorrow it's jihad for your land. The noisy public demonstrations were the opening salvo in the creation of an Islamic state where you are. Hamas equals Jihad. Jihad equals ISIS, ISIS is Islamic State. Islamic State can be anywhere. It has come to you. This is only the beginning. You have let them in, and they are there to stay. It's time for you to leave, or challenge them.

"Political correctness" is preventing the international community from doing anything about it. For too long it has been unacceptable to speak of anything *"Islamic,"* or *"Jihad,"* even when radical Islamic terror organizations, and those that support them, use these words openly. Others support them but remain silent, for now. It's their cause, you see.

In many Western countries you cannot put the words *"Islamic Jihad"* together for fear of arrest. And heaven forbid you should add the word *"terrorist"* to *"Islamic Jihad,"* even though your country may call Hamas and Hezbollah terrorist organizations. In Islamic countries jihadists are not called *"terrorists."* They are called *"heroes."* The dead ones are called *"martyrs."*

The West denies the evidence; mumble their explanation, carefully avoiding inflammatory words to avoid being accused of Islamophobia, while those wishing to impose their will do so openly.

Compare their political correctness against yours, and tell me who is winning the mind games for the narrative?
This is why an Israeli Jew can say things clearly, while you are officially gagged from speaking the truth out of fear of being called Islamophobic.

So let me introduce you to what Hamas really stands for. Here is the infamous Hamas Charter in all its racist, anti-Semitic threats. As you read it, tell yourself that this is the Palestine that your government, politicians, media and marchers will impose, because this will be the rogue state that the international community insists on releasing onto the world.

I have highlighted some of the more hideous aspects of this Palestinian manifesto;

THE HAMAS CHARTER

Article One: The Ideological Aspects; **"The Islamic Resistance Movement draws its guidelines from Islam;** *derives from it its thinking, interpretations and views about existence, life and humanity; refers back to it for its conduct; and is inspired by it in whatever step it takes."*

Article Three: Structure and Essence; **"The basic structure of the Islamic Resistance Movement consists of Muslims who are devoted to Allah** and worship Him verily [as it is written]: "I have created Man and Devil for the purpose of their worship" [of Allah]. Those Muslims are cognizant of their duty towards themselves, their families and country and they have been relying on Allah for all that. **They have raised the banner of Jihad** in the face of the oppressors in order to extricate the country and the people from the [oppressors'] desecration, filth and evil."

Article Six: Peculiarity and Independence; **"The Islamic Resistance Movement is a distinct Palestinian Movement which owes its loyalty to Allah,** derives from Islam its way of life and **strives to raise the banner of Allah over every inch of Palestine.** "

Article Seven: **The Universality of Hamas;** *"Hamas is one of the links in the Chain of Jihad in the confrontation with the Zionist invasion...* It links up with the setting out of the Martyr Izz a-din al-Qassam and his brothers in the Muslim Brotherhood who fought **the Holy War in 1936;** it further relates to another link of the Palestinian Jihad and the Jihad and efforts of the Muslim Brothers during the **1948 War,** and to the **Jihad operations of the Muslim Brothers in 1968 and thereafter."**

"The time will not come until Muslims will fight the Jews (and kill them); until the Jews hide behind rocks and trees, which will cry: O Muslim! There is a Jew hiding behind me, come on and kill him!"

Article Eight: The Slogan of the Hamas**;** *"****Allah is its goal,*** *the Prophet its model, the Qur'an its Constitution,* ***Jihad its path and death for the case of Allah*** *its most sublime belief."*

Article Eleven: **The Strategy of Hamas: Palestine is an Islamic Waqf;** "The Islamic Resistance Movement believes that **the land of Palestine has been an Islamic Waqf throughout the generations and until the Day of Resurrection**, no one can renounce it or part of it, or abandon it or part of it. No Arab country nor the aggregate of all Arab countries, and no Arab King or President nor all of them in the aggregate, have that right, nor has that right any organization or the aggregate of all organizations, be they Palestinian or Arab, because Palestine is an Islamic Waqf throughout all generations and to the Day of Resurrection."

Article Thirteen: **Peaceful Solutions, [Peace] Initiatives and International Conferences;** "[Peace] initiatives, the so-called **peaceful solutions, and** the **international conferences to resolve the Palestinian problem, are all contrary to the beliefs of the Islamic Resistance Movement. For renouncing any part of Palestine means renouncing part of the religion**;"

Article Fourteen: **The Three Circles;** "The problem of the **liberation of Palestine** relates to three circles: the **Palestinian, the Arab and the Islamic**. Each one of these circles has a role to play in the struggle against Zionism and it has duties to fulfill. It would be an enormous mistake and an abysmal act of ignorance to disregard anyone of these circles. **For Palestine is an Islamic land**..."

Article Twenty-Two: **The Powers which Support the Enemy;** "The enemies have been scheming for a long time, and they have consolidated their schemes, in order to achieve what they have achieved... They also used the money to take over control of the Imperialist states and made them colonize many countries in order to exploit the wealth of those countries and spread their corruption therein... **They obtained the Balfour Declaration and established the League of Nations in order to rule the world by means of that organization**. **They also stood behind** World War II, where they collected immense benefits from trading with war materials and prepared for the establishment of their state. They inspired the establishment of the United Nations and the Security Council to replace the League of Nations in order to rule the world by their intermediary... **There was no war that broke out anywhere without their fingerprints on it."**

Article Twenty Seven: The Palestine Liberation Organization; *"The PLO is among the closest to the Hamas, for it constitutes a father, a brother, a relative, a friend... Our homeland is one, our calamity is one, our destiny is one and our enemy is common to both of us... PLO has adopted the idea of a Secular State, and so we think of it. Secular thought is diametrically opposed to religious thought... Therefore,* **in spite of our appreciation for the PLO** *and its possible transformation in the future,* **we cannot substitute it for the Islamic nature of Palestine by adopting secular thought, for the Islamic nature of Palestine is part of our religion. Anyone who neglects his religion is bound to lose."**

Article Thirty-One: **The Members of Other Religions Hamas is a Humane Movement;** *"Hamas is a humane movement, which cares for* **human rights** *and is committed to the tolerance inherent in Islam as regards attitudes towards other religions. It is only hostile to those who are hostile towards it, or stand in its way in order to disturb its moves or to frustrate its efforts.* **Under the shadow of Islam it is possible for the members of the three religions: Islam, Christianity and Judaism to coexist in safety and security.** *Safety and security can only prevail under the shadow of Islam...* **The Nazi Zionist** *practices against our* people will not last the lifetime of their invasion, for 'states built upon oppression last only one hour, states based upon justice will last until the hour of Resurrection.'"

Article Thirty-Two: The Attempts to Isolate the Palestinian People; "**World Zionism** and Imperialist forces **have been attempting,** with smart moves and considered planning, **to push the Arab countries**, one after another, **out of the circle of conflict with Zionism**, in order, ultimately, to isolate the Palestinian People. Egypt has already been cast out of the conflict, to a very great extent through the treacherous Camp David Accords, and she has been trying to drag other countries into similar agreements in order to push them out of the circle of conflict. **Hamas is calling upon the Arab and Islamic peoples to act** seriously and tirelessly in order **to frustrate that dreadful scheme** and to make the masses aware of the danger of coping out of the circle of struggle with Zionism... Their scheme has been laid out in the **Protocols of the Elders of Zion... Leaving the circle of conflict with Israel is a major act of treason...** Hamas regards itself the spearhead and the avant-garde. It joins its efforts to all those who are active on the Palestinian scene, but more steps need to be taken by the Arab and Islamic peoples and Islamic associations throughout the Arab and Islamic world in order to **make possible the next round with the Jews, the merchants of war.** "We have cast among them enmity and **hatred till the day of Resurrection**. As often as they light a fire for war, Allah extinguishes it. Their effort is for corruption in the land, and Allah loves not corrupters." Sura V (Al-Ma'idah—the Table spread), verse 64."

Article Thirty-Four: **Confronting Aggressors throughout History;** "**Palestine is the navel of earth**, the convergence of continents, the object of greed for the greedy, since the dawn of history. The Prophet may Allah's prayer and peace be upon him, points out to that fact in his noble hadith in which he implored his venerable Companion, Ma'adh ibn Jabl, saying: 'O Ma'adh, Allah is going to grant you victory over Syria after me, from Al-Arish to the Euphrates...'"

Article Thirty-Five; "*Hamas takes a serious look at the defeat of the Crusades at the hand of Saladin the Ayyubid and the rescue of Palestine from their domination; at the defeat of the Tatars at Ein Jalut where their spine was broken by Qutuz and Al-Dhahir Baibars, and the Arab world was rescued from the sweep of the Tatars which ruined all aspects of human civilization. Hamas has learned from these lessons and examples, that* **the current Zionist invasion had been preceded by a Crusader invasion from the West; and another one, the Tatars, from the East**. *And exactly as the Muslims had faced those invasions and planned their removal and defeat, they are* **able to face the Zionist invasion and defeat it.** *This will not be difficult for Allah if our intentions are pure and* **our determination is sincere**; *if the Muslims draw useful lessons from the experiences of the past, and extricate themselves for the vestiges of the [western] ideological onslaught; and* **if they follow the traditions of Islam.**"

If you thought that Palestinian Jew hatred was restricted to Hamas and their Islamic Jihad, think again.

The revised **Palestinian National Charter** of 1968, otherwise known as "*the Palestinian Covenant*" denies Israel's right to exist. Here are some of its highlights;

"**Palestine, with the boundaries under the British mandate, is the homeland of Palestinian Arabs and is indivisible.**" (Articles 1 and 2);

"The Jews who lived in Palestine before the Zionist immigration are considered Palestinian." (Article 6);

"Armed struggle is the only way to liberate Palestine. Thus it is the overall strategy, not merely a tactical phase. The Palestinian Arab people assert their absolute determination and firm resolution to continue their armed struggle and to work for an armed popular revolution for the liberation of their country and their return to it. They also assert their right to normal life in Palestine and to exercise their right to self-determination and sovereignty over it." (Article 9);

"Commando action constitutes the nucleus of the Palestinian popular liberation war. This requires its escalation, comprehensiveness, and the mobilization of all the Palestinian popular and educational efforts and their organization and involvement in the armed Palestinian revolution. It also requires the achieving of unity for the national (watani) struggle among the different groupings of the Palestinian people, and between the Palestinian people and the Arab masses, so as to secure the continuation of the revolution, its escalation, and victory." (Article 10);

"The partition of Palestine and the founding of Israel are entirely illegal since they violated the will of Palestinians and the principle of self-determination included in the United Nations Charter." (Article 19);

"The Balfour Declaration and the British mandate for Palestine are null and void." (Article 20);

"The Palestinians reject all solutions which are substitutes for total liberation of Palestine." (Article 21);

*"**Zionism,** associated with international imperialism**, is racist**, expansionist and colonial, and Israel is the instrument of the Zionist movement."* (Article 22).

"Fighters and carriers of arms in the war of liberation are the nucleus of the popular army which will be the protective force for the gains of the Palestinian Arab people." (Article 30);

Following the signing of the Oslo Accords, and due to Israeli Prime Minister, Yizchak Rabin's strident objections, Yasser Arafat wrote letters to President Clinton and Prime Minister Blair in January 1998 explicitly listing the articles of the Charter referred to in the PNC's 1996 vote. The articles identified by Arafat as nullified called for Palestinian unity in armed struggle, deny the legitimacy of the establishment of Israel, deny the existence of a Jewish people with a historical or religious connection to Palestine, and label Zionism a racist, imperialist, fanatic, fascist, aggressive, colonialist political movement that must be eliminated from the Middle East for the sake of world peace. While this was seen as progress in some quarters, other Palestinian officials contended that the Charter had not yet been amended.

Arafat declared an end to terror, but continued the Palestinian terror campaign against Israeli civilians. The provisions for including Hamas and Islamic Jihad into the PLO have yet to be verified.

Fatah was the party of Yasser Arafat. It is the party of Mahmoud Abbas. **The Fatah Charter** is as troubling as the Palestinian National Charter. Its provisions include the following articles;

Article (4) *"**The Palestinian struggle is part and parcel of the world-wide struggle against Zionism**, colonialism and international imperialism."*

Article (5) *"**Liberating Palestine is a national obligation** which necessities the materialistic and human support of the Arab Nation."*

Article (6) *"UN projects, accords and resolutions, or those of which undermine the Palestinian people's right in their homeland are illegal and rejected."*

Article (7) *"**The Zionist Movement is racial**, colonial and aggressive in ideology, goals, organization and method."*

Article (8) *"**The Israeli existence in Palestine is a Zionist invasion** with a colonial expansive base, and it is a natural ally to colonialism and international imperialism."*

Article (9) *) "**Liberating Palestine and protecting its holy places is an Arab, religious and human obligation.**"*

Article (12) *"**Complete liberation of Palestine, and eradication of Zionist economic, political, military and cultural existence.**"*

Article (13) *"Establishing an independent democratic state with **complete sovereignty on all Palestinian lands, and Jerusalem is its capital city,** and protecting the citizens' legal and equal rights without any racial or religious discrimination."*

Article (17) *"**Armed public revolution is the inevitable method to liberating Palestine.**"*

Article (19) *"**Armed struggle is a strategy and not a tactic**, and the Palestinian Arab People's armed revolution is a decisive factor in the liberation fight and **in uprooting the Zionist existence, and this struggle will not cease unless the Zionist state is demolished and Palestine is completely liberated.**"*

Article (20) *"Achieving mutual understanding with all the national forces participating in the **armed struggle to attain the national unity**."*

Article (22) *"**Opposing any political solution offered as an alternative to demolishing the Zionist occupation in Palestine**, as well as any project intended to liquidate the Palestinian case or impose any international mandate on its people."*

Article (23) *"**Maintaining relations with Arab countries** with the objective of developing the positive aspects in their attitudes **with the proviso that the armed struggle is not negatively affected.**"*

Article (24) *"**Maintaining relations with all liberal forces supporting our just struggle in order to resist together Zionism** and imperialism."*

Article (25) *"**Convincing concerned countries in the world to prevent Jewish immigration to Palestine as a method of solving the problem.**"*

The importance of the Charter to the Palestinians cannot be exaggerated. To the Palestinians, it is virtually their secular Koran. There remains to this day clauses in the Charter that still declare the establishment of Israel to be illegal and void and call for armed resistance until all of Palestine is liberated.

When Palestinian Arabs determine that *"The PLO will strive to strengthen its solidarity with the Socialist countries, and with forces of *liberation and progress throughout the world, with the aim of frustrating all the schemes of Zionism, reaction, and imperialism"* this offers little hope for peace, especially as we see the anti-Israel actions of the *"Socialist countries"* mentioned in their declaration.

If all this was not enough we have the utterances of the leaders of the Palestinian Authority. These, we are told, are Israel's pragmatic and moderate peace partners. With appreciation for the work of Itamar Marcus and Palestinian Media Watch, let's take a peep at some examples of what they are telling their own people in their own language.

PA minister legitimizes murdering Israelis by saying a 3.5 million shekel fine imposed by Israel upon murderer of a one-year-old infant and his father is *"delegitimizing the* **[Palestinian]** *national resistance";*

Ali Sa'ada, a terrorist prisoner who murdered a father and his one-year-old baby, was fined 3.5 million shekels by Israel. That fine is *"delegitimizing the* [Palestinian] *national resistance,"* says Prisoners' Affairs Authority Director and PA Parliament Member Issa Karake. According to Karake, who holds the rank of minister, the killing of one-year-old Israelis is legitimate *"resistance."*

PA official paper glorifies planner of Munich Olympic Games massacre Abu Daoud:
"His name shone brightly in the German city of Munich in 1972..." Al-Hayat Al-Jadida," July 6, 2010.

Palestinian leaders like to talk to their people in code. One example came in January 2014 when **Mahmoud Abbas**, the leader of the

Palestinian Authority, embraced a singer on a live TV show who sang the words; *"By Allah, oh traveling bird, I burn with envy. My country Palestine is beautiful. Turn to Safed and then to Tiberias, and send regards to the sea off Acre and Haifa. Don't forget Nazareth, the Arab fortress, and tell Beit Shean about its people's return. My country Palestine is beautiful."*

The message in this song, sent by Abbas to the viewers in Arabic, was that no matter what is said about a two-state solution, the ultimate plan is for there to be one Palestine in place of Israel.

Sometimes, Palestinian leaders have loose tongues and let things slip. On June 8, 2014, **Ihab Al-Ghussein,** former Hamas spokesman, posted on his Facebook page;

> *"***You know what Mahmoud Abbas says behind closed doors?*** He says: 'Guys, let me continue saying what I say to the media.* ***Those words are meant for the Americans and the occupation*** *(i.e., Israel),* ***not for you [Hamas]****. What's important is what we agree on among ourselves. In other words,* ***when I go out*** *[publicly]* ***and say that the*** *[PA]* ***government is my*** *[Abbas']* ***government and it recognizes 'Israel' and so on, fine - these words are meant to trick the Americans.*** *But we agree that the government has nothing to do with politics (i.e., foreign relations). The same thing happened in 2006, he [Abbas] said: 'Don't harp on everything I tell the media, forget about the statements in the media."*

Saeb Erekat is, in effect, the Palestinian Authority Foreign Minister and often speaks in the name of the PA. On December 2, 2014, on official PA TV he said, *"In brief, we cannot accept the Jewish state – Israel as a Jewish state – not today, not tomorrow and not in a hundred years, because whoever accepts Israel as a Jewish state agrees to change his history, his narrative and even his religion."*

Dr. Mahmoud Al-Habbash, the Supreme Shari'ah Judge and Mahmoud Abbas' advisor on Religious and Islamic Affairs, said in the official PA daily newspaper, Al-Hayat Al-Jadida, Oct. 22, 2014, that selling or handing over lands and real estate in Jerusalem and all of Palestine to the Israeli occupation or settlers constitutes treason and a violation of Islamic law. Al-Habbash emphasized that according to Islamic Shari'ah law, the entire land of Palestine is *waqf* (i.e., an inalienable religious endowment in Islamic law) and is *"blessed land, and that it is prohibited to sell, bestow ownership or facilitate the occupation of even a millimeter of it."*

The official Palestinian media often calls **Israel** *"the occupied interior."* **It refers to Israeli Arabs as** *"Palestinians of the Interior"* or *"Palestinians of '48"* meaning Arabs living in pre 1948 Palestine which is yet to be liberated. **It sometimes calls Israel** *"the 1948 territories."*

The Palestinian Authority constantly depicts a world without Israel in their media. The official PA daily, Al-Hayat Al-Jadida, Aug. 3, 2014, ran a piece saying that "*Israel is a completely artificial state without historic or moral roots.*" It went on, *"As long as it exists, it will only produce things that are against humanity."* It called Israel's Prime Minister, Benjamin Netanyahu *"a descendant of the Nazis who worships Hitler's path and imitates him in all the Holocausts he has perpetrated."*

The **Al-Hayat Al-Jadida** newspaper, June 25, 2014, said that **Jews never ruled Judea and Samaria, but even if they did, the Israelites of the Bible were in fact Arab tribes and not related to Jews of today.**

Secretary-General of the Islamic-Christian Council for Jerusalem and the Holy Places, Hanna Issa, said that, despite all the archeological evidence that Israel *"never saw or knew any Jewish civilization or antiquities."*

Mahmoud Al-Habbash, Abbas' Advisor on Religious and Islamic Affairs, said, *"The* **Palestinians have been on this land for 5,000 years.***"*

Palestinian children's TV programs claim that all of Israel will be replaced by *"Palestine."* The Palestinian Authority Ministry of Culture teaches children not to recognize Israel. Their official media claim that Israel's creation was *"a crime against humanity"* and *"an international conspiracy."* It also calls Israel a *"monstrosity"* and a *"crime unprecedented in history."*

Mahmoud Abbas leads the Ramallah-based Palestinian incitement against Israel and the glorification of violent attacks and terror against Israelis. Evidence is clear that this led to a series of provocative knifings, drive-by vehicular attacks against pedestrians, and shootings including the deadly attack at the Kehitlat Bnei Torah synagogue on November 18, 2014, that left four Jews at prayer dead, and the attempted murder of Rabbi Yehuda Glick outside the Menachem Begin Heritage Center in Jerusalem on October 29, 2014. Glick was hit by four bullets at close range but miraculously survived. The 32 year old Arab gunman, Mutaz Hijazi, was later killed in an exchange of fire with police who came to his home to arrest him.

Not only did Mahmoud Abbas not condemn the attempted murder of the rabbi but, on November 3, he sent a condolence letter to the terrorist's family. An official statement was published in the Palestinian Authority newspaper, *Al-Hayat Al-Jadida*, which read, *"President Abbas expressed his anger and his condemnation of the abominable crime committed against Martyr Mutaz Hijazi, who was murdered last Thursday by the killing and terror gangs of the Israeli occupation army."*

This is just a tiny portion of the ideology spewed by the Palestinian Authority, Israel's purported peace partner's industry of lies.

Can anything else be expected of Mahmoud Abbas, the Palestinian figurehead who's 1984 Doctorate in Holocaust denial, disinformation and lies positioned the Nazis and Zionists in cahoots in the mass-murder of European Jews. His book *"The Other Side: The Secret Relationship Between Nazism and Zionism"* was the precursor for transposing the Palestinian Arabs partnership with Hitler and Nazi Germany to one of portraying Jews killing Jews to appease the Nazis. The Abbas thesis is somewhat confusing. He claims that by preventing the rescue of Jews and cooperating with the Nazis, this somehow led to the formation of a Jewish national home in Palestine.

Mahmoud Abbas called the murder of six million Jews at the hands of the Nazis a *"Zionist fantasy."* He claimed the gas chambers in the Nazi concentration camps where never used to kill Jews but only to clean and disinfect them. In his book, Abbas said that David ben Gurion and Adolf Hitler were *"good friends."*

Is it any wonder that Israel looks at the Palestinian leadership with jaundiced and untrustworthy eyes?

*

Hamas is part of the web of global political Islam. President Obama called the Paris terror carnage as a *"senseless attack,"* but it made perfect sense to political Islam.

Political Islam, of which Hamas is a part, is motivated by religious zeal, a zeal that fuels itself on the hatred of Jews personified by Israel the Jewish State, but also against America and the West generally as being *"the infidels."*
This religious zeal is the trunk from which the branches of political Islam grow.

The same political/religious fervor engulfs much of the Muslim world as it spreads in secular Europe and America. With it comes intolerance of Israel as the Jewish state, and hatred of Jews and the West generally.

As Charles Hill, a diplomat in residence at Yale University and a former ambassador wrote in a Politico blog, *"Political Islam's very purpose is not only to be incompatible with modernity, but also to oppose it, demolish it and replace it in every regard."*

*

The abduction and murder of three Jewish teenagers by Hebron-based Hamas terrorists preceded the Hamas rocket assault on Israel. The Arab slaughter of Jews in Hebron is nothing new. Back in 1929, urged on by false rumors and libels incited by the mufti of Jerusalem, Arab Jew-haters massacred sixty seven Jews in Hebron. Homes, Jewish businesses and synagogues were destroyed. When the background is one of constant incitement, as it is today with the Palestinians, violence is the end result. Nothing has changed in more than eighty five years.

*

In the 2014 Gaza conflict, Israel's I.D.F. discovered a more entrenched defense/attack system in Gaza than anticipated. This demanded a more robust military response to overcome and destroy the Hamas offensive capabilities, an offensive infrastructure that was almost entirely, and purposely, grounded in civilian areas. In such warfare, casualties are inevitable. A media that had been silent over civilian casualties caused by American, Britain, and coalition forces in other conflicts, where considerably more civilians were killed than in Gaza, now screamed from the rooftops over Gaza casualties, pointing an accusing finger at Israel, ignoring the crimes of the Hamas enemy that was the prime cause of all the death and destruction.

Western media fell afoul of the Hamas media strategy. It fell afoul of the blood libel that Israel targets Palestinian children. It was this media reporting, biased by lack of context, which became the dry tinder that anti-Semitic haters eagerly lit their anti-Zionist bonfire. It reminded me of a long history of Jews being burnt at the stake, condemned by false charges and accusations. It was this lethal journalism and perceived anti-Israel reporting that resulted in the explosion of rage on the streets of Europe.

*

Children in the south of Israel have become accustomed to responding to rocket attacks. It happens so often that they are inured to the procedure. There is no procedure, however, to the threat that, one day, they could be killed or kidnapped by monsters coming out of the ground at them. It's difficult for adults to contemplate this nightmare, let alone have kids fear such a fate.

Rocket attacks from the air and terrorists coming out of the ground are something that Britons never need to contemplate although, in a way, it happened. Despite that nation surrounded by a highly effective moat, and the Englishman's home being his castle, it failed to protect them from domestic terror attacks.

In London on 7 July 2005, terrorists went into the Underground to explode their deadly backpacks while others came out of the underground to blow up a double-decker bus. One would have thought this would make the average Londoner empathize with the horrors that Israel faced when Palestinian terrorists burrowed death tunnels under the homes and kindergartens of innocent Israelis, as well as attacking them from the air. Apparently it didn't, when one compares the numbers that demonstrated against Israel to those who rallied in support.

Radicalization will breed more home-grown terrorists in Britain. They will succeed, despite the remarkable success records of British intelligence services, the police and security forces. Sadly, it will take future tragedies to bring Brits to appreciate the Israeli situation.

*

A quick glance at the distorted reporting of the 2014 Gaza conflict makes it crystal clear that much of the Western media are more into sensationalism and shallow news reporting than context or truth. Although it is common knowledge that journalists lost their virginity in Gaza when forced by Hamas stringers to only cover what they permitted to be covered, they parachuted into the Strip with their editors' guidelines in their back pocket. This manual contains the edict that Israel is the oppressor and Gaza is Palestinian occupied land. So it was with rare exceptions that the media had little trouble echoing the bullet points given to them by their Hamas hosts. In the main, they did not go in search of the truth. They simply honored their deadlines by spouting Hamas-supplied information about Israeli criminality.

This, of course, fed into the public psyche and into media-sensitive official responses. A White House and the State Department tuned in to public reporting and perceived sentiment, accused Israel of *"totally indefensible"* and *"disgraceful"* targeting of an UNWRA school, when no such attack was conducted by Israel. Furthermore, had Israel done so it would have been absolutely defensible, because that school had been the location of Hamas attacks against Israeli targets.

Hysterical accusations amplified in the media helped whip up institutions with a poor history of anti-Israel bias.
The UNHRC threatened to prosecute Israel for suspected crimes. It overlooked the obvious litany of international crimes and breaches of law perpetrated by Hamas in their unprovoked violence against Israeli civilians. More importantly, it ignored, hopefully to its peril, the crimes committed on United Nations properties and by United Nations staffers in the Gaza Strip in support of the Islamic terror regime's warfare against civilians.

It is in Israel's interest to stop playing defensive in its public diplomacy and go on the offensive. It has justice and truth of its side. It should not be embarrassed to prosecute United Nations organizations of involvement in crimes. It has overwhelming evidence of such crimes. It should publicly accuse bodies such as the UNHRC of hypocrisy, and prove to the world why this organization is in basic breach of its raison d'etre, namely to honestly and fairly speak up for those who are suffering, in massive numbers, from human rights crimes and abuses. It refrains from doing so because its chamber has become a sealed room, protecting the main perpetrators of humanities worst crimes and abuses.

One of the heinous defects of the United Nations has been the operations of the UNWRA whose only purpose in life in to perpetuate, into its fifth generation, the fallacy of a Palestinian refugee-hood. No matter that almost all so-called Palestinians are born in other countries, they are deliberately kept stateless, in many cases, to maintain the unrealistic notion of a *"law of return"* to an Israel they reject. While sixty million refugees are catered for under another UN organization, UNHRC, the world allows the Palestinian to have their own exclusive agency. This agency, UNWRA, has no intention of removing the stigma of refugee-ship from the shoulder of those in its care. It assists the Arab regimes to keep these oppressed people as pawns in a political game. As such, UNWRA is a radicalizing and destabilizing force in a violent region. Israel should lobby governments to have this issue reconstituted and have UNWRA disbanded.

Israel must educate and lobby major media outlets on ways to broadcast facts and truth relating to Israel's position in a dangerous and rejectionist region. It needs to help them to understand and explain context in reporting and journalism. This was singularly lacking during the 2014 Gaza conflict. It is vitally important because media coverage informs public opinion and forms the mindset of influential decision makers.

*

Ari Shavit, Ha'Aretz journalist and someone from the left of the Israeli political spectrum, once wrote, *"Twenty years of fruitless talks have led to nothing. There is no document that contains any real Palestinian concession with Abbas' signature. None! There never was, and there never will be."*

*

Two states, or any state?

Professor Shlomo Avneri, a long-time proponent of a two-state solution, has lost faith in it. In an article he wrote in August 2014 he said, *"Those of us who supported Oslo - and who still think it was the right step - must recognize that salvation won't come from the Palestinians. They're genuinely uninterested in a solution of two states for two peoples because they're unwilling to grant legitimacy to the Jewish right of self-determination."*
Indeed, it is the perpetuation of this denial that has been at the heart of the Arab-Israeli conflict for far too long.

This sad state of affairs affected even Shimon Peres's eternal optimism. In a significant admission to the BBC he said, *"I find it difficult to explain today withdrawal from Gaza or justify future withdrawal from the West Bank."*
Shimon Peres has been the champion of Israel surrendering land for peace.

Hillary Clinton, not a right-wing rabble rouser, said, *"So what I tell people is, yeah, if I were the prime minister of Israel, you're damned right I would expect to have control over security on the West Bank."*

There is widespread recognition by people not grounded in brainless altruism that it would be reckless for Israel to surrender land, including the heights of Judea and Samaria overlooking sensitive population centers and major national infrastructure facilities, that could end up in the hands of Hamas, either by the ballot or bullet.

*

Authors are not supposed to express emotion when writing books like this, but of all the accepted Palestinian-statehood lies, the one about 1967 borders really annoys me.

I was once on a social media TV show debating with 22 year old Ahmed from Amman, Jordan. He was born in Amman and studies at a university there, yet he calls himself a Palestinian. He claims he came from a West Bank village, despite the fact that he has never been there. When challenged on this he said that his grandfather and father left this village in 1948. He vehemently talked of the *"illegal occupation"* of his family home. I asked him who illegally occupied his home between 1948 and 1967. He waffled. I forcefully reminded him that the West Bank wasn't called the West Bank until after 1948 when the Jordanian army crossed from the east side of the Jordan River and invaded Judea & Samaria, driving back the nascent Israel Defense Force, known at the time as the Haganah.

The Jordanians tried to annex this territory but this wasn't recognized by the international community. Nor was it sanctioned by the Arab League. In other words, it was illegally occupied, along with east Jerusalem, by the Jordanians.

On air, I asked Ahmed if his grandfather or father had ever protested the illegal occupation of this home or village between 1948 and 1967. No answer. I asked him why his family did not return there during this period. After all, the Jordanians had driven out most of the Jews. Again - no answer.

Here was an Arab family that remained silent, even acquiescent, to the Jordanian occupation of their home. They had no concern to declare their Palestinian identity during this period. This is rather strange behavior for a so-called people, or even for this individual Arab family that failed to return to their home on land that had been conquered, indeed occupied, by the Arab army of Jordan. Surely they should have returned home? Instead they remained in Jordan and did nothing to claim an artificial nationhood until after the Jordanians once again attempted to drive the Jews into the sea in 1967, and once again lost. Only then, did they develop a false narrative of Palestinian sovereignty.

Here is a typical example of a young man who adapted a family history that ignored the country into which he was born to claim an identity which he has no rights and identify a cause in which his family had never challenged when Arabs invaded land not theirs.

Today, the 1967 nonsense has become an accepted mantra by those who should know better but who are determined to ram home what they see as the only show in town, namely a Palestinian state located over a fictitious border plus the Gaza Strip. Everything is thrown into this simmering pot, everything from the falsehood that Israel occupied a Palestinian land, built homes *"illegally"*, settled the land *"illegally"*, oppressed the *"indigenous"* Palestinian people *"illegally"* and this *"injustice"* must be redressed by Israel withdrawing from all of this territory. The bogus thought that this misinterpretation of past military armistice lines could serve as a template for Israeli peace with a rejectionist Palestinian leadership bent on further devious conquest based on their own narrative incitement and violence, is perverse. So let's re-examine the 1967 lines through the eyes and pens of the authors of the UN Security Council Resolution 242, which was unanimously adopted on November 22, 1967.

To begin with, one must appreciate that this resolution followed yet another war of aggression launched by Jordan against the State of Israel. Truth be told, 1967 lines are a myth. They have absolutely nothing to do with 1967. They are, in fact, positions where Israeli and Arb forces stopped fighting at the end of Israel's War of Independence in 1949, not 1967.

Let me state it clearly, Israel's wars of self-defense have important implications in international law as it applies to territorial acquisition, in addition to Israel's longer standing legal claims to the land.

UN Resolution 242 is often quoted by promoters of the Palestinian cause as a cornerstone of their statehood bid, but the significant point to take from this issue is that nowhere in 242 is a Palestinian state ever mentioned.

As a continuum to this, Jerusalem is not mentioned and, by virtue of these two missing items and as a third significant feature, there is no reference to Jerusalem, nor is there any other location referred to in this UN resolution to be recognized as a Palestinian capital.

Let's look carefully at what the main authors of the United Nations resolution had to say about the wording and their intentions.

On June 12, 1974, Lord Caradon told the Beirut *Daily Star*, *"I know the 1967 border very well. It is not a satisfactory border. It is where the troops had to stop. It is not a permanent border. It would have been wrong to demand that Israel return to its positions of June 4, 1967, because those positions were undesirable and artificial...They were just armistice lines. That's why we didn't demand that the Israelis return to them and we think we were right to do so."*

Ambassador Arthur Goldberg, another of the authors of Resolution 242, also confirmed that, *"historically, there never have been secured* or recognized boundaries in that area," and that the armistice lines did not answer that description.

President Lyndon Johnson predicted in September 1968 that, *"It is clear that a return to the situation of 4 June 1967 will not bring peace."*

Trying to establish a Palestinian state on 1949 armistice lines is beyond problematic for Israel. They were referred to as *"Auschwitz Lines"* by then Israeli Foreign Minister, Abba Eban. It is patently absurd and dangerous to impose this *"peaceful"* solution on Israel, particularly with the current character of the Palestinian leadership, as it would not result in peace.

*

What is happening when a liberal democracy is ditched by liberal democracies in favor of yet another rogue regime in the Middle East without consideration of the inevitable end result?
This is what happens when Europe and America decide to ram through the gears to establish a Palestinian state in the expectation that the direct way to peace is the best way.

Simply put, they are fed up with the slow painstaking process to a two state solution which is, for them, the only game in town, and they are determined to push it through come what may.

And they call this professional diplomacy. It is nothing of the sort. It is mindless meritocracy of the most dangerous kind. It cannot be said too frequently. It is all too similar to the appalling methods applied by Western politicians that launched Hitler on his rampage. It is the same appeasement to satisfy the beast, the same altruistic foolery that threw Czechoslovakia under the bus.

Now its Israel's turn.

How grimly familiar! How fatally predictable!

No amount of objection will save Israel from a Czech fate. The idiots in charge of the mad house have decided. This is their road map to hell.

*

I reject the notion that all Israel has to do to achieve permanent peace is comply with international wishes and Palestinian demands that Israel should withdraw to an armistice line drawn at the end of a war in which Jordan tried to annihilate Israel. This is a deception devoutly to be wished by Israeli detractors and naïve diplomats.

Israel pursues peace, but does so without detaching itself from the harsh truth of our adversaries. To pursue peace with a detachment to the reality that surrounds us is dangerous. It could be fatal. A sober, responsible, and cautious approach is essential. This, rather than rush into a solution on demand devoid of certainties or security guarantees.

*

Whatever temporary relief British Jews may have gained from rallying in support of Israel during the summer was badly squashed by the statement made by Labour leader, Ed Miliband, at the Labour Party Conference in Manchester. Statements made by Miliband and his Shadow Foreign Minister, Douglas Alexander, at the Conference on Monday, September 22, 2014, were appalling for their one-sided bias against Israel.

Although they condemned *"Hamas rockets and the terrorization of civilian populations"* the only use of the word *"illegal"* was to refer to Israeli building, and the word *"immoral"* was only for settlements, which they described as being done *"on other peoples land."*

No consideration was given for a view that the land belongs, both historically and legally, to Israel under international law dating back to 1922 and beyond. No mention of the fact that this is enshrined in the United Nations Charter, including the reference to *"close Jewish settlement"* of the land. All that, and more, was wiped away by a Labour leadership that ignores facts and history, overlooks Palestinian crimes and rejectionism, in favor of condemning Israel of criminality.

Further, they denounced Israel's need to enter Gaza for what they called *"an Israeli invasion...to perpetuate the cycle of violence, tragedy, and loss of innocent life."*

No mention of the necessity to eradicate the Palestinian terror attack tunnels, to denude Hamas of their rocket stockpile, or to eradicate one thousand two hundred Gaza-based terrorists who threatened and murdered Israeli civilians for decades.

Their moral equivalency tilted so radically that their language reflected a world in which Palestinians were naughty for firing rockets and for murdering Israeli civilians, including babies and teenagers, while Israel was criminal for executing its right of self-defense.

They made the usual trope of *"occupation"* and *"illegal settlements."*

Let Miliband and Alexander go back to the statute books and do some revision. Let them start by reading the League of Nations Mandate for Palestine, then proceeds to the UN Charter Article 80. They should finish off by reading the wording of the Oslo Accords to which Britain was a witness and guarantor. All these preserve and define Israel's legitimacy to act in the territories, particularly in what is known as Area C. Let them then say if Israel is at fault of both the Accords and even the Geneva Convention by providing homes, education facilities, transport systems, access and employment to the local inhabitants.

Instead, their blind, dogmatic, left-wing, failed Two-State notion has fossilized the Israel-Palestinian conflict for far too long. Demanding that Israel surrender more territory is not a potion for peace. It is a remedy for further violence. Israel sees what Miliband fails to see, that an Israeli withdrawal from Judea & Samaria will follow the pattern of our evacuation from Gaza. Israel removed every Jew, soldier and civilian from every settlement. Israel handed over a thriving and profitable agricultural paradise to the Palestinians and, in return, got suicide bombers, rockets, and terror tunnels. Can Miliband guarantee that this will not happen should Israel listen to his ill-advice and withdraw from the Samarian and Judean hills, leaving Hamas to take over the West Bank, by ballot or by bullet, as they did in the Gaza Strip?

Britain may lurch to the left in the next general election but the vast majority of Israelis totally distrust Palestinian intentions and deeply cynical of politicians such as Miliband.

If Miliband wants peace let him task his Labour Friends of Palestine to reform Hamas and persuade the Fatah-led Palestinian Authority to recognize the right of the Jewish people to live in peace in the Land of Israel. For, if there is a monster in the room, it is not an Israeli building a home in Maale Adumim or Ariel, it is the monster of Hamas terrorism, the rejectionism of Mahmoud Abbas, and the rabid anti-Semitism of them both that is the major obstacle to peace.

Based on recent statements by Miliband and Alexander, a future Labour-led Britain can contribute nothing to peace, neither for Israel, nor for the Palestinians.

But the problem is more global. Anyone reading the League of Nations Mandate can see the legitimacy for Israel to turn waste land into state land after proper investigation and procedures to ensure that none of this land is private land. This it did in early September 2014, when it decreed that 940 acres of land in what is known as the Etzion bloc is be state land. This created an outcry from the European Union whose spokesman, Michael Mann, said that the EU *"would not recognize any changes to the pre-1967 borders, including with regard to Jerusalem, other than those signed by the parties."*

Putting aside the point that, if Israel chooses, it can transfer state land to Palestinians should it decide to do so under the framework of an amicable and permanent peace agreement, Mr. Mann makes the inevitable mistake of so many diplomats who think they know what they are saying. The EU is in such a hurry to make their own definition of which territory belongs to who that they fall over themselves with their misuse of language and words. Mr. Mann should be reminded that the 1967 lines were never *"borders"*. They were never demarcation lines dividing two countries. Neither has there been any law or resolution that decrees that this line must be the border between Israel and any other state in the future. On the contrary, the facts were that the so-called 1967 lines were armistice lines drawn when fighting ended between an aggressive Jordanian army and the defending Israeli army in 1967.

*

Let me throw another challenge. Who says that a future Palestinian state should be based in Judea & Samaria?

Surely, for those who only have the best interests of the Palestinians at heart, and for a sensible, reasonable, permanent solution to the Israeli-Arab, Israeli-Palestinian, conflicts, a better solution is surely the one proposed, surprisingly, by Egyptian President Abdel-Fattah el-Sisi who offered a large section of the vast Sinai Peninsula linked to the Gaza Strip to form a large contiguous land mass for Palestinian sovereignty?

His suggestion was quickly withdrawn but it is worthy of serious consideration.

His proposal would give the Palestinian Arabs 1,600 square kilometers of land removing the problem of national density that the West Bank and Gaza would cause them. This infinitely larger territory would be rich in agricultural, tourism, industrial and residential potential.

Compared to the impossible density and lack of access to the sea that a West Bank solution would create, a Sinai-Gaza landmass must surely touch the hearts of all those who really feel for the betterment of the Palestinians. There is sufficient land to resettle any Palestinian refugees who may choose to be part of their new homeland. As part of such a peace deal, it could be possible for Arabs living in cities in Judea & Samaria to remain and have official Palestinian identity. It may even be possible to have towns with exclusive Arab citizenship in the West Bank to be declared as being federated to a Palestinian entity based in the Sinai-Gaza, and the remaining waste and public land retained as Judea and Samaria in Israel, therefore removing the notion of the so-called 1967 line demarking any division between Israel and Palestine.

The idea of a Palestinian state in the Sinai was proposed back in 2006 by Giora Eiland who was then the director of the Israeli National Security Council. He proposed it as an alternative to the deadlocked two-state dogma. As he put it at that time, *"the maximum that the State of Israel can offer the Palestinians is far smaller than what the Palestinians will be prepared to accept."* This has always been one of the core problems of the two-state based on the restricted territory in which the two sides currently find themselves.

A broader vision is necessary, and the Egyptian president proved he has a statesman-like political horizon. The advantages are clear. It would resolve the Israeli-Palestinian conflict. It would provide for proper independence and sovereignty for the Palestinians, security and more breathing space for Israel, and it will help the Palestinians solve their refugee problem in a way that would not adversely affect Israel and its character as a Jewish and democratic state. Such a solution would easily lead not only to mutual recognition between Israelis and Palestinians under the auspices of the Egyptians, but almost certainly from the Jordanians, and meet with the approval, encouragement, and investment of the international community.

*

For Hamas, human rights are unimportant except as a propaganda weapon to be used by their supporters not against them and their horrendous abuses but against their Zionist enemy. Any lie, in the name of *"human rights"* will do if it weakens support for Israel.

*

When blanket condemnation of Israel occurs, as it did during and after the 2014 Gaza conflict, it is beholden for Israel supporters to face down and challenge the accusations. We have seen progress with people who have said *"Enough of the lies and bias!"*

In mid-October 2014, over sixty Jewish students at Cambridge University angered by their teachers who egregiously accused Israel of being guilty of horrendous crimes condemned their professors calling them *"misguided and myopic."*

In a letter signed by the students they attacked a statement signed by fifty five members of the university teaching staff calling it as showing *"a severe lack of nuance surrounding the complexity of the Arab-Israeli conflict."* The students claimed the teachers' statement was also *"un-academic."*

Calling out the discrimination displayed by the teachers, the students wrote *"We condemn these academics for singling out Israel…which has been deemed by this group to be the only country in the world worth criticizing."*

The Cambridge students said it was *"almost laughable"* to suggest that the Gaza war and the conflict between Israel and the Palestinians absolves anyone of the immorality of singling out Israel as these academics did. They then listed world conflicts about which the academics had been silent. They also highlighted the hypocrisy of the teachers who claim to have concern for the humanitarian condition of the Palestinians yet had nothing to say about the thousands of Palestinians who have been killed and millions displaced in Syria.

In a smart academic equivalence to the courses led by the teachers, the Jewish students mentioned the legal issue of Palestinian war crimes in their rocket fire against Israeli civilians, the philosophers who committed moral hypocrisy by condemning Israel without a mention of Palestinian terrorism, and the historians who should teach that *"the blockade of Gaza was the result of the Hamas eviction of Fatah government officials and the ensuing rocket attacks, and not the cause."*

The teachers' statement perversely demanded an end to *"the persecution of critics of Israel within academia."* In response, the Jewish students called for an end to the victimization of Israeli supporters on campus and in the media which, they wrote, *"continued the theme of discrimination by these academics."*

Over in America, the summer Hamas-Israel conflict blurred the line between anti-Zionism and anti-Semitism, particularly on college campuses.

A pro-Israel student at Temple University was punched in the face by a member of Students for Justice in Palestine (SJP) who called him a *"baby killer," "Zionist pig"* and *"kike."*

The Hillel International branch at Temple expressed its concerns for the safety of students on campus with Hillel professionals and counselors from the university's counseling center. Phil Nordlinger, the director of the branch, said at the time he was working to ensure a climate of civility *"where our students feel it is safe to celebrate their Jewish identities and show support for Israel."*

A student at another college, Elliott Hamilton at Pitzer College in California, wrote in an op-ed for JNS.org that the Temple incident didn't come as a surprise to him.

"SJP historically bullies pro-Israel students and invites vehemently anti-Semitic speakers to campus under the pretense of 'dialogue.'"

Things got so bad that the Brandeis Center issued a resource guide called *"Fact Sheet on the Elements of Anti-Semitic Discourse"* to educate both students and campus officials on the difference between legitimate criticism of Israel and hate speech.

Kenneth Marcus, the president of the Louis D. Brandeis Center for Human Rights Under Law, said to JNS.org, *"We want university administrators to understand that much of the anti-Israel protest that we see on college campuses is really not just about politics. In fact, it has roots in ancient and medieval Jew hatred."*

Jacob Baime, the executive director of the Israel on Campus Coalition, said that Students for Justice in Palestine *"don't do anything to bring people together. They don't do anything to actually help Palestinians. Not only do they not accept the notion of two states for two peoples, but if you ask a representative of SJP whether Israel has the right to exist as a Jewish state, they won't acknowledge it – they won't even answer the question generally."*

Baime said that his ICC encourages students to *"try to deescalate a situation"* like Temple.

In the face of tremendous provocation, the pro-Israel side is exhibiting a tremendous amount of decorum, but is that too much decorum? StandWithUs CEO, Roz Rothstein thinks that, *"we need to point the finger at anti-Semitism and bullying, and not accept it as commonplace."*

She agreed with Hamilton. *"While SJP has the right to express their opinions, in accordance with free speech, in many cases this is really about bullying."*

StandWithUs defines the difference between legitimate criticism of Israel and anti-Semitism based on Natan Sharansky's 3 D's – demonization, delegitimization, and double standards.

*

A vote was taken in the British Parliament on October 2014 which favored Palestinian statehood by 274 votes to 12. This was symbolic as it was a back-benchers motion, but it was, nevertheless, significant.

The Britain government's statement following this vote was not reassuring. It said will only recognize a Palestinian state *"at a time of its choosing"* and when it will *"best help to bring about peace."* It should have said when the two parties agree and sign a permanent peace agreement. It didn't.

What is deeply troubling is what the British Parliament didn't say but leapt off the pages of Israeli newspapers the same day as the UK vote was being reported.

The PLO General-Secretary, Yasser Abed Rabbo, announced that the Palestinian Authority will ask the United Nation Security Council to issue a resolution declaring a Palestinian state based on pre-1967 lines.

This is what happens when countries like Britain and Sweden blunder blindly to a Two-State solution without taking the consequences of their overly simple resolutions into account.

By January 2015, the UN Security Council complexion changed to one that overwhelmingly detests Israel. Neutral countries are being replaced by anti-Israel countries with no ties to with Israel, nations such as Venezuela and Malaysia. This leaves Israel dependent on an American veto in a chamber that is stacked against it.

The other headline contained the real danger for Israel by naïve or cynical voting for Palestinian statehood by altruistic countries with no responsibility for their liberal actions.

What these countries are saying is that Israel must withdraw to indefensible borders, they will allow Palestinian society to elect their own government and let Israel take the consequences if it turns out to be hostile to the Jewish state. This is how they jeopardize the safety and security of the people of Israel.

If they have their way, we will have Hamas on the streets of Jerusalem, commanding the heights over Ben-Gurion Airport and the central, low-lying coastal plain where eighty percent of our population live and the location of much of our sensitive and essential national infrastructure.

*

The Palestinian Authority Religious Affairs Minister Mahmoud al-Habbash is a study in Palestinian narrative where facts get - how shall I put it? - distorted. I selected this gentleman because he can be perceived as moderate, or neutral, in Palestinian political terms, even to the point of courage. He was born in the Nusseirat refugee camp in the Gaza Strip. As a young man, he excelled in Islamic studies and was active in Hamas, eventually becoming a preacher in Hamas-affiliated mosques in Gaza. However, to his credit, in 1994, he left the organization, an act for which he is hated by many in the Hamas leadership. The animosity is mutual. He moved to Ramallah. Many of Habbash's Facebook entries are criticisms of Hamas. He attacked the Hamas leadership for not paying their electricity bills, for stealing taxpayers money, accused them of preventing Gaza's citizens from leaving the Strip and, in one entry he vowed that Gaza's citizens would soon be liberated, although he did not mean by Israel.

Although Habbash left Hamas, he refused to join Fatah. Despite having been given the religious affairs ministry, he is resented by many senior Fatah leaders as an outsider and as a former Hamas activist. He was untouchable, however, thanks to his special relationship with the PA president, Mahmoud Abbas, whose life he saved by tipping him off about a Hamas plot to assassinate him when his motorcade visited Gaza in 2004.

His position made him a political asset to Abbas. As a man who defected from Hamas, Fatah's most serious political opponent, when Habbash criticized Hamas from his pulpit in his Friday sermons, with Abbas and other ranking Fatah leaders in attendance, and covered on official Palestinian television, his words carry extra weight. In a sermon, given in July 2013, for example, in front of Abbas, he attacked Hamas for its "impulsive" strategy of armed struggle and praised the PA leadership's *"sense of responsibility toward the nation"* in signing the Oslo Accords, the peace agreement with Israel.

It is here we get to the Palestinian language of distortion, even with this *"balanced"* personality who compared Arafat's signing of the Oslo

Accords to *"The Treaty of Hudabiyyah,"* which has huge implications for Israel and their relationship and lack of trust with the Palestinian leadership today.

Mohammed, the conqueror of Medina, was prevented from entering into Mecca by the controlling Quraish pagans. After much negotiation, a truce was signed March 628 AD. One condition that was struck out of the agreement was the part where Mohammed presented himself as *"the Messenger of God."* This was unacceptable by the pagans of Mecca. Some of the conditions were that both parties would resist from making war with each other for ten years. During this time both parties would be safe, neither would injure each other, or cause secret damage, but behave with honor. Whoever entered into a covenant with Quraish could do so, and whoever entered into a covenant with Mohammed could also do so.

Many of Mohammed's Muslim followers looked on this agreement as a humiliation. The humiliation was contained in the condition that imposed that anyone embracing Islam without the permission of the people of Quraish must be returned by Mohammed to Quraish, but whoever renounces Islam among Mohammed's followers will be allowed to join Quraish without harm.

"Then whoever will it, let him believe, and whoever wills it, let him disbelieve." [18:29]

This degree of Islamic tolerance was very short-lived.

Mohammed presented it as a victory by declaring that, on his way back to Medina, he had a vision which said, *"Verily We have given thee a victory, a very clear victory."* To convince his followers he promised them rich future rewards, *"...and He sent down peace of reassurance on them, and hath rewarded them with a near victory and much booty that they will capture". (*Qur'an 48:18-19). So, after signing a peace agreement with Quraish, Mohammed offered his people rich pickings and booty in the future.

While it is recorded that one of Mohammed's men, a person named Banu Bakr, joined the Quraish and attacked the Muslims at a place called Al-Watter, the Quraishans sent a delegation to Medina to petition Mohammed to maintain the truce, offering him compensation. But, by this time, two years after the Hubadiyyah treaty, the Muslims had gathered strength and Mohammed led them to conquer Mecca.

Mahmoud al-Habbash insists that Islamic history records that Muslims maintain respect for signed agreements. However, Yasser Arafat signed the Oslo Accords and then, after he returned to Ramallah, he restarted his terrorism against civilians which resulting in over one thousand dead Israelis.

Shortly after signing the peace agreement with Rabin on the White House lawn in 1993, Arafat, during a visit to Johannesburg, gloated publicly, *"This agreement, I am not considering it more than the agreement which had been signed between our Prophet Muhammad and Quraish, and you remember the Caliph Omar had refused this agreement and considered it 'Sulha Dania'* [a despicable truce]. *But Muhammad had accepted it and we are accepting now this [Oslo] peace accord."*

Jews in particular have an aversion to the brutal reign on Mohammed, which to Jewish historians is alarmingly similar to the inhuman practices of Islamic State in Syria and Iraq.

When Mohammed conquered Medina, the booty included the public beheading of eight hundred men and boys and the enslavement of their girls and women. He destroyed the last remaining Jewish tribe of Qurayzah at the Jewish city of Khaibar. After first taunting the Jews, he then attacked and slaughtered them. Celebratory cries of *"Jews! Jews! Remember Khaibar!"* rang from the street of Europe to the streets of Miami during the 2014 Gaza conflict by Muslims as Hamas hurled their rockets at Israeli cities.

Habbash says it's permissible under Islam to make peace with Israel. He left Hamas because their attachment to violence to achieve a political end. He believes that negotiations and coexistence are the way to peace. *"If both sides come with open hearts I believe it is possible to reach an agreement."* But what open heartedness is there when Habbash refuses to recognize Israel as a Jewish state. According to him, this contradicts his *"historical facts"* such as *"the historical right of the Palestinians"* in places such as Jerusalem.

Palestinians such as Habbash cannot bring themselves to recognize a Jewish narrative that gives the Jewish people a special status and place in the land of Israel. Doing so would annul the Palestinian narrative of their ties to the same land. This is the crux of the conflict that, even after an Israeli withdrawal from the land demanded of them by the Palestinians today, would still leave a weeping wound and a conflict on whatever land is left for Israel to occupy.

The difficulty they have in accepting Israel as the nation state of the Jewish people, as written in so many treaties and resolutions, is that it would force them to reject their own national narrative that encompasses all of what once was Palestine, from the river to the sea. So Israel in any place would be a burning issue without resolve for a

Palestinian entity unable to surrender their *"national narrative."* Signing an agreement forcing Israel back to 1967 lines and surrendering Jerusalem as its eternal capital would be like signing the Treaty of Hubadiyyah, an agreement to be torn up at a time of convenience for future conquest to capture territory inaccessible to them today.

Jerusalem is a perfect example of the Habbash-style denial of history. When asked about the Western Wall of the Temple, or the Kotel as it is also known to Jews, his answer is, *"What is the Kotel? Maybe you mean al-Bureq wall?"* referring to the mythical horse that, according to the Koran, was a creature from heaven that conveyed Mohammed, in his dream, from Mecca to what is referred to *as "the farthest mosque"* without actually mentioning Jerusalem. According to Islamic tradition this is the wall that Mohammed was said to have ties his horse. Of course, this begs the question, who built this wall, if Mohammed was the founder of Islam?

By denying the origins of this structure even *"moderate"* Muslims like Habbash maintain the conflict not only against Israel but against Jews and Christians forever. His *"open heart"* is unable to accept and share a Jerusalem that has never been a sovereign city linked to Palestinians. His version of the "Palestinian narrative" is a fiction rooted in the desire for conquest over the unbelievers, and no evidence to their rich and recorded history, not even the stones of the Temple Mount, placed there by the Jews of old under the sovereignty of a Jewish kingdom, will sway him otherwise.

The decent Habbash does not believe there was a Temple where Jews prayed despite the clear archeological evidence. When asked, as the Palestinian religious affairs minister, would he allow Jews to pray in Jerusalem after the establishment of a Palestinian state and after an

Israeli withdrawal from east Jerusalem (hence, the Old City), he said that everything could be discussed according to their religious principles, according to their belief, and according to their religious rights. In other words, Jews would be driven out of the Old City of Jerusalem and away from their ancient holy sites by the Palestinians as they were by the Jordanians between 1948 and 1967, when Israel succeeded in liberating Jerusalem once more.

It is this delusional denial that emphasizes the hopelessness of a peace agreement with the current Palestinian leadership in Ramallah. And this is before we take into consideration the real possibility that Habbash's prime adversary, Hamas, takes over the Palestinian government, by ballot or bullet, and hoists its flag over the ramparts of Jerusalem.

*

The killing of Jews has less to do with the creation of a Palestinian state and a lot more to do with a blood cult against Jews.

*

Hamas flags flying over Jerusalem.

Mahmoud Abbas said, on 11 November 2012, that Palestinians *"would continue the march until victory when Palestinian flags are hoisted over the walls of the Old City of Jerusalem and its mosques and churches."*

As if this thought wasn't bad enough, notice he did not say anything about synagogues, or other Jewish holy places. In case you were wondering, this has nothing to do with his respect for our sacred sites.

He hasn't got any, if we are to believe what official Palestinian TV News is saying.

The Palestine Media Watch NGO, headed by Itamar Marcus, exposed an item that the Palestinian Authority denounced the existence of any Jewish history in Jerusalem. In this report, they claimed that the Jewish Temple *"exists only in the minds of radical organizations."*

Not only do they deny Jewish identity to Jerusalem and the land, they actively reject and destroy all evidence and facts placed in front of them. In its place, they invent an ancient Palestinian history unprovable by any physical evidence. The Palestinian Authority, from Abbas down, accuses Israel of stealing Palestinian heritage when confronted with the evidence of Jewish history. So what hope is there for mutual understanding and recognition? There is none.

What do Palestinian flags flying over Jerusalem mean in real estate terms? And what are the potentially explosive repercussions of such a move? Would they be hoisted over the Temple Mount, the Western Wall, David's Citadel or the Hurva Synagogue, all inside the Old City?

They have said they do not recognize such places. Will you be willing to see Palestinian, even Hamas, flags flying over the walls of the Old City and the Zion Gate? Apparently, those who support the division of Jerusalem would. They naïvely think this would herald peace.

The battle for real estate comes down to this. Can you see Hadassah Hospital and the Rockefeller Museum under the sovereignty of a Palestinian Authority, possibly led by Hamas? Will Christians, worldwide, tolerate having the Garden of Gethsemane and the Church of the Holy Sepulchre in the hands of the Palestinians, probably

Hamas? Do they care, at all, who will be the future guardians of their holy shrines? How about the Mount of Olives? And here's the clincher. Even if Israel were to be naïve enough to hand over this real estate to Palestinians, will we be able to live with ourselves, will be able to live, when Hamas takes over the feeble Palestinian Authority and rule over these vital assets in the heart of Jerusalem?

What would we have sacrificed for peace when that day comes, as it inevitably will? Will we see the Islamic flag, alongside the Palestinian one, flying over sacred Jewish and Christian sites, announcing yet another conquest in their regional and global crusade?

At that point in time we will realize, too late, that our *"peace gesture"* was, in reality, our surrender and submission to their will.

In that day, will the Hebrew University be renamed the Islamic University? Surely it is better to live with their *"Nakba"* than to perpetrate our own?

As if this wasn't bad enough, in June 2012, an Egyptian cleric close to the newly elected President Morsi, in an amazing display of Islamic chutzpah, claimed Jerusalem will be the capital of Egypt under Muslim Brotherhood rule. Safwat Hagazy said on Egyptian religious Annas TV,

"Our capital shall not be Cairo, Mecca, or Medina. It shall be Jerusalem, with Allah's will. Our chant will be 'millions of martyrs will march towards Jerusalem!'"

I wonder what the Palestinians think about their new capital overrun by an emerging Egypt?

What was meant is that Jerusalem is to be the center of an Islamic global Caliphate, achieved on the back of the Palestinian movement, even if they have to conquer it by force. He proved this by adding, *"Yes. We will either pray in Jerusalem, or we will be martyred there!"*

Masked rioters have already been seen carrying the green Hamas flag through the streets of Jerusalem. Better to give it peacefully to the Palestinians and avoid the bloodshed, we are told. No self-respecting Jew would tolerate this heinous scenario.

All this is not to say we should cease striving for a solution to the Palestinian problem, if only to get them off our backs. It may take the form of a Two-State Solution. It may take other forms. Clearly, after decades of failure, it will require creative, even original, thinking. Perhaps a Two-State Solution is not the answer? Despite the overwhelming opinion that this, and only this, is the only game in town, it is obviously not happening, despite the tremendous pressure being put on Israel. How can it be, given our negotiating partner? Who, on the other side, can deliver a final and permanent peace acceptable to Jews and to clear thinking Christians, even if Israel were to give them everything they want? Who, in fact, speaks for the Palestinians – all the Palestinians? Answer - no one.

So let's stop dreaming and get real. Let's not waste time trying to persuade a weak, cowardly, rejectionist, and devious leader of a Palestinian minority who, according to local elections in the West Bank, failed to secure majorities in any of the main towns and cities, including Ramallah. Abbas refuses to recognize the Jewish state and live in peace alongside us. And Hamas, the popular choice of the Palestinian street, is infinitely worse. Palestinian Arabs, beyond Abbas's parochial parish area, have no intention of settling for anything less than the elimination of the Zionist entity. Let's be brutally honest, even Abbas shares that dream, despite rhetoric to the contrary.

It is clear, from their public incitement and declarations, that none of them have any desire to live alongside Israel in peace and harmony. On the contrary, as we recently witnessed they really want to kill us.

A people whose bible doesn't mention Jerusalem once, a people who, when they pray in Jerusalem, do so with their backsides facing the Temple Mount and the Dome of the Rock, cannot claim Jerusalem as a capital based on religious grounds, despite their protests.

In truth, they want it as a statement of conquest, to plant their flag to displace the Jewish infidel's sovereignty over Jerusalem. It's less about having their state. It's more about destroying our state and planting their victory flag over Jerusalem.

Planting a flag is a sign of sovereignty, but sovereignty over what? A state, or a staging post? Here's what Yasser Arafat said back in 1993;

"...the Palestinian state is within our grasp. Soon the Palestinian flag will fly on the walls, the minarets and the cathedrals of Jerusalem. Since we cannot defeat Israel in war, we do this in stages. We take any and every territory that we can of Palestine, and establish sovereignty there, and we use it as a springboard to take more. When the time comes, we can get the Arab nations to join us for the final blow against Israel."

Interesting to note that he said this on the same day he signed the Declaration of Principles on the White House lawn with President Clinton and Israel's Yitzchak Rabin.

Such is the deception of the Palestinians. Can we believe that Mahmoud Abbas, raised in the spirit of Arafat, is any different? Jerusalem is the springboard to the rest of Israel.

Mahmoud Abbas holds to the same desire as Hamas who recently declared, during their 2014 missile attack on Israel;

"We are announcing a war against the sons of apes and pigs, which will not end until the flag of Islam is raised in Jerusalem."

With this is mind, for Israel it is time for crisis management, not crisis solution. In politics, as in business, you should only enter into crisis solutions when you are absolutely sure that everyone gathered around the table is ready, honest, and capable of delivering an acceptable permanent agreement. Do we have that with the Palestinians? No. Do we know who will control the Palestinians next year? No. Are any of those European parliaments or United Nation member states ready to guarantee Israel's security when things go wrong? No.

Despite everything, given a referendum and a flexible and committed Palestinian leadership, the majority of Israelis would readily accept a pragmatic and guaranteed end of conflict agreement. Nobody can claim this to be true about the other side. Crisis solution, therefore, is out of the question when the opposing adversary is a minority representative of a fractious society and has proven to be incapable of uniting his people around him. Hence, crisis management and original alternatives must be the order of the day.

When politicians and diplomats fail to face the reality of what is at stake here but call on an Israeli withdrawal to insecure borders to accommodate this type of Palestine their talk is simply inane and should be ignored.

*

It's a hackneyed trope of Holocaust revisionism in service of the Palestinian cause to equate Hamas-controlled Gaza with the Warsaw Ghetto. This portrayal is designed to gain sympathy for the Arabs in the Gaza Strip. It also equates Israel, the Jewish State, as the new Nazis.

This inappropriate Holocaust imagery, a desecration of the memory of the Holocaust is, in itself, a form of anti-Semitism. As British writer Howard Jacobson aptly put it, *"It is to wound Jews in their recent and most anguished history, and to punish them with their own grief. Its aim is a sort of retrospective retribution, canceling out all debts of guilt and sorrow, It is as though, by a reversal of the usual laws of cause and effect, Jewish actions of today prove that Jews had it coming to them yesterday...Instead of saying the Holocaust didn't happen, the modern, sophisticated denier accepts the event in all its terrible enormity, only to accuse the Jews of trying to profit from it, either in the form of moral blackmail or downright territorial theft. According to this thinking, the Jews have betrayed the Holocaust and become unworthy of it, the true heirs to their suffering being the Palestinians."*

It seems that not even the memory of the genocide of European Jewry is sacrosanct on the continent which allowed it to happen.

*

In August, 2014, nearly two hundred Hollywood actors and directors, including Arnold Schwarzenegger and Sylvester Stallone, signed an anti-Hamas petition in which they wrote "we *stand firm against* ideologies of hatred and genocide which are reflected in Hamas' charter, Article 7 of which reads, 'There is a Jew hiding behind me, come on and kill him!'"

It's sadly disappointing that action heroes from Hollywood get it but apparently European politicians, who claim to be working hard for Middle East peace, don't.

*

The UN *"independent, international Commission"* was once chaired by William Schabas, professor of International Law at Middlesex University, before he was deposed because of his connections with the PLO. He is on record saying he would like to see Prime Minister Binyamin Netanyahu put on trial at the International Criminal Court for his complicity in Operation Caste Lead. He apparently wasn't aware that Netanyahu wasn't in office at the time. Why allow facts to confuse the objective? This is the United Nations; there's no limit to how low the UN can go in its attacks on Israel.

The UNHRC is occupied territory. It is controlled by corrupt third world regimes who abuse its platform to promote their self-serving and hypocritical agendas. They have no right to this territory. Their traditions don't embrace human rights. They don't speak its language.

For its own sake, the Council must be liberated by leaders of the free world so it can fulfill the mission for which it was created. Gross violations of human rights go uninvestigated and unpunished because corrupt bigots have hijacked and continue to occupy the body created by the international community to protect and enhance human rights.

I'm not a lawyer and even I see through this transparent and flagrant abuse of authority to promote the UNHRC's warped political agenda.

This is not a Commission created in good faith but a charade intended to stage a show trial for the sole purpose of discrediting Israel.

By its actions, the UNHCR bestows its blessing on the tidal wave of anti-Semitism currently sweeping streets and campuses around the world. It is complicit in the movement to demonize and delegitimize Israel with a view to creating the public opinion to justify Israel's annihilation.

*

Israel looks on Europe with utter dismay.

Political tremors are starting to be felt across Europe.

In Britain, we see the rise of an emerging independent party, UKIP, which is Euro-sceptic and takes a corrective line on the UK's unbridled open-door immigration policy.

In France, the Socialist Hollande looks likely to be replaced by the center-right Sarkozy.

The left-wing Swedish government barely lasted three month before being forced to abandon a failed leadership. This gave them sufficient time to rush through a *'Palestine'* vote which may be overturned by an incoming center-right government.

Across Europe, voters are objecting to poor economic and immigration policies. They are offended by the rise of crime perpetrated by immigrants they had welcomed into their once decent countries.

Cultural changes are making their countries unrecognizable to the indigenous population, and not to their pleasing.

One prominent reason for the political swing has been politicians pandering to Islamic sensitivities at home. This is causing pause and division among their populations. The recent outbreak of symbolic parliamentary voting for an ill-defined Palestinian state is one outward expression of politicians catering to a rising constituency against which their grassroots citizenry are rebelling.

The swing in the polls reflects a desire to return to an old patriotism of long lost national values, lost in the mire of multiculturalism brought on by uncontrolled immigration against a background of recession and poor economic performance.

They are in search of a once-was national character. A yearning to return to something past will not save them from the reality of what they now have. However, we will see European nations shift, possibly polarize, as populations demand that their voices are heard above the growing needs and demands of strong minority and troublesome migrants and left-wing anarchists.

But will these changes come in time to save a sinking Europe from the misguided immoral decisions already being taken by a largely Socialist fractured continent?

One nation outside of Europe that is suffering from European misguided policies is Israel.

From an Israeli perspective, it looks at Europe as a landmass that feels itself in need to cater to an unruly Muslim population that offers their politicians votes but on the other hand can, and does, cause problems and violence if their causes are not addressed. This expressed itself with displays of violent anti-Semitism that left local Jews vulnerable.

Countries, one after another, fall prey to the lobbying of left-wing fringe groups allied to a Palestinian agenda by the introduction of anti-Israel resolutions. One after another, nations fall like dominoes not wishing to appear out of step to an ill-considered mantra of Palestinianism that contradicts European commitments to a permanent solution of the Israeli-Palestinian conflict that must be settled only by the two parties involved, without any external unilateral moves that may endanger or foreclose such an outcome.

The Oslo Accords, signed on the White House lawn between Israel and Palestinian leader Arafat called for mutual recognition, something that it totally lacking from Hamas, the leading political body of Palestinian Arabs, or from the rejectionist Mahmoud Abbas and his Palestinian Authority. The notion of *"two states for two peoples"* has been totally rejected by the Palestinians.

Europe has ignored this. Why? It is not something irrelevant.

An end to terrorism is yet another condition for peace. Can anyone truly say that an end of terrorism has been achieved following the grotesque Palestinian rocket attacks that erupted out of the Gaza Strip last summer with the horrendous sight of Palestinian terrorists coming out of the ground by Israeli farms and villages, intent to capture or kill huge numbers of Israeli civilians including women and children?

Yet, on December 17, the European Court of Justice removed Hamas from the EU list of terrorist organizations. This, just days after the

Hamas leadership had celebrated in Gaza by parading their rockets and suicide bombers, vowing to eradicate the Jewish State of Israel.

Israel's Prime Minister summed up the feeling of all Israelis and Jews when he responded, *"It seems that too many in Europe, on whose soil six million Jews were slaughtered, have learned nothing. But we in Israel, we've learned. We'll continue to defend our people and our state against the forces of terror and tyranny and hypocrisy."*

The hypocrisy was aimed squarely at a Europe that fails to support the only liberal democracy in the region but bends over backwards to establish a state that will, in all likelihood, be headed by an Islamic terror group or by a rejectionist body with a shared motivation to remove Israel as part of a *'liberating Palestine'* agenda.

Europeans need to be asked, if Hamas is not a terrorist organization, what is?

As European parliaments fall, one by one, to a *'Palestine'* vote, and its court cannot understand what constitutes a terrorist organization if it is cloaked in Palestinian clothes, no other issue brought the Israeli parliament into unison as the European court's decision.

Wall to wall condemnation was heard across Israel's divergent political parties against the European Court of Justice whose decision demonstrates the loss of a moral path, in the words of MK Naftali Bennett.

Former Justice Minister, Tzipi Livni, reminded Europe that Hamas is *"an extreme Islamic religious terrorist organization that must be fought with all force."*

Islamic extremists and terrorists must not be allowed to exploit the freedoms they enjoy in Europe (and America). But, sadly, they are being allowed to exploit those freedoms.

Clearly, Europe today does not have the stomach, or the political will, to fight Islamic terror with all its force, if at all.

What hope can there be when a senior Swedish politician said that Muslims traveling from Sweden to the Middle East to commit mass murder and rape with the Islamic State terrorist organization are *"victims of violence"*, according to Anna Kinberg Batra, in an interview with the newspaper *Expressen* in early February 2015?

As Knesset Speaker, Yuli Edelstein said, the European Union *"must have lost its mind!"*

This is clearly the case. It's a question of whether the winds of political change in Europe will arrive in time to save itself and Israel from the damaging tsunami of current political moves.

*

Professor Irwin Cotler points to the lack of global outcry against Hamas as a subtle form of anti-Semitism, since that group's charter calls for the eradication of the Jewish people, as listed in this book's chapter, Fighting Hamas. *"How do you combat terrorism when you are not prepared to identify the perpetrator?* Cotler asks.

Cotler characterized the month of December 2014 as a tipping point for the international vilification of the Jewish people. This was the month in which the United Nations General Assembly passed twenty resolutions targeting Israel and only four targeting all other countries.

"Israel is portrayed as the enemy of all that is good and the repository of all that is evil."

In December, the European Parliament rejected the proposal for a working group on anti-Semitism. In the same month the European Court of Justice removed Hamas from its list of terrorist organizations, this after all that had transpired out of Gaza during the summer of 2014.

Along with condemnations from other global bodies these moves, according to Professor Cotler, dangerously constitute the *"laundering of delegitimization of Israel under universal public values."*

"The preoccupation with Israel has the effect of sanitizing other evils," he said giving the examples of countries such as Iran, Venezuela, Saudi Arabia and others. *"None of these countries dented the international radar screen."*

*

World should enforce tough conditions for peace on the Palestinians.

Softness and generosity is getting us nowhere.

In early December, the head of the International Red Cross in Israel, Jacques de Maio, said at an Institute for National Security Studies conference that the world was holding Israel to double standards when it comes to war crimes allegations.

A year earlier, the Dutch Foreign Minister, Frans Timmermans, said that Europe was judging Israel by double standards.

Then, at the 2014 December Jerusalem Conference, the Danish Ambassador to Israel demanded that Europe should apply a double standard to Israel.

Enough already! It's time we told these diplomats to put Israel aside and begin applying tougher standards on the Palestinians. After all, they are the ones demanding support for statehood. The support for their demand must come with stringent conditions. It isn't. Instead, the world community gives them a free pass - a get-out-of-jail free card, if you will. They can commit whatever crimes they choose and the world community continues to give them their love, support and money. It's absurd! It's obscene, as the Palestinian crimes include corruption, violence, terror, human rights abuses and war crimes.

It's time to get real. Stop the softness and generosity. It's getting us nowhere. It's time the world take a hard look at the Palestinian leadership and started imposing firm conditions for their political support and funding.

Let's begin with the demand that they cut out their racial anti-Semitism. Tell them that they don't get a cent as long as both the Hamas and PLO Charters contain their heinous articles about Jews. What do their references about killing Jews, and a perverse Islamic view of what is a Jew, have to do with Palestinian self-determination, except perhaps for their stated condition that a Palestine must be Judenrein – Jew free? This again must give the international community pause. But apparently it doesn't. This is shameful! Not only will then not allow a Jew to be a Palestinian citizen, but they also refuse to recognize Israel as the nation state of the Jews, despite the fact that this legitimate claim is conditioned in the League of Nations Mandate that forged not only Israel, but is enshrined in Article 80 of the founding United Nations Charter. The world, therefore, has a legal obligation to insist that any state bordering on Israel recognize the national character of Israel, its neighbor.

Would European parliaments that voted to support a Palestinian state be so willing to accept such a state if it is controlled by an unrepentant Hamas? According to a Palestinian opinion poll released on December 9, 2014, the majority of Palestinians canvassed supported Hamas. This is not unusual. It's a fact that, according to all Palestinian polls and elections, between 64%-74% of Palestinian Arabs have always preferred Hamas to Fatah or any other political party.

So, taking the history of Hamas who usurped power in a bloody coup d'état in Gaza, a Hamas that is affiliated to the Muslim Brotherhood, a rabidly Islamic regime that kills its opponents, builds a terror infrastructure, has a Charter calling for killing Jews and the destruction of Israel, has launched repeated terror and rocket wars against Israel, and is officially recognized as a terrorist organization by most of the Western world, is this really the Palestine that European politicians desperately want to see created in the Middle East?

Either by the ballot or by the bullet, Hamas will take over any Palestinian state. This is inevitable, and it has been caused by an international community that has not only failed to allow Israel to eradicate this terror regime but has, over the years supported and financed the development and strength of this violent and brutal organization, both directly and indirectly.

When one looks dispassionately at Israel on the one hand, a truly liberal democratic country that has given so much to the world in its generosity in times of crisis and its talented innovative benefits to mankind, and a corrupt, violent, racist, rejectionist Palestinian entity on the other hand, surely it is time to take a realistic look at the conflict and begin to concentrate on reforming the Palestinian leadership and society to a culture of pragmatism and flexibility, if not liberal democratic values.

No peace is possible until the international community puts its weight behind changing the face of Israel's adversary and taking responsibility for transforming it into a genuine and reasonable peace partner.

Israel made peace with two past adversaries. It happened when pragmatic and reasonable leaders took the courageous step to openly recognize Israel and officially accept its right to exist. Sadat of Egypt paid with his life but the agreement with Egypt has stood the test of upheavals and terror, as has the agreement with Jordan despite the Islamic and Palestinian storms that sweep the area.

*

Jews, Israel, and the Palestinian cause.

British historian, Paul Johnson, wrote, *"To the Jews we owe the idea of equality before the law, both divine and human; of the sanctity of life and the dignity of the human person; of the individual conscience and so of social responsibility; of peace as an abstract ideal and love as the foundation of justice, and many other items which constitute the basic moral furniture of the human mind. Without the Jews it might have been a much emptier place."*

Why is it that so many despise the collective Jew in Israel, denying them credence that is so evident that the Jewish state is based and practices the morality that Johnson admires? Not only that, but it extends a compassionate hand to those that the anti-Israel critic support, a hand that is violently rejected by people who fail Johnson's test time and time again.

Where is the morality of those who hit on Israel in support of a cause that is based on the sanctity of death, indignity to those who do not conform, abuse of individual conscience, peace on intolerable terms, hate as a motivational force, a form of justice that victimizes minorities, and denies the Jew any place in their midst. The world will be an emptier place should this type of society prevail.

*

When the West Bank becomes Hamastan will the Left be so keen on a Palestinian state?

The Left, of whatever stripe, is falling over itself to promote the Valhallah of Palestine. Whoever promotes Palestine today promotes the rise of Hamas. It's as inevitable as storms after strong winds.

They may not do this intentionally, but this will be the result.

From radical Marxists to Social Democrats to Laborites, they are all keen to see the dawn of an Arab Palestine.

Despite all being anti-nationalists, they have all devoted their political capital (hardly an appropriate word for the grey economy of Socialism) and clout to cultivate a Middle East in their image, one that will labor in the socialist tradition.

All of them fail to learn from history when leftist activism destabilized a country or a region and left them with serious egg on their faces. They never get the glory they seek. They are among the first to be dragged off the streets and never come back. But like clowns in a deadly circus, they keep on pratfalling.

It happened when Iraqi Communists plotted an Iraqi world post-Al-Bakr, and ended up being dragged away by Saddam's henchmen.

It happened when they lined up in support of the Ayatollah in removing the Shah from power in Tehran, and got blown away for their troubles. In Iran, the Marxist Tudeh Party reckoned the *"positive"* politics of Khomeini outweighed the negatives, and gambled wrong. Surely, they though, he wouldn't impose a rigid theocracy on the populace once they helped him achieve power? Sure, he would sweep away the corrupt nepotism and capitalism of the Shah and grant the people economic reforms. He did, but without them. The Marxists were taken away, tortured, executed, and disappeared, with all the rest.

Communists are not queasy about mass killings for a cause. One only has to look at its history to see this is true. It's just a matter of who are doing the killing and when Palestinian's are doing it can be justified by their Soviet-style propaganda. As for who is doing the dying, if it's Israelis it can be as easily excused away as was when thousands of Jews were killed under Communism. Blame it on the Jewish deviousness, how they control the world, anything else that defames and demonizes them sufficiently to have them removed.

The radical left has employed highly successful sophisticated marketing to clothe a vindictive political agenda anti-Semitic in its exclusivity of Israel for targeting, anti-Semitic in its use of language, anti-Semitic as exposed by several of its perpetrators in their speech and comments, anti-Semitic in that they target their local Jews for collective guilt by association with Israel, the collective Jew.

They have seduced the more moderate left and liberals with an emotive narrative that appeals to the soft heart of pacifists and anyone who feels sympathy for an underdog, and their dog in this fight are the Palestinians. Their hyper-activism allows them to infiltrate committees of similar leaning ilk, bodies like trades unions, local political councils, church groups, and up into the left wing of the halls of power.

They are clever. With few exceptions they prefer not to establish glaringly provocative political parties. Instead they slow-drip their tainted propaganda into the life-blood on the mainstream Labor, Social Democrats, Liberal parties in Europe and have them do their bidding. So you see European parliaments adopt resolutions calling for a Palestine without ever discussing what Palestine they are voting for. And all the parliaments that fall like dominoes for this empty-headed motion are all left-wing. It was the newly elected Social Democrats of Sweden to be followed by the Labor side of the Houses of Parliament.

It was no accident that former Labor leader, Lord Prescott, was heard to talk about Israel's *"indiscriminate"* bombing of Palestinian territory was a *"war crime"* and that Gaza was a ghetto in July 2014. The fact that Israeli bombing was targeted and not *"indiscriminate,"* that it was not a *"war crime,"* and that Gaza is NOT a ghetto had nothing to do with Prescott's adopted political line which is tainted with emotional untruths against Israel and had nothing to say about thousands of Palestinian rockets falling on Israeli civilian centers, or armed Palestinian terrorists appearing suddenly out of attack tunnels by Israeli villages and farms.

The Irish lower house, strongly influenced by the Sinn Fein, closely associated with the IRA, an Irish terrorist organization that wreaked havoc across Ireland and mainland England, also adopted support for Palestine with explosive language with some Irish delegates accusing Israel of *"genocide."* Would an IRA-based political party be concerned about the rise of Hamas in Palestinian politics? Hardly likely.

Here, Mick Wallace, in an anti-Semitic deliberate misreading of history said, *"In 1948, the Jews expelled, massacred, destroyed and raped in that year, and generally behaved like all the other colonialist movements operating in the Middle East and Africa since the beginning of the 19th century…What is happening today is not very different."*

Today, they don't know they're looking through spectacles so blurred with murky past failures that they again promote a leftist fantasy that will bring to power the Palestinian Ayatollahs of Hamas dressed in modern garb. Hamas, the Palestinian Muslim Brotherhood. Hamas, the Palestinian Baath Party that will certainly reject the West, reject Zionism and capitalism, as these leftists desire, even as Hamas leaders stash the cash in far-off bank accounts. They'll certainly be anti-American. That will please the supportive radical left, but it will also brutally destroy any ideology they see as challenging their brand of totalitarianism, as occurred so often in the past.

Why should Palestine end up any different from any of the past causes the left so passionately supported from Cuba, to Saddam, to the Ayatollahs, even to Gaddafi in Libya, who the left looked on as introducing a Socialist revolution?

What can possibly be the fate of a Palestine wedged between Israel, Egypt, Jordan, and Syria with little natural resources and no desire for a technocrat government to drag this new state into the 21st Century? What Palestine do these left-wing European parliamentarians think they are helping to establish? Clearly it is one that will be unable to adequately answer the needs of its people. A feeble Abbas/Fatah led leadership is doomed to fall. They blew away the technocrat talent of Prime Minister, Sayim Fayad, gone under the squalid jealousies and intrigues of corrupt Fatah politicians.

What hope will a weak, greedy, and impotent Palestinian bureaucracy have in attracting meaningful foreign investment sufficient to cover their welfare costs and pay their bills? What happens when they become yet another Middle East basket case? Can anyone see a Palestine doing a better economic job than Jordan?

And, when angry Arab voices rise again it will be mighty Hamas who will march into power by the ballot, or the bullet.

The incomplete rise of Palestine, looking for the inevitable scapegoat of their own Naqba, will again find it in Israel as propaganda for their ongoing cause. They have to draw attention away from their political failings. Tragically, it can go no other way. The power struggle is too strong. The prize is too powerful. The result will be more turmoil, more violence, and more bloodshed in an unresolved conflict.

One thing we have learned to our cost, whenever a regime fails, whenever political movements crash and Jews have been anywhere to be seen, they are the ones to blame. It works for the Arabs and the Palestinians, so why should they surrender this card when their incompetence is on the line?

They'll always have the left to bail them out of their failures, and use Israel as the Jewish whipping boy.

*

The major world problem is one of radical Islam rejecting all that is not Islamic. Palestinian rejection of a Jewish state in the Middle East is an echo of that world problem.

*

Fighting Hamas and radical Islam on the campus.

In a discussion with London's *Jewish Chronicle* mentioned in the chapter on *Fighting Anti-Semitism,* David Cameron addressed the root cause of the British security threat, he said, *"This means going after the poisonous ideology of Islamist extremism that perverts the Islamic faith in an attempt to justify the most sickening barbarism and brutality."*

"This is why we have banned extremist preachers, increased the resources available for programs that prevent radicalization, and why we are getting extremist material taken down form the internet."

I have no doubt that he and his Home secretary, Theresa May, has read and taken note of the research on radical Islam on UK campuses done by The Center for Social Cohesion which was published in a 2010 document which contained the names of UK universities where radicalization was allowed to penetrate its *"poisonous ideology"* under the noses of deans, faculty heads, and the British authorities in the name of free speech and pluralism. The list of major British seats of learning where radicalism festered and influenced impressionable students is shamefully long.

As Douglas Murray of the Henry Jackson Society noted in the report's foreword, *"Islamic extremism on campuses not only continues unabated, it continues – as this report demonstrates – to flourish."*

Extremist speakers are regularly invited onto campus to address and influence students. This has led to a number of students and graduates committing acts of terrorism or convicted of terrorist related offences. The report lists many of them. They include *Ahmed Omar Saeed Sheikh*, a student at the London School of Economics who masterminded the kidnapping and beheading of Daniel Pearl in 2002.

Omar Sharif, radicalized at King's College, took part in the suicide bombing at Mikes Place in Tel Aviv in 2003. Several students became members of Al-Qaida.

Yassin Nasari, a student of the University of Westminster, was arrested at Luton Airport in 2006 with a blueprint of the al-Qassam rocket used by Hamas against Israeli towns in his luggage. He also had documents about weapons training and martyrdom in his computer hard-drive, as well as recordings of lectures given by extremist clerics.

Among the invited radical campus speakers, *Haitham al-Haddad* openly supports Hamas and called for the abolition of Israel and the removal of all Israelis from the land.

In 2007, *Riyadh ul-Haq*, speaking on the topic of Israel called on Muslims to *"be willing to sacrifice anything that may be required of us."* Advocating the need to *"liberate"* the Al-Aqsa mosque that sits on Jerusalem's Temple Mount he said, *"We are willing to die in the process,"* and *"we will consider it an honor and a privilege to shed our blood"*. He also said, Allah has promised that Islam will, *"prevail over all other religions, even though the disbelievers may dislike it."*

Included in ul-Haq's academic rants were these anti-Semitic words, *"The Jews don't have to be in Israel to be like this. It doesn't matter whether they're in New York, Houston, St Louis, London, Birmingham, Bradford and Manchester. They're all the same. They've monopolized everything: the Holocaust, God, money, interest, usury, the world economy, the media, political institutions... they monopolized tyranny and oppression as well as injustice. A Jew is generally allowed to kill a non-Jew without fear of punishment, repercussions, neither in this world or the hereafter."*

As a result of comments made by *Daud Abdullah,* who openly called for jihad against Israel, the then Communities Minister, Hazel Blears, cut British government ties with the Muslim Council of Britain of which Abdullah was the deputy secretary-general. He rejected all Middle East peace initiatives in favor of violent jihad to eradicate Israel.

Azzam al-Tamimi was prevented from accepting invitations to speak on UK campuses because of his inflammatory views. A supporter of Hamas and Hezbollah and an advocate of violent jihad, he said when appearing on BBC's *Hardtalk* he was willing to carry out a suicide attack in Israel. *"Sacrificing myself for Palestine is a noble cause. It is the way to pleasing my God and I would do it if I had the opportunity."*

Al-Tamimi did speak in 2006 on the campus of SOAS (School of Oriental & African Studies) at the University of London where he repeated his support for terrorism against Israel in the most anti-Semitic terms. He also spoke on the campuses of Birmingham and Nottingham as well as to the Federation of Student Islamic Societies.

Thus radicalism, anti-Israel and anti-Semitic rhetoric is spread in the UK academic world.

Louise Ellman M.P. said of Al-Tamimi in Parliament that, *"This is not a man of peace. He and his arguments incite hatred against Jews."* Yet, such is the character of these people that has student bodies lining up to invite them to speak on their campuses.

SOAS and the London School of Economics were funded by the Libyan dictator Muammar Gaddafi.

In America, Islamic imams and Muslim Student Associations are closely associated with appearances on campuses. The Muslim Student Union at the University of California, Irvine, in 2004, sponsored a week of campus activity labeled *"Tragedy in the Holy Land; 56 years of Terrorism."* They invited Amir Abdul Malik Ali, the Imam of Masjid Al-Islam in Oakland, and Mohammed al-Asi, a radical Islamic cleric from Washington, DC. to speak.

Also at the University of California during the infamous *Israel Apartheid Week* annual campus farce, Malik-Ali said, *"The architects of the financial crash are Alan Greenspan, Zionist Jew, Geithner, Zionist Jew, Larry Summers, Zionist Jew."*
This anti-Semitic statement was featured in the 2011 Daniel Greenfield authored document *"Muslim Hate Groups on Campus."* Greenfield's research identifies and names Muslim hate groups together with their leftist allies that propagate anti-Israel, anti-Zionist activity that often lapses into typical anti-Semitism.

Malik Ali claimed that Zionism was a white European colonizing movement that was racist by nature and that those who consider themselves Zionists are therefore white supremacists. He said that he was speaking about *"Zionist Jews,"* not *"righteous Jews,"* and claimed that his speech wasn't anti-Semitic but rather anti-Zionist.

In an earlier visit to Irvine, at the invitation of the Muslim Student Union, Ali gave a lecture titled *"America Under Siege: The Zionist Hidden Agenda,"* he called Zionism a mixture of *"chosen people-ness and white supremacy,"* and claimed that the Iraqi war was in the process of *"Israelization"* and that Zionists had *"Congress, the media and the FBI in their back pocket."* He also said that, *"the Israelis knew about and were 'in-control' of 9-11"* and that it *"was staged to give an excuse to wage war against Muslims around the world."*

In February 2004, the Students for Justice in Palestine and the Third World Forum sponsored a presentation by Dr. Jess Ghannam at the University of California-San Francisco. Ghannam, a University of California-San Francisco professor and outspoken pro-Palestinian activist, has repeatedly accused Israelis of practicing racism, apartheid, and *"ethnic cleansing."*

At the talk, according to one attendee, Ghannam characterized the Israeli-Palestinian conflict as an issue of white Jews vs. non-white Arabs, calling Israelis and Americans *"racists, white masters, and oppressors."*

Such is the template for the radical anti-Israel lurid rhetoric in place of academic research on too many campuses in support, not of a peaceful Palestine alongside Israel, but for the removal of the Jewish state.

HamasOnCampus.org was set up by a group of students from different campuses across the USA and Canada. They represent both Jews and non-Jews, left and right, liberal and conservative. They claim to value freedom of speech, women's rights and human rights and use these values to challenge those using increasingly radical behavior and rhetoric by Hamas supporting organizations on campus. They highlight the extensive connection between the Muslim Student Association (MSA), Students for Justice in Palestine (SJP), and radical Islamic organizations such as Hamas. By employing Al-Qaeda tied speakers to other radical speakers both the MSA and SJP have had a chilling effect on the safety of Jewish students on campus.

According to HOC, SJP is Hamas on campus. Students have to contend with numerous radical Islamic campus organizations that share speakers, financial ties, and coordinate activities with other Hamas affiliated bodies. *"Beneath the public facade of the SJP's anti-Israel rhetoric, is a radical Islamic organization that has been guided from the beginning to be Hamas on campus."*

Tactics used by radical Islamists include portraying Hamas in pleasant pastel colors while denigrating anyone who gets in their way. John Esposito of the Islamic Networks Group, a who's who of radical Islamic apologists and activists that flood campuses and other auditoriums, once famously presented the Hamas terrorist organization as engaging in *"honey, cheese-making, and home-based clothing manufacture."* On the other hand, this Georgetown professor in a Huffington Post article blamed *"hard-line Christian Zionists"* for Islamophobia in America.

While American Jewish students were celebrating Rosh HaShana (the Jewish New Year) in September 2014, immediately after the Hamas summer assault on Israel, a leading anti-Zionist organization on campus *American Muslims for Palestine* (AMP) called for *An International Day of Action* to *"make Free Palestine and Ending the Siege on Gaza part of campus education by holding teach-ins, rallies, sit-ins, civil disobedience, and push for BDS activities."*

Their interpretation of the 2014 Gaza conflict, which began and was maintained by an incessant rocket bombardment of Hamas rockets in to Israeli towns and villages including six ceasefire breaches by the Palestinian terror group, was caused when *"Israel launched an unparalleled brutal assault against the Palestinians of Gaza."* Such is the deliberate misinterpretation of facts for anti-Israel propaganda purposes. They can echo much of the faulty media reporting to portray Israel and the bully Goliath and Hamas as an underdog David.

The Anti-Defamation League, America's Jewish community's watchdog organization for anti-Semitism and civil liberties abuses, says AMP can be traced directly back to Hamas through the now defunct Islamic Association for Palestine (IAP). (The IAP, among other things, printed and distributed Hamas literature calling for a global jihad against Jews.)

Clearly Jewish students feel intimidated by the powerful, well-funded, multiple anti-Israel groups that are hyper-active on American campuses. The under-funded pro-Israel students are simply unable to counter the massive weight of events and theme-based and very public exhibitions and demonstrations that attract attention. Out of fear, Jewish students increasing gather in undisclosed locations to discuss counter strategies. Open events have been infiltrated by radical elements, who are allowed to enter in the name of free speech but who use such free speech rights to close down pro-Israel forums.

During the Second Intifada that Jewish Agency for Israel head Natan Sharansky, then deputy prime minister, realized how dire the situation on campuses was for Israel. *"The most important battleground for the future of the Jewish people is on the campuses,"* Sharansky said, and his team worked to come up with a plan to bolster their Israel engagement efforts on North American campuses.

At the height of the Gaza conflict, JAFI had already begun training its 2014 team of 66 campus Israel Fellows, which are based out of Hillel Houses on 111 campuses throughout North America. All the fellows completed army service and university study and signed on for up to two years on campuses where they aim to *"empower student leadership and create Israel-engaged campuses."*

The Israel Fellows program is the poster child for a successful JAFI-Hillel partnership on campuses. Recently this cooperation was given much more permanence and prominence with the establishment of a separate Israel Education and Engagement department.

Sharansky said the emphasis on Israel engagement is a direct about-face from Hillel International's stance during the Second Intifada. *"During the Second Intifada Hillel was doubtful if it would be good for them to have Israel activity. Today we are partners and practically every Hillel wants an Israel Fellow because they have realized we cannot keep people Jewish without a strong connection to Israel."*

Birthright-Israel Taglit agreed to give Hillel International a list of names and email contacts of former trip participants still on campuses. And Hillel has been in contact with them, trying to engage them, get them into Hillel for meals or social activities — and recruit them in the struggle against anti-Israel sentiment.

In merging all the Israel programs available from JAFI and Hillel on campuses, and at the same time leveraging human resources such as Birthright and Masa alum, a larger, smarter team that can utilize the expertise of both Hillel and JAFI professionals has been created.

StandWithUs in Israel, under the excellent leadership of Michael Dickson, runs an Israel Fellowship program on six of the major campuses throughout the country. StandWithUs trains Israeli university students who have completed their army service to become capable advocates for Israel. Chosen from over 2,000 applicants, StandWithUs Israel Fellows attend lectures by experts in academia, international affairs, public diplomacy, politics, and history, and they develop innovative programs that reach an increasingly wider audience worldwide. These young leaders represent the best and the brightest and are groomed to become Israel's future ambassadors and leaders. Graduates are placed in internships, where they become the *"human face"* behind the headlines as they speak about Israel and often end up in high-level positions in academia, government, business, medicine, and the media in Israel and abroad. After graduation, they form an alumni network and help recruit future applicants for the program. The StandWithUs Israel Fellowship is one of the most sought-after fellowship programs in Israel. It is endorsed by the Israeli Ministry of Foreign Affairs and the National Union of Israeli Students. Recently, they opened a new center in the heart of Jerusalem.

Over in the States, with a generous grant from Rita and Steve Emerson, the StandWithUs Emerson Fellowship is a prestigious one-year fellowship program that recruits, trains, educates, and inspires pro-Israel college students to become an elite cadre of leaders on college campuses across North America. StandWithUs Emerson Fellows form a network of trained pro-Israel student leaders, chosen from over 50 campuses, who utilize their skills and energy to drive and inspire their peers to run effective pro-Israel events and bring Israel's message to their campuses. Among their program responsibilities, fellows hold leadership positions within pro-Israel student groups, run four to six programs on their campuses throughout the year, write articles for local media outlets, and attend training seminars in Los Angeles, CA.

Meanwhile, a counter Jewish student movement calling itself *"Open Hillel"* is determined to deny Hillel International guidelines, by inviting contrary voices including journalist Peter Beinart, anti-Israel BDS supporting Judith Butler who thinks that Hamas and Hezbollah are social progressive movements, and executive director Rebecca Vilkomerson of Jewish Voice for Peace, a group that holds gruesome *"Die-In"* campus demonstrations in which students lie on the ground pretending to be dead Palestinians.

As such, Open Hillel are enablers, enabling those with an anti-Israel agenda to spread their influence into the realm of Jewish students while the base-groups that promote people like Butler and JVP refuse to allow pro-Israel proponents to have their say at their events. As such, this is a one-sided battle in which Jewish organizations like Open Hillel give ground instead of holding ground in an affirmative support for the Jewish state.

By inviting speakers hostile to Israel by using a Jewish identity they provide cover for vicious anti-Israel voices that may, for the occasion, paint a softer emotional tone to their hatred.

While Jewish groups like Open Hillel and JVP may talk about *"inclusiveness"* and *"nuance"* they invite the intolerant other, while demanding the Jewish community to tolerate pro-BDS groups and leading advocates for Israel's destruction, while many Open Hillel and JVP leaders are intolerant of pro-Israel voices that they dislike.

According to Holly Bicerano, who resigned as Open Hillel Campus Outreach Coordinator out of protest over what was going on within that group, disclosed, *"Open Hillel leaders decided—shamefully—to form a committee in order to address the issue of anti-normalization in Open Hillel. The anti-normalization campaign strives to end joint discussions and programs between Jews and Palestinians unless they subscribe to the BDS movement."*

Aiden Pink, writing in *The Tower*, had similar observations about Open Hillel. *"Open Hillel phrases their intentions in the context of a free and unfettered debate (hence "open"), their events, speakers and partners actually seem to be far more interested in institutionalizing a set of radical opinions—and browbeating the mainstream into accepting it: That far from being a lonely liberal democracy facing daunting challenges from without and within, Israel is actually an illegitimate, oppressive, colonial state that might be better off not existing; and that Jewish students cannot truly understand it without teaming up with extreme pro-Palestinian groups"*

Pink's impression, coming out of attending an Open Hillel conference, was, *"My clear sense at the conference was that they—rather than Hillel International—are the ones attempting to forcibly impose a monolithic discourse. And it is the promotion of this kind of discourse—*

disingenuous, postmodern, radical, and often hateful—that is one of the biggest threats facing the future of Jewish communal life."

Zack Stern, founder of JStreet Watch, asks, *"Should the Jewish student center welcome chants that call for the destruction of the Jewish state and individuals who justify terrorism? 'Open Hillel' thinks it should."*

In the *Arutz Sheva* article *"Open Hillel only advocates for anti-Semitism"* Stern opined that *"'Open Hillel' has a right to support whatever it wants, but it should not lie about its motives, 'Open Hillel' is nothing more than a group of students advocating for anti-Semitic messages at what is supposed to be a place where Jewish students can go to avoid an already (in many cases) anti-Semitic atmosphere on campus."*

The Jewish Agency, which already reaches 111 campuses throughout North America, has a huge backlog of dozens more that have requested urgent help. Cash-strapped Israeli and Jewish institutions are unable or unwilling to match the tsunami of anti-Israel activism on the campus.

Until the Israeli government and its various ministries really wake up to the fact that Israel is losing the war on the campus battleground the students will have to fight with their backs against the wall, out-gunned and out-numbered by a well-funded, well organized adversary determined to see the end of the Jewish state.

*

Palestinian sympathy eases Western guilt – but this is no reason to punish Israel.

When the conflict was Arab-Israeli wars it was too global a perspective for the West to dabble in corrective morality. At the time, however, it was bon ton for leftists and liberals to support Israel, a tiny nascent socialist state that had been attacked by five Arab armies. Israel was *"flavor of the month"* and roundly applauded for its spectacular military victories.

It was, I believe, the confluence of two significant factors that drove the Western elites, particularly the left-wing section of that constituency, to abandon the Jewish state and dump their post-colonialism, post-Holocaust guilty conscience on to Israel.

After repeated and embarrassing military defeats the Arabs began to promote Yasser Arafat as the leader of a new Palestinian movement. Adopting the name of Palestine as his cause, they allowed Arafat, the first modern-day Islamic arch-terrorist, to spearhead a Pan-Arabism targeting Israel as the epitome of the West that they hated. He was their terror proxy where conventional warfare had failed them.

Initially, Arafat saw himself as the champion of Pan-Arabism. He even went so far as to deny a Palestinian aim in his fight against Israel. In a 1970 interview with Italian journalist, Arianna Palazzi, he said, *"The question of borders doesn't interest us. Palestine is nothing but a drop in an enormous ocean. Our nation is the Arabic nation. The PLO is fighting Israel in the name of Pan- Arabism. What you call Jordan is nothing more than Palestine."*

What Arafat said was, and still is, factually, legally, and demographically true with the vast majority of people living in Jordan calling themselves *"Palestinians"*. The *"Palestinian people"* is an anthropological fabrication. This was admitted by Feisal Hussein after the Oslo Accords when he said that this cause was a *"Trojan Horse"* to conquer Israel.

Palestinism became the hook on which the Arabs, the Muslims, the radical left, and the European intellectual elite, hung their animus of anti-Western, anti-capitalist, anti-colonialist, all the *"anti's"* that fed off European guilt for their past history. One *"anti"* was anti-Semitism. The guilt attached to this was their anti-Semitism had been exposed by the atrocities that are an end product of this type of hatred. As such, it went dormant for decades, waiting to re-emerge as criticism of Israel and support for the Palestinian cause. It merged with the noisy actions of a well-funded, well-organized radical campaign. Triumphant from tactics employed to overthrow the white regime in South Africa, they adopted more of the same in their next experiment, namely the elimination of Israel.

At the same time, Israel turned away from the socialism of the Labour Party. It was a time to liberate and capitalize their economy, the success of which can be seen in the emergence of Israel as *"The Start Up Nation."* But the rejection of socialism was an anathema to the Western left, especially the more aggressive and radical wings who are tireless in plotting and planning a world in their image. They had by now added a *"human rights"* element to their argument. By craftily airbrushing out deeply felt Arab hatred of Jews, backed by Palestinian violence and terror that targeted citizens of the Jewish state, they sold a fraudulent picture of oppression when facts on the ground showed that Israel was acting in defense of its people against the assaults of a hateful enemy positioned just minutes away. Their arguments, however, were a soft sell to a shallow thinking public opinion whose knee jerk reaction is to support the perceived underdog.

Undoubtedly, Europe can boast peaceful open borders but, for all their enlightenment and intellectual superiority, they still suffer from a collective guilt conscience. Europe is still shackled to Nazi crimes. In a post-Holocaust era, they fashioned a doctrine designed to prevent further genocides. They failed in this noble mission. Massacres occur with alarming regularity. Not only have been unable to prevent them from happening, they have failed to stop them once they begin.

Decades later they misinterpret and misapply Geneva conventions to conflicts unrelated to the intentions of the original Geneva drafters. One prime example is the Israeli-Palestinian problem. Some use Geneva-talk. They finesse expressions such as *"occupation"* and *"illegal settlements"* when there is equal, perhaps better, legitimacy for a different Israeli opinion. *"Transfer of population into occupied territory"* is applied to Israel, but not to Turkey in Cyprus. *"International law"* is quoted where none exists.

Repeating a fallacy does not make it kosher no matter how many times the international community tells the lie. When Europeans construct false claims into an automatic denunciation of Israel they should remember that this is an artificial machination. No matter how hard they try to push it up the hill it will not fly. It is not built on fact or truth.

European guilt goes way beyond Auschwitz regrets. They have a stained history of colonization, exploitation, and oppression of foreign lands to live down. Third World poverty and starvation, past and present, can be laid at their, and America's, door. Their shame will not be redeemed by imposing their guilt factors into resolutions and sanctions that victimize Israel. Instead, they should stop their utopian altruism and false morality, or at least tether it to a realistic political policy that takes into account decades of Palestinian violence, terror, and incitement for a world without the Jewish state. It may take two to tango, but Israel and Palestinian Arabs may dance more harmoniously if the band leader played an honest tune.

Rushing a Palestinian state will not guarantee it to be the new democracy in the Middle East, no matter how hard they wish it to be true. On the contrary, steamrolling Israel underfoot will produce a rogue regime bent on its declared ambition to eliminate the Jewish state.

Middle East countries do not share the European mindset, not in morality, and not in democracy. The West must understand the mindset of the Arab and Muslim world before they impose their liberal, democratic, values on a region that has zero tolerance for such niceties. Forcing Israel, the only liberal democracy in the area, to behave European, while giving a free pass to a rejectionist, rigid, and intolerant adversary, is not the path to peace. It will be as useless and immoral as it has been with all the other genocides and massacres that have been perpetrated since the last Holocaust of the Jewish people.

Such a disaster will not swathe a Western guilt complex. On the contrary, such a mistake could lead the Jewish people into yet another ghetto from which they will be unable to effectively defend themselves.

This historic fate would have echoes of the past and only increase the guilt of a world that has always failed its Jews.

*

The lies they tell at Christmas.

The spirit of Christmas soured that cold, wet, winter of 2013 in London's Piccadilly. The bright festive scene of decorative trees and twinkling colored lights lit up the stores and arcades, but a malevolent shadow blanked out the entrance to St. James's Church. It took the form of a monstrous wall whose image spelt division and bias and a false narrative that ran counter to my understanding of the spirit of love and goodwill to all.

It took the false form of Israel's security barrier that keeps out murderous terrorists but was presented as Israeli oppression of Palestinian Arabs.

Palestinian leader, Yasser Arafat, had defied the Christian tradition in Bethlehem, which had been respected and upheld when under Israeli authority, by appointing a Muslim governor and engineered a Muslim takeover of the city council. He then put his stamp on this town by converting the Greek Orthodox monastery, next to the Church of the Nativity, into his official Bethlehem residence.

At great risk to his life, Pastor Naim Khoury, of the Bethlehem Baptists Church, exposed the developing threats to Christians within the territories controlled by the Palestinian Authority. *"People are always telling Christians to convert to Islam."*

His ministry is based on love and non-violence. He is also a strong advocate for Zionism based on God's land covenant with Israel through Abraham.

Because of his views, his church has been bombed fourteen times, and he has been shot three times. He has been threatened by the

Palestinian Authority to close the doors of his church which they consider as *"illegitimate."*

This brave Christian priest needs and deserves the active support of church leaders worldwide. Instead, they boycott him and pick on Israel for their wrath, ignoring the human rights crimes of the Palestinian leadership whom they openly support. How twisted is that?

Elias Freij, the Christian mayor of Bethlehem at the time of the Oslo Accords in 1993, warned Israeli Prime Minister, Yitzhak Rabin, to maintain control over his town. *"Bethlehem will become a town of churches devoid of Christians if you transfer control to the Palestinian Authority."*
Israel caved in to international pressure, and the mayor's warning became the current Christian nightmare.

The St. James's Church charade failed to mention the fear that pervades the shrinking Christian population. The fear of attack by Muslim Palestinians personified by Joseph Canawati whose sister, her husband, and three children have fled to America.

"I want to leave but nobody will buy my business. I feel trapped. We are isolated," he complained. The Piccadilly church leaders turn a deaf ear to his please.

Or the fear of death at the hands of non-Christian Palestinians in Bethlehem such as that felt by Jeriez Moussa Amaro whose two sisters, Rada aged 24 and Dunya aged 18, were gunned down by Muslims in their own home. Their crime was to be young, attractive, and wear Western clothes and no veil.

Sami Qumsieh, the general manager of *"The Nativity,"* the only Christian television station in Bethlehem, has received death threats and visits from armed gunmen. As he said, *"As Christians, we have no future here."*

How sad it is that St. James Church, the British Methodist Church, and many other Christian leaders are so blindsided in their pursuit of a perceived Jewish enemy that they fail to come to the rescue of, or campaign for, their co-religionists persecuted by those who they actively and expensively support.

If a section of Israel's security barrier has been built close to Bethlehem, it is there to hold back this dangerous Palestinian hatred and terror that has spilled out of Bethlehem and wreaked its death and violence on Israelis.

Since the Hamas takeover in Gaza, Christians have fled in droves from the Strip. Incited by Islamic calls for action, Muslim Palestinians murdered their Christian neighbors. One victim was Rami Ayad.

Rami Ayad, 31, was the manager of The Teacher's Bookshop, the only Christian bookstore in Gaza, operated by the Palestinian Bible Society. In addition to selling Bibles and Christian books, it offered computer classes and an Internet cafe. The bookstore was attacked several times.

Two months before the murder, a man entered the bookstore and asked Rami why he was not a Muslim.
"Because I believe in Jesus," Rami replied.
"I know how to make you become a Muslim," the man said, and left.

Two days before the murder, the taxi driver who took Rami home from the bookstore noticed that they were being followed by a car. It parked on the street outside his house, waited for Rami to get out of the taxi, and then drove away. Rami didn't recognize the driver, but he did note that he had a beard. On Saturday, he left the bookstore at four in the afternoon. Two hours later, he called his wife and told her that he might be late. That was the last time anyone heard from him. On the morning of the next day his body was found on a street in Gaza City, shot in the head and stabbed in the chest.

Ibrahim, Rami's brother, says, *"I want to find out who killed my brother, and then I will take my family and go away from here."*

The Palestinian Authority and Hamas have grafted Shariah Law into their Charters and constitution. In such an unwelcoming environment is it any wonder that Christians feel threatened and flee?

But once a year, at Christmas, the Palestinian leadership cynically trot out a deformed tale of Jesus for political and propaganda purposes. Their tale is not one of peace and goodwill to all men. Rather it is one of Jew-hatred achieved by hijacking the Christmas message and converting Christ into a Palestinian.

Disturbingly, those who persecute Christians are encouraged and supported by cliques of replacement theologists who become their *"useful idiots"* in a malevolent hate campaign against the Jewish state.

Christian replacement theologists have aligned themselves with Islamic replacement theologists. Both want to remove the Jewish presence in the land in favor of a Palestinian state in its place.

One example of where this ought to clash up against Christian origins is the stubborn pronouncements of Palestinian leaders that there never was a Jewish Temple on the Temple Mount in Jerusalem. This place is the central location of Jewish holy sovereignty in their ancient, and now modern, capital. This alone should cause Christian leaders and activists pause. Any Jew or Christian acknowledges that the Temple was a reality, not just a biblical fable. It shapes the foundation of both religions. Even Jews, who do not hold Jesus as a messiah, accept that Jesus made pilgrimages to Jerusalem and to the Jewish Temple to pray and to preach to the people outside of the holy center. He did so as a Jew, not as a Palestinian messenger. So why do they pursue a fraudulent Kairos Palestine Document while abandoning the Old Testament, which is the underpinning of their own faith? Take the British Methodists as a prime example of a faith that has lost its way.

British Methodists attempted to turn their anti-Israel boycott campaign into a consumer product questionnaire posing loaded questions that led selected receivers into giving anti-Israel answers.

In an article I wrote I questioned just how far the Methodists had strayed from the guiding principles of their founding fathers, John and Charles Wesley. These brothers deeply believed in the Old Testament commitment of the return of the Jews to the Holy Land. It was enshrined in several of their hymns;

"Oh that the chosen band might now their brethren bring
And gathered out of every land present to Zion's King.

Of all the ancient race not one be left behind
But each compelled by secret grace his way to Canaan find!

We know it must be done for God hath spoke the word
All Israel shall their Saviour own to their first state restored.

Rebuilt by His command Jerusalem shall rise
Her Temple on Moriah stand again, and touch the skies."

How far they have drifted from these sentiments to the dogma of today says more about the Methodists than it does about the Jewish state.

Since I wrote these words back in 2013 even more churches have been destroyed and Christians slaughtered and oppressed at the hands of Muslims in the Middle East, including in the Palestinian-controlled areas, and into Africa.

Israel is the one sure nation in which Christians can find refuge and the freedom to worship?

If Christians have a savior in the Middle East it is Israel.

Instead, Israel is demonized with lies among many Christian communities and charities.

In Ireland, the Palestinian Solidarity Campaign sold Christmas cards showing the Three Wise Men denied entry into Bethlehem by a security barrier. Another card featured a Madonna and Child draped in a Palestinian flag, thereby falsely politicizing the nativity scene.

In the UK, there were two public demonstrations outside churches, in Liverpool and in London, portraying a fraudulent message that brutalized Israel.

The Amos Trust distributed a *"Bethlehem pack"* to present churches and Christians with a warped perception of Bethlehem at their Christmas events. Of course, they failed to mention the flight of Christians from Bethlehem since Israel handed over control of this once Christian town to the Palestinian Authority. Since then the Christian population dropped from over 80% to less than 12%. Instead, they prefer to promote the Mahmoud Abbas version of the Christmas story. His message is that Jesus was a Palestinian.

"In Bethlehem, more than 2000 years ago, Jesus Christ was born, a Palestinian messenger who could become a guiding light for millions around the world. As we Palestinians strive for our freedom, two millennia later, we do our best to follow his example."

Ignoring the fact that Jesus was not a Palestinian messenger, what *"example"* of this *"Palestinian messenger"* are Palestinians following? Suicide bombers, rockets against civilians, knifings, kidnappings and murders, plane hijackings?

Abbas goes on, *"Our prayers are with the churches and mosques of Jerusalem which remind the world of the Arab identity of our occupied capital."*

Abbas speaks of churches and mosques, but what of synagogues and Jewish temples? He failed to mention them. No place in Abbas's manger for a Jew. The identity of Jerusalem was originally Jewish, but Abbas denies the Jewish Temple to which the Jewish Jesus came each year to pray. For Abbas it did not exist, tippexed out as he did to the Holocaust. To acknowledge this would be to acknowledge the true Jesus as a Jew who made his pilgrimage to the Jewish capital in Jerusalem on the Jewish holy days.

When was Jerusalem ever a Palestinian capital? Never!

In that statement, Mahmoud Abbas exposes that any Palestinian state will be *'Judenrein,'* clear of Jews because, according to Abbas, Jews have no history or heritage there. Is this the character of a *'Palestine'* that many Christian leaders support and work to achieve?

How elastic is the figure of Jesus. Christian usurers have bent and misshaped their savior until he is no longer recognizable.

It is amazing to me that certain strands of Christianity share and thrive of this falsehood.

As with the Methodists, hateful words and actions of church leaders say more about them that it does about Israel, the one nation in the Middle East where the Christian population has grown in numbers.

I wrote an open letter in response to a Catholic preacher, Stephen Pritchard, who endorsed an anti-Israel Christian exhibition in Liverpool and who refused to allow an Israeli Jewish perspective on this event;

"Someone sent me an email regarding the refusal of Stephen Pritchard to have an Israeli perspective on an exhibition in Liverpool that demonizes Israel's essential security barrier.

It is particularly hurtful and troubling that he does so during the Christmas period.

I am not a Christian. I am a Jewish Israeli, but I would have thought that any caring and practicing Christian would have adopted an open heart, especially at this spiritual time.

If you are able to bring my message to Mr. Pritchard and to others, it would be one of my role as the founder of the Netanya Terror Victims Organization, and my personal experiences of Palestinian terror, by helping the victims of those who have, and are still suffering from the handiwork of Palestinian terrorists in my hometown.

Pritchard may recall that Jesus, born on Christmas was a Jew that celebrated Passover. In Netanya, my small coastal town perched on the clifftops of the Mediterranean Sea, we experienced the horrendous Passover Massacre when a Palestinian suicide bomber entered the Park Hotel and destroyed the lives of people, including two Holocaust survivors, who had gathered to also celebrate the Jewish Passover.

We are located eight miles only from the Arab town of Tulkarm, a fifteen minute car ride from the main shopping mall that suffered two separate suicide bombings, one of which almost killed my wife.

These were just three of the many deadly attacks on innocent civilians perpetrated in my hometown by the Palestinians from locations under Palestinian-control that Prichard promotes.

Tulkarm became a hotbed of Palestinian terror. Netanya lost over fifty of its citizens to their murderous attacks. More than three hundred others suffered physical and psychological damage.

That was when Israel decided to build a security barrier. Since the erection of that fence no one in my town has been killed or injured by Palestinian terrorists.

So, to have Pritchard promote the notion that our life-saving barrier is somehow a brutal act is shamefully wrong, and to have Pritchard refuse to hear the Israeli truth is troubling.

I ask the question, what is it in Pritchard that he will not allow the voice of truth to filter into his public event? I leave his conscience to answer.

May I wish reasonable and open-minded Christians a very Happy Christmas, and may people like Pritchard use this season to do some much needed soul searching."

*

In the name of Mohammed.

The greatest threat to Jews today comes not from Nazis or Communists but from an Islam that has remained what it was in the days of Mohammed.

When Jews are targeted and killed in the name of Islam, and in the name of Mohammed, no American president can convince us we are not really being slaughtered in the name of that religion.

We Jews have long memories, memories of persecution and massacre, massacres like the beheading of eight hundred Jews by Mohammed himself after his conquest of Medina.

The fact that the Qurayza Jews had not participated in the battle of Medina did not prevent the "prophet of peace" from taking pleasure in their slaughter. This was his trophy prize and a way of paying his jihadists with sex slaves and property.

Mohammed had the Jews brought in batches to a dug trench where he sat with Aisha, his 12 year old sex bride. When one woman went crazy from witnessing the slaughter, Aisha wrote,

"I will not forget that she was laughing extremely although she knew that she would be killed." (Abu Dawud 2665).

Boys as young as thirteen were beheaded if they had reached their puberty. The Muslims ordered them to drop their pants and if they had pubic hairs they had their throats cut (Abu Dawud 4390).

The estimate of the number of Jews beheaded at Medina range from 400 to 900. The girls and women were given to Mohammed's men for sexual pleasure or servitude. The Jews did not have weapons, but their properties and chattels were divided out and some of their women were sold as slaves in the market.

If all this sounds frightening familiar, given the horrors of Islamic State, it is because they are reliving the source of Mohammed and Islam.

Just as Islamic State spread from country to country so did Islam. The following year, Mohammed won the battle for Khaibar. The Jews there, knowing of the fate of their brethren in Medina, fought hard but when Khaibar fell they were slaughtered or sold into slavery.

The cries of *"Jews! Jews! Remember Khaibar!"* still ring out on the streets of Europe and Miami as a warning that Islamic anti-Semitism is alive and killing today.

The Jews of the Arabian Peninsula were prosperous and influential due to their diligence.

An Islamic scholar, Alfred Guillaume recorded, *"The prosperity of the Jews was due to their superior knowledge of agriculture and irrigation and their energy and industry. Homeless [Jewish] refugees in the course of a few generations became large landowners in the country, [the* refugees who had come to the Hijaz when the Romans conquered Palestine] controllers of its finance and trade.... Thus it can readily be seen that Jewish prosperity was a challenge to the Arabs, particularly the Quraysh at Mecca and ... [other Arab tribes] at Medina."

Influence did not prevent their slaughter. Diligence and ingenuity are useless unless supported by a strong defense and security. Jews must never let themselves be deceived, as they were with entreaties from Mohammed before the battle of Khaibar. Israel must not let its guard down for a non-promise of peace and recognition.

In short, when Jews condemn those who kill in the name of Mohammed, do not call us Islamophobes, for we know from whence we speak.

*

In 2013, Saudi Arabia donated ten million dollars each to the universities of Harvard and Georgetown to advance Islamic studies and general understanding of the Muslim world. These donations clearly have strings attached.

Qatar, a prime supporter and financier of the Hamas terror organization, donated $14.8 million to the Brookings Institute in 2013 where Martin Indyk is their Middle East expert. Does this influence Indyk's position on Israel which has been highly critical in recent times?

On the other hand, Rudy Giuliani, mayor of New York during 9/11 firmly rejected a ten million dollar gift from the same Saudi donor because it was conditional on him and the United States *"adopting a more balanced stance toward the Palestinian case."*

Giuliani continues to hold a strong pro-Israel view as he sees the dangers to Israel from regimes wallowing in oil and money but lacking in the liberal democratic values of the Jewish state.

There can be no doubt that the money to universities and think tanks from the Islamic world is in direct proportion to the detrimental teachings and policy statements coming out of these institutes that are increasingly anti-Israel.

*

ADDITIONAL INSIGHTS INTO FIGHTING HAMAS.

France: Importing conflict from, and exporting problems to, the Middle East.

It came as a surprise for Israel's leadership that at the UN Security Council, France voted in favor of Palestinian statehood. This was contrary to the positions held by the United States, Australia and Great Britain.

The French vote should primarily be seen as one more gesture made toward its Muslim population: Muslims massively supported the candidacy of François Hollande in the 2012 French presidential elections.

The French vote at the UN is a small part of far larger and more complex processes occurring in France and elsewhere within Europe. On Bastille Day, July 14, 2014, while Operation Protective Edge was taking place, Hollande announced that the Israeli-Palestinian conflict would not be imported [to France.] The previous day French Prime Minister Manuel Valls had already stated that France would never tolerate having the Israeli-Palestinian conflict imported to French soil, via verbal violence or actions. The main reason behind these repeated declarations was the slate of attacks on French synagogues and other Jewish targets by Muslims.

These statements distorted the French reality. Hollande and Valls should have said something more truthful, to the effect of, *"We will not let the Muslim aggressions against the Jews continue. French anti-Semitism in 2014 was even more severe and more prevalent than in previous years. The attacks on the synagogues were, yet again, extreme acts of violence by Muslims against Jews and Jewish targets in France."*

The local anti-Semitic incidents largely began to manifest after the year 2000, almost immediately after the beginning of the second intifada.

Before that, some Middle Eastern Muslims had already made their intentions known. In Paris in 1982, for instance, at the Jewish-owned kosher-style Goldenberg restaurant, six people were killed, most probably by the Arab Abu Nidal group.

The remarks of Hollande and Valls regarding *"importing the conflict"* implied that the two so-called French *"proxies"* of the Palestinian-Israeli conflict, namely, Muslim immigrants and French Jews, were fighting each other. This is not the case.

For the past 14 years there has only been unilateral aggression, with most violence coming from one distinct direction: Muslims. Well before the start of the Protective Edge campaign, Sammy Ghozlan, the president of the National Bureau for Vigilance against Anti-Semitism in France, was quoted as saying that the vast majority of physical attacks in France against Jews are committed by Muslims.

The *"import"* of the Middle East conflict and the ensuing increase of anti-Semitism in France had already commenced much earlier. The potential for Muslim aggression against the Jews was already present the moment France allowed millions of Muslims to immigrate, unselectively. A 2014 Anti-Defamation League study showed that Algeria, Tunisia and Morocco are among the 10 countries with the highest percentage of anti-Semites in the world. Immigrants from these countries brought their culture with them to France, and for some of them, that included their anti-Semitism. Polls confirm the disproportionately large level of anti-Semitism among French Muslims as compared to the general population.

The Jews were the first and foremost targets of the aggressors, but certainly not the only ones. By the autumn of 2005, major violent disruptions and acts of vandalism had broken out all over France. The rioters were either all Muslim or almost all Muslims. Hooligans and criminals of North and West African descent destroyed not only thousands of cars, but also large amounts of other public and private property.

These disturbances had nothing to do with either the Palestinian-Israeli conflict or with any Muslim-Arab identification with the Palestinians.

The riots were anti-French in nature, did not focus particularly on the Jews, and were a result of an immigration policy which France should have never allowed. The size of the immigrant population alone could have easily indicated to the various governments that France could not possibly integrate them into French society.

The issue of importing conflicts however, is much wider than France.

The massive immigration from Arab and Muslim countries has brought about increased and more extreme anti-Semitism in many other Western European nations. Not only is the number of anti-Semitic incidents in which Muslims are involved disproportionately larger than the percentage of those involving the local population, but the most severe of such incidents are often perpetrated by Muslims.

Another social ill imported with part of the immigrant population is the marked tension between various groups of immigrants and between immigrants and native populations within several countries. For example, in 2007 in Doetinchem, the Netherlands, all-night violence broke out between dozens of Kurds and Turks.

In July 2014, there was a pro-Islamic State demonstration in The Hague.

In October 2014, 60-70 Kurdish protesters occupied part of the Dutch Parliament in The Hague, demanding international action to defend the Syrian town of Kobane against IS fighters.

The main country of conflict nowadays, however, seems to be Germany.

Along with the support for Islamic State among some German Muslims also came protests against this terrorist group, particularly by Yazidi and Kurdish immigrant groups in Germany, who were acting in solidarity with their home communities. In August 2014 in Herford, Germany, 300 Yazidi immigrants from Syria and Iraq protested Islamic State actions against their communities. During the demonstration they were attacked by pro-IS supporters. Earlier in the day, a Yazidi restaurant owner and a 16-year old were attacked and wounded by Islamic State supporters for displaying a poster advertising the anti-Islamic State demonstration. There were also over the years conflicts in asylum centers between Christians and Muslims.

In October 2014 there were violent clashes in the German cities of Celle and Hamburg. In Celle there were also clashes between Yazidi and Chechen Muslim immigrants. In Hamburg, an initially peaceful protest by Kurdish immigrants turned violent when Salafist Muslims confronted them.

In addition, certain German extremists have joined the *"imported battle."* They demonstrate under the banner *"Hooligans against Salafists."*

In the absence of Salafist demonstrations, they confront the police in the meantime. This was the case when 4,000 football fans and members of a neo-Nazi organization confronted police, causing major riots in Cologne, Germany. The authorities faced great difficulties in containing the situation.

All this, however, pales in comparison to current reactions to German immigration. A new group called Pegida, *(Patriotic Europeans against the Islamization of the West)* marched against Muslim immigration and against having public funds support immigrants in the town of Dresden. Only a minority of the over 15,000 Pegida supporters there were neo-Nazis. The remainders were ordinary citizens.

What can one conclude from all of this? Once again, the Jews were the first to suffer, this time from Europe's unselective immigration policies. Yet now the negative consequences of unselective Muslim immigration have assumed completely different dimensions.

And as far as the recent French UN vote and France's political stance are concerned, the French authorities may give futile excuses for the way they voted. The prime reason, however, is related to the massive number of unselectively imported Muslims in France. In order to please them, the current French government is supporting the establishment of a Palestinian state, and thus exporting its domestic problems to the already much-troubled Middle East.

Manfred Gerstenfeld is the former Chairman of the Jerusalem Center for Public Affairs and recipient of the Lifetime Achievement Award of the Journal for the Study of Anti-Semitism.

The next two articles are from the pen of Martin Sherman...

The Arabs' war against the Jews: Root causes & red herrings

"Our forces are now entirely ready not only to repulse any aggression, but to initiate it ourselves, and to destroy the Zionist presence in the Arab homeland of Palestine. The Syrian army, with its finger on the trigger, is united. I believe the time has come to begin a battle of annihilation."
– Hafez Assad, then Syrian defense minister, later president, May 20, 1967.

"We will not accept any... coexistence with Israel. The existence of Israel is in itself an aggression...against the Palestinian people." – **Gamal Abdel Nasser, President of Egypt, to the international media, May 28, 1967.**

"The existence of Israel is an error which must be rectified. This is our opportunity to wipe out the ignominy which has been with us since 1948. Our goal is clear – to wipe Israel off the map."
– Abdul Rahman Arif, President of Iraq, May 31, 1967.

The Arabs have been waging war against the Jews and their presence in the Land of Israel for over a hundred years; they have been waging war against the Jewish political sovereignty for almost seven decades.

The war has ebbed and flowed over the years, but as I have pointed out in recent columns, we are entering a new, and particularly menacing, phase of ongoing Arab aggression aimed at the annihilation of the Jews and their nation-state. Rabbi Shmuley Boteach wrote... *"It's open season on the Jews of Israel."*

Diagnosing root causes & red herrings.

If the Jews are to prevail in this brutal assault to drive them out of their ancestral homeland, if they are to preserve their national independence, it is essential that they diagnose the true reasons for Arab aggression, and distinguish misleading red herrings from real root causes.

After all, if the diagnosis is flawed, the prescription for remedy will be similarly flawed – even fatally so.

Sadly, if we judge by the tenor of public discourse in Israel today, there is little ground for optimism.

One senior public figure after another – not only on the Left of the political spectrum – have come out with declarations that have ranged from regrettably inappropriate, through hopelessly unfounded, to dangerously counter-productive.

From the President Reuven Rivlin to veteran Police Chief, Yohanan Danino, statements explicitly alleging or insinuating that the Jews' own conduct – such as exercising their right of access to religious sites or legislative initiatives to codify in law the values reflected in the Declaration of Independence – precipitated, or at least, exacerbated, recent Arab butchery of innocent Jews in the streets, on the roads, inside synagogues, and at building sites across the country.

Apart from a resurgence of a shtetl mentality that Zionism was supposed to eradicate, such unfortunate proclamations reek of the *"soft racism"* of low expectations for the Arabs, and a craven desire to avoid upsetting non-Jews that is dangerously detrimental. These personages hopelessly conflate red herrings with root causes – and in so doing, promote misguided policies and foster the very problems they mean to contain.

What the Jews are, not what they do.

Only the moronic or the malevolent could seriously contend that Arab animosity toward the Jews is a result of anything the Jews do.

No matter what the Jews do, they are assailed for what they don't; and no matter what they don't do, they are assailed for what they do. If they do not concede to Arab demands, they are accused of being intransigent. If they make far-reaching concessions, they are berated for those not made.

As the introductory excerpts show, Arabs harbor a burning Judeophobic hatred, and a blatant Judeocidal desire to annihilate the Jewish state infuses the entire Arab world – from Iraq through Syria to Egypt. This obdurate enmity had nothing to do with the policies of the Jewish state, but with its very existence.

For these bellicose proclamations all predate the 1967 Six Day war. They were all made before any Jewish presence in Judea-Samaria (a.k.a. the "West Bank"); before *"occupation"* and *"settlements"* – the perennial buzzwords for rallying anti-Israeli sentiment – had any practical relevance or conceptual significance.

It was before there was any access for Jews on the Temple Mount, or any legislative initiative to declare Israel a *"Jewish state."* It was a time when Jewish holy sites in the Jordanian-controlled *"West Bank"* were desecrated, made into public urinals or converted into goat sheds; when Jewish cemeteries were defiled and Jewish gravestones uprooted to be used as construction materials; when, under the Hashemite monarchy, Jordanian snipers lurked atop the walls of Jerusalem's Old City, randomly picking off civilians going about their business on the Israeli-controlled western side of the city.

The mortal sin of existence.

Yet despite this, on March 8, 1965, fully two years before the outbreak of the 1967 war (!), long before Israel controlled a square inch of territory now claimed as *"Palestine,"* long before any *"radical right-wing rabbi"* could offend Arab sensibilities or ignite Arab rage with *"rabid religious rhetoric,"* Egyptian president Gamal Abdel Nasser laid out the Arabs' bloodcurdling objective: *"We shall not enter Palestine with its soil covered in sand, we shall enter it with its soil saturated in blood."*

Not to be outdone in the expression of sheer savagery, Yasser Arafat's predecessor as PLO chairman, Ahmad Shukeiri, crowed in a somewhat premature expression of triumph, a few days before the crushing Arab defeat: *"The Arabs... will not flinch from the war of liberation...This is a fight for the homeland – it is either us or the Israelis. There is no middle road... We shall destroy Israel and its inhabitants and as for the survivors – if there are any – the boats are ready to deport them."*

It is clear, therefore, that the Arabs cannot countenance Jewish existence itself – or at least, the existence of a sovereign Jewish political entity. They unequivocally state and actively strive to fulfill their stated intention: *"The* [very] *existence of Israel is in itself an aggression;* they *"will not accept any... coexistence with Israel"* since *"the existence of Israel is an error which must be rectified."*

'The establishment of the state of Israel is entirely illegal'.

The same implacable refusal to accept any form of Jewish national independence is clearly reflected in the founding documents of all Palestinian political organizations.

Thus, Fatah's constitution declares its goal to be the total *"eradication of Zionist economic, political, military and cultural existence,"* which it pledges to achieve by *"armed struggle*[which] *will not cease unless the Zionist state is demolished"*; the Hamas Charter candidly asserts: *"Israel, by virtue of its being Jewish and of having a Jewish population, defies Islam and the Muslims,"* cautioning that the Day of Redemption will not come *"until Muslims fight the Jews* (and kill them); *until the Jews hide behind rocks and trees, which will cry: O Muslim! there is a Jew hiding behind me, come on and kill him*; while the Palestinian National Covenant declares: *"The partition of Palestine in 1947 and the establishment of the state of Israel are entirely illegal, regardless of the passage of time,"* denying that *"Jews constitute a single nation with an identity of its own,"* since *"Judaism" is not an independent nationality."*

But this adamant inflexibility is by no means confined to documents alone. It epitomizes the unequivocal positions of the current leadership of the Palestinian-Arabs – including the allegedly moderate Mahmoud Abbas and his PLO.

Breathtaking duplicity and double standards.

The PLO's response to the proposed *"Jewish state"* legislation (*The Jerusalem Post*, November 25, 2014) should be extremely edifying for anyone at all open to being edified.

According to the PLO, the bill *"is a racist political decision to complete the theft of Palestinian land and rights,"* and *"the so-called historic homeland of the Jewish people is a racist and ideologically exclusionary attempt to obscure the Palestinian historic narrative and abolish Palestinian existence."*

With a breathtaking display of hypocrisy and double standards, Abbas, who has unabashedly and consistently proclaimed that any Palestinian state must be entirely Judenrein, had the temerity to declare that the initiative to codify Israel's status as a Jewish state in law *"places obstacles in the way to achieving peace."*

There you have it. The prospect of a Jewish state is a racist obstacle to achieving peace on the basis of the two-states-for-two-peoples principle, but the exclusion of all Jews from a Palestinian one, is not? Hmmm.

It is against this background of uncompromising rejection by Abbas and the PLO of any permanent acceptance of, or possible reconciliation with, some arrangement that would allow the Jews national sovereignty in land the Arabs perceive as theirs, that Israel's policy options should be evaluated.

Corroborating breaking news.

The Arabs' war against the Jews has taken on many forms and configurations. When one method proved ineffective, another was adopted – fedayeen insurgency, conventional warfare, terrorist attacks, suicide bombings, rockets and missiles at civilian targets.

All were tried. All failed to bring about the demise of the Jewish nation-state. We are entering a new phase: Ideological incitement to provoke individuals, or small unorganized groups, to commit acts of slaughter, and to foster insurrection among Arabs with Israeli citizenship.

But before considering how this should be dealt with, one must grasp that none of the manifestations of Arab endeavor to eliminate the Jewish state were a result of provocation on the part of the Jews – not *"occupation"* (there was no *"occupation"* prior to 1967), not settlements (there are no settlements in Gaza), not Jewish access to the Temple Mount, not any legislative initiative to declare Israel what it is – a Jewish state. Rather, they are all rooted in the abiding hostility and hatred that Arabs harbor for the Jews, or, at least, for Jewish sovereignty.

And consistent with this, breaking news came while this column was being composed of a massive terrorist plot, initiated from Hamas headquarters in Turkey that was uncovered and thwarted by the security services.

The Post reported that the terrorists planned massive attacks against Jerusalem's main Teddy soccer stadium, the capital's light rail system, car bombings, and kidnappings of Israelis in the West Bank and elsewhere.

Significantly, the terror network began operating at the end of August 2014 – well before MK Moshe Feiglin's visits to the Temple Mount or MKs Yariv Levin and Ayelet Shaked submitted their proposal (based on former Kadima MK Avi Dichter's initiative) for *"Jewish state"* legislation.

None of those are the real reason for Arab violence against Jews – only opportunistic excuses, sadly endorsed by many Jews.

Ruthless resolve, not reticent restraint.

The Arabs cannot be appeased or placated into abandoning their quest to eradicate Jewish national sovereignty. Each gesture of conciliation will only fuel further demands for additional such gestures.

They can only be deterred from pursuing their design, or – should deterrence fail – be defeated in doing so. Anything else is a dangerous delusion, which will result in tragedy.

Tough measures – punitive and preemptive – are called for. Arab communities must be saturated with intelligence collection efforts – whether conducive, consensual or coercive.

Challenges to Jewish sovereignty must be met with stiff penalties, including deportation and loss of citizenship/residency for offenders and their dependents. The Jews must convey an unambiguous message to the Arabs – on both sides of the Green Line – that they will not brook any challenge, domestic or foreign, from within its borders or from without, to their national sovereignty and political independence.

Unless the Jews convey the unequivocal message that any such challenges will be met with overwhelming force, they will increasingly be the victims of such force at the hands of their Arab adversaries. There may be those who find this prescription excessively harsh.

Sadly, the only way the Jews can avoid living permanently by the sword is to convey convincingly to the Arabs that they have the resolve to do so. I invite everyone to consider the alternative.

Only Arab despair can bring any hope for peace.

Something rotten in the state of Denmark?

"Something is rotten in the state of Denmark." – William Shakespeare, Hamlet, Act 1, Scene 4,

"Israel should insist that we discriminate [against it], that we apply double standards [to it], this is because you are one of us." – Jesper Vahr, Danish ambassador to Israel, at The Jerusalem Post Diplomatic Conference on December 12, 2014.

"The difference between stupidity and genius is that genius has its limits." – Albert Einstein.

The Jerusalem Post Diplomatic Conference took place in Israel's capital with an impressive lineup of prominent public figures – including the present and the previous presidents and the US ambassador.

The real fireworks, however, took place in the panel discussion dealing with relations between the EU and Israel.

Ignorant buffoon or disingenuous bigot?

The furor was set off by an inane remark by Denmark's ambassador, Jesper Vahr, who in the space of a few short minutes managed to bring discredit to himself, his country and its diplomatic service, and to reveal himself to be either an ignorant buffoon or a disingenuous bigot. I imagine some unkinder souls might hold that the two (buffoon and bigot) are not necessarily mutually exclusive.

In response to allegations that Israel was being treated unfairly by the EU, Vahr eagerly rushed to confirm them, and proffered a startling *"rationale"* (for want of a better word) for why Israel should warmly endorse this openly confessed European bias. He declared: *"There is the allegation that Europe is applying double standards, discriminating. Let make this point. I think Israel should insist that we discriminate [against] you; that we apply double standards."*

According to Vahr, Israel should embrace this bias *"because you are one of us."*

Referring to events in the other Mideast countries and the values they reflect, the Nordic envoy informed us that *"those are not the standards that you are being judged by. It is not the standards that Israel would want to be judged by. So I think you have the right to insist that we apply double standards – put you on the same standard in the European context."*

Soft bigotry of low expectations.

In response to this barefaced display of European arrogance and blatant bigotry of low expectations, the discussion moderator, The Jerusalem Post's Herb Keinon, asked, with perhaps more courtesy than was called for: *"But isn't it kind of patronizing to Palestinians to say we hold Israel to a higher standard than we hold you?"*

Vahr's less-than-convincing reply was that Israel was the much stronger party in the conflict with the Palestinians and hence it was only natural that Europe engage *"our long standing partner* [Israel] *in a different fashion than we engage others."*

This position is manifestly absurd – on a number of levels.

First, there seems no way to interpret it other than condoning weakness as a license – or at least, an excuse – for moral depravity, or at least moral inferiority, regardless of the merits of the case of the stronger party, or the lack thereof of the weaker party.

Infuriating hypocrisy.

In the case of Israel, this attitude is particularly infuriating and hypocritical.

For over the last two decades, Israel has made gut-wrenching concessions to the Palestinians. Invariably, the justification for these concessions has been presented as Israel's overwhelming strength, which could be brought to bear, should those concessions be exploited against it by the Palestinians. Yet, when those concessions have been exploited, and Israel has been compelled to use its strength to redress the situation, it has been excoriated for the use of *"disproportionate force"* – despite the fact that it was precisely that very preponderance (i.e. *"disproportionality"*) of force that was invoked as the reason for making the concessions in the first place.

Perversely, instead of Israel's strength being a restraint against Palestinians excesses, it is presented as the justification for tolerating those excesses.

But the self-righteous hypocrisy goes even deeper.

Instead of what one might have expected, i.e. that an allegedly like-minded Europe would rally round Israel, as one of its own, besieged by a sea of animosity, Europe is mobilizing to impose the will of Israel's tyrannical, Judeophobic foes on it – despite the fact that their societies reflect the diametric negation of values the EU purports to cherish.

Rather than trying to propagate the values it claims to represent, Europe is blatantly threatening to advance their negation. Instead of supporting those who uphold common values, Europe is threatening to beleaguer those who do.

Impudence and arrogance.

But beyond the hypocrisy, European censure of Israel radiates a misplaced impudence and arrogance.

As Nathan Gelbart, head of Keren Hayesod Germany, who also participated in the discussion, remarked: It is easy for us Europeans to give Israel advice, having neighbors like Belgium, Luxembourg and San Merino...or even Denmark.

As painfully obvious as this might seem, its significance is lost on many. After all, for Israel, it is not only a matter of being judged by a divergent set of values, not applied to its adversarial neighbors. It is also a matter of being subjected to the divergent values of those adversaries.

But fairness and decency require Israel's responses not only be judged by the values expected of it, but in view of the values of its adversaries, to which it is subjected and with which it has to contend to ensure its security and survival.

Policies that may well be appropriate/effective in contending with adversaries who share *"European values"* may well be hopelessly – even, perilously – inappropriate/ ineffective in contending with adversaries who do not.

In this regard, Western democracies have allowed themselves far more moral latitude than they apparently deem appropriate for the Jewish state – even when they have been called upon to contend with threats far more remote and far less menacing to their survival/ security than Israel is facing. But more on that in a moment.

Not a double, but a singular, Israel-only, standard.

Ambassador Vahr's remarks elicited a robust response from my colleague, the Post's Caroline Glick.

With an understandable burst of righteous rage, she resoundingly rebutted the ill-conceived concoction of allegations-cum-clarifications-cum-apologetics the hapless Danish envoy offered as the European position on the conflict.

But perhaps the most telling point she made was that Israel was not being judged by double standards, but by a singular standard that no other nation on the planet is expected to live up to.

The point is not that Israel is being judged by criteria different to those applied to the gory tyrannies that abound in the region; it is that Israel is being judged by standards different to those that Western democracies, and the EU, judge themselves.

No other nation on earth is called on to show such understanding for its sworn enemies, to display such largesse toward the demands of those openly dedicated to its destruction, to exercise such restraint against those overtly committed to its demise, to expose it children to such risk to satisfy the will of foes who, time after time, have proven they cannot be trusted.

Holding Israel to such standards is not holding it to double standards, but, as Glick correctly points out, to a singular – Jews-only – standard.

Stone throwing residents of glass houses?

After all, Israel has been harshly condemned for inflicting undue civilian casualties, the use of *"disproportionate force,"* the quarantine of Gaza, the interception of vessels such as the Mavi Marmara.

However, even setting aside for the massive destruction inflicted on the civilian populations of the Axis powers by the Allies in WWII, there seems little room for the West to sanctimoniously pontificate to Israel.

Indeed, in recent decades, the West, including nations comprising NATO, has responded militarily to situations in the Balkans, Afghanistan, and Iraq far more harshly than Israel has, even when the threat to its own domestic populations has been far less tangible than those menacing Israeli civilians.

Yet, although the forces of Western democracies have, in far-flung theaters, thousands of kilometers, from their homelands, inflicted vast numbers of civilian casualties, engaged in massively disproportional responses, imposed far more punishing embargoes, conducted far more *"non-compliant boarding"* of vessels in international waters, they have never been subject to the same degree of censure – and certainly not been threatened with sanctions – as Israel has.

It seems it is only the Jews who are called upon to adhere to standards and impose constraints on their freedom to defend themselves that are far more stringent than those observed, not by the brutal regimes of the Mideast, but by the liberal *"European-compliant"* regimes of the West.

NATO in the Balkans.

During early 1999, in the Balkans, in just under 80 days of intensive, high-altitude – some would say, indiscriminate, but certainly imprecise – bombing by NATO forces, including the use of cluster bombs, inflicted hundreds of civilian Serbian casualties. Serbian estimates are 2,500 dead. NATO bombs hit hospitals, old-age homes, market places, schools, passenger trains on bridges, buses cut in half while crossing ravines, and convoys of fleeing refugees – all this in a military campaign during which not one single civilian in a single NATO nation was ever threatened by Serbian action.

When questioned on the issue of civilian casualties, then-NATO spokesman Jamie Shea stated: *"There is always a cost to defeat an evil. It never comes free, unfortunately. But the cost of failure to defeat a great evil is far higher."* Sounding like a carbon copy of IDF spokespeople explaining Israeli action in Gaza, he insisted that NATO planes bombed only *"legitimate designated military targets"*; and if civilians died it was because NATO had been forced into military action.

Adamant that *"we try to do our utmost to ensure that if there are civilians around, we do not attack,"* Shea emphasized that *"NATO does not target civilians... let's be perfectly clear about that."*

In contrast to the thousands of civilians killed or wounded, the hundreds of thousands of civilians displaced and the tens of thousands civilian homes destroyed, there were fewer than 700 deaths reported among Serbian military personal. No NATO combat casualties were reported.

Disproportionality anyone?

'...that's more children than died in Hiroshima.'

In Afghanistan, where military action was undertaken in 2001, in response to a single terrorist attack, on a single NATO member, precise estimates of civilian deaths are difficult to come by. Most assessments, however, put civilian deaths at more than 20,000.

To give a sense of comparative *"proportionality"* of responses, relative to Israel's population size, the number of fatalities incurred by the US in the 9/11 attacks would be barely equivalent to fatalities Israel incurred in two of the almost 200 suicide attacks it suffered in the bloody days of the 2000-2005 second intifada.

In Iraq, the number of recorded civilian deaths since the 2003-invasion due to direct war-related violence is approaching 150,000, in a military campaign which was launched without any overt aggression being directed against the US or its citizens.

But prior to the 2003 armed strike against Saddam Hussein, a crippling US-led UN embargo was enforced against Iraq – far more destructive than the quarantine placed on the terrorist enclave of Gaza. To gauge the devastating effect this had on Iraqi civilians, consider the following chilling extract from a Leslie Stahl interview on 60 Minutes (May 12, 1996) with Madeleine Albright, then-US ambassador to the UN, later secretary of state in the Clinton administration, on the effect the sanctions were having on the Iraqi population: Stahl: *"We have heard that a half-million children have died. I mean, that's more children than died in Hiroshima.... Is the price worth it?"* Albright: *"I think this is a very hard choice, but... we think the price is worth it."*

Now imagine if an Israeli politician had displayed such callousness...

Breaking news – Hamas off terror list.

The General Court of the European Union in Luxembourg accepted a petition by Hamas to have itself removed from the EU's list of terrorist organizations.

In light of this, how lame the words of Italian ambassador to Israel, Francesco Maria Talo, seem, when toward the end of the Jerusalem Post Diplomatic Conference debate, he appealed: *"Please don't say we are helping terrorists. We want to avoid... help[ing] terrorists; there are rules within our countries to avoid this so we are sticking to international law."*

Really, Mr. Ambassador?

Martin Sherman is the founder and executive director of the Israel Institute for Strategic Studies. He is a regular contributor to the Jerusalem Post opinion column.

International condemnations: Nu, so what.

On January 19, 2015, the European Parliament proclaimed its support for recognizing Palestinian statehood.

So did the parliament of Luxembourg. (Previously it was the Portuguese, French and Swedish legislatures.) Simultaneously, the High Contracting Parties of the Fourth Geneva Convention gathered in Switzerland to condemn Israel – only the third time the signatories have met since 1949, and each time only to deal with Israel. And the EU court removed Hamas from the European list of terrorist organizations.

Now the Security Council is about to take up a Palestinian resolution demanding Israeli withdrawal from the West Bank within two years, or else. Secretary of State John Kerry has declined to say that the US will veto this.

Left-wing pundits and politicians are in a tizzy, warning that these initiatives should set off *"loud alarm bells"* in Jerusalem. It's a diplomatic tsunami, they say. And I say: Nu, so what! So they condemn us. So they *"recognize"* make-believe Palestinian statehood. Nu, so what! We've been there before. Israel will get past this round of condemnations too.

Israel and the Jewish world fret far too much about vacuous resolutions that ceremoniously pronounce upon Palestinian political rights. We need to remind ourselves of Prime Minister David Ben-Gurion's mordant dismissal of international opinion and institutions. *"Ooom, shmoom,"* was his scornful ditty, which is a play on words using the UN's Hebrew acronym, and Israeli slang for nullity.

The *"Ooom"* (UN) is *"shmoom"* (insignificant).

Ben-Gurion then added that what counts is what the Jews do, not what the goyim say.

What counts is Aliya, the Israeli birth rate, building starts in Jerusalem, the strength of our military, the tone and tenor of our educational, cultural and legal institutions, the Jewish and democratic fabric of our society, the depth of our belief and loyalty to Jewish and Zionist principles. That's what really counts.

Everything else – our foreign and diplomatic relations and our standing in the international community – will fall into place if we Israelis are united and confident in our creed.

Having said that, it is obvious to any sane Israeli citizen or statesman that Israel need not needlessly provoke the world into outrage, nor spurn the importance of maintaining decent ties with the governments in Washington, Ottawa, London, Paris, Bonn, Moscow and more. It's not comfortable to be in this situation. You can't deny that the cumulative weight of all these unfriendly resolutions is corrosive to Israel's standing.

Thus Israel cannot callously dismiss international opinion. *"Ooom shmoom"* should not be Israel's approach. But Israel also needn't obsess with worry over recent developments. It shouldn't go running to hide in panic because a few foreign parliaments lent their hand to Mahmoud Abbas's campaign to shift the Israeli-Palestinian conflict from the negotiating room to the court room.

Jews have not been liked for several thousand years. Our collective effort to build a Jewish state is not liked much more either. The world has been opposed to core Israeli diplomatic and security policies throughout this country's existence, from the very beginning. Nevertheless, Israel has survived all the condemnations and threats of isolation.

The State Department reproached Israel for capturing the Galilee and the Negev in 1948. The UN condemned Israel for invading Sinai in 1956. It condemned Israel's 1967 *"aggression,"* and excoriated Jerusalem's reunification. It raked Israel over the coals for annexation of the Golan Heights. It fulminated against Prime Minister Menachem Begin's bombing of the Iraqi nuclear reactor, and of Beirut, etc., etc. The US, by the way, was party to all these condemnations.

The UN and other international bodies have blasted us for the assassination of master PLO terrorist Abu Jihad and many other critical, anti-terror operations abroad. This includes Israeli interdiction of strategic armament shipments from Iran to the Islamic armies on our northern and southern borders.

The UN has slap-happily censured Israel for defending itself against Hamas and Hezbollah – in the first and second Lebanon wars, and for operations against Hamas in Gaza in 2009, 2012 and 2014.

The UN annually condemns Israel for (reportedly) building a nuclear weapons capacity, and lambastes Israel for a load of other fabricated evils (from stealing Palestinian water to destroying Palestinian archeology). The International Criminal Court declared the security fence illegal.

The UN Security Council has adopted more than 150 anti-Israel resolutions since 1967. (The US vetoed about 50 others.) Nu, so what? None of this should come as any surprise.

As for the current diplomatic campaign against Israel: Internationalizing the conflict and criminalizing Israel was always a central Palestinian strategy, and Mahmoud Abbas has made this centerpiece of his decade as Palestinian dictator. He decided more than four years ago to abandon the track of serious negotiations with Israel, and instead to maximize the window of grace he has with US President Obama to increase international pressure on Israel.

But, of course, none of this will get the Palestinians very far, despite the unpleasantness for Israel.

No series of condemnatory international resolutions will change the realities on the ground. And the reality is that there is no sovereignty for the Palestinians without negotiated Israeli cooperation, and without much greater Palestinian willingness to compromise.

There is no mini-state or maxi-autonomy for Palestinians (which is really what we're talking about) without overall Israeli security control in the entire area west of the Jordan River – and this requires a strong and permanent Israeli military imprint in all areas of the West Bank and along the borders. There is no Palestinian state possible without circumscribing maximalist Palestinian demands for a division of Jerusalem or for refugee return. There can be no Palestinian state possible without compromise over settlements, and without Palestinian recognition of Israel as the national homeland of the Jewish People.

Unfortunately, UN and European resolutions that pronounce upon contours and timetables for Palestinian statehood without taking into account these realities, only stiffen the resistance of Abbas (and Hamas) to making the sort of concessions that are required for peace.

On the contrary, such diplomatic muckraking only emboldens and radicalizes the Palestinians, and pushes any realistic arrangements far down the road.

And it forces Israelis to say, alas, ooom shmoom.

David Weinberg is the director of Public Affairs at the Bar Ilan University's Begin-Sadat Center for Strategic Studies. He is also the Israel office director of Canada's Center for Israel and Jewish Affairs, and the senior advisor to the Israel office of the Tikvah Fund. He is a columnist with the Israel HaYom newspaper and the diplomatic columnist at the Jerusalem Post.

Matti Friedman's speech at the BICOM dinner in London on January 26, 2015.

One night, several years ago, I came out of Bethlehem after a reporting assignment and crossed through the Israeli military checkpoint between that city and its neighbor, Jerusalem, where I live.

With me were perhaps a dozen Palestinian men, mostly in their thirties – my age. No soldiers were visible at the entrance to the checkpoint, a precaution against suicide bombers. We saw only steel and concrete. I followed the other men through a metal detector into a stark corridor and followed instructions barked through a loudspeaker.

"Remove your belt. Lift up your shirt."

The voice belonged to a soldier watching us on a closed-circuit camera. Exiting the checkpoint, adjusting my belt and clothing with the others, I felt like a being less than human and understood for the first time how a feeling like than would provoke someone to violence.

Consumers of news will recognize this scene as belonging to the Israeli occupation of the West Bank, which keeps the 2.5 million Palestinians in that territory under military rule, and has since 1967. The facts of this situation aren't much in question. This should be an issue of concern to Israelis, whose democracy, military, and society are corroded by the in equality on the West Bank. This, too, is not much in question.

The question we must ask, as observers of the world, is why this conflict has come over time to draw more attention than any other, and why it is presented as it is. How have the doings in a country that constitutes 0.01 percent of the world's surface become the focus of angst, loathing, and condemnation more than any other?

We must ask why Israelis and Palestinians have become the stylized symbol of conflict, of strong and weak, the parallel bars upon which the intellectual Olympians of the West perform their tricks – not Turks and Kurds, not Chinese and Tibetans, not British soldiers and Iraqi Muslims, not Iraqi Muslims and Iraqi Christians, not Saudi sheikhs and Saudi women, not Indians and Kashmiris, not drug cartel thugs and Mexican villagers. Questioning why this is the case is in no way an attempt to evade or obscure reality, which is why I opened with the checkpoint leading from Bethlehem. On the contrary – anyone seeking a full understanding of reality can't avoid this question. My experiences as a journalist provide part of the answer, and also raise pressing questions that go beyond the practice of journalism.

I have been writing from and about Israel for most of the past twenty years, since I moved there from Toronto at age 17. During the five and a half years that I spent as part of the international press corps as a reporter for the American news agency The Associated Press (AP) between 2006 and 2011, I gradually began to be aware of certain malfunctions in the coverage of the Israeli story – recurring omissions, recurring inflations, decisions made according to considerations that were not journalistic but political, all in the context of a story staffed and reported more than any other international story on earth.

When I worked in the AP's Jerusalem bureau, the Israel story was covered by more AP news staff than China or India, or all of the fifty-odd countries of sub-Saharan Africa combined. This is representative of the industry as a whole.

In early 2009, to give one fairly routine example of an editorial decision of the kind I mean, I was instructed by my superiors to report a second-hand story taken from an Israeli newspaper about offensive T-shirts supposedly worn by Israeli soldiers. We had no confirmation of our own of the story's veracity, and one doesn't see much coverage of things US Marines or British infantrymen have tattooed on their chests and arms. And yet T-shirts worn by Israeli soldiers were newsworthy in the eyes of one of the world's most powerful new organizations.

This was because we chose to hint or say outright that Israeli soldiers were war criminals, and every detail supporting that portrayal was to be seized on. Much of the international press corps covered the T-short story. At around the same time, several Israeli soldiers were quoted anonymously in a school newsletter speaking of abuses they had supposedly witnessed while fighting in Gaza. We wrote no fewer than three separate stories about this, although the use of sources whose identity isn't known to reporters is banned for good reason by AP's own in-house rules. This story, too, was very much one we wanted to tell. By the time the soldiers came forward to say they hadn't actually witnessed the events they supposedly described, and were trying to make a point to young students about the horrors and moral challenges of warfare, it was, of course, too late.

In early 2009, two reporters in our bureau obtained details of a peace offer made by the Israeli Prime Minister, Ehud Olmert, to the Palestinians several months before, and deemed by the Palestinians as insufficient. The offer proposed a Palestinian state in the Gaza Strip and the West Bank with a capital in shared Jerusalem. This should have been one of the year's biggest stories. But an Israeli peace offer and its rejection by the Palestinians didn't suit OUR story. The bureau chief ordered both reporters to ignore the Olmert offer, and they did, despite a furious protest from one of them, who later termed this decision *"the biggest fiasco I've seen in 50 years of journalism."* But it was very much in keeping with not only the practice at AP, but in the press corps in general. Soldiers vile T-shirts were worth a story, anonymous and unverifiable testimonies of abuses were worth three, and a peace proposal from the Israeli Prime Minister to the Palestinian President was not to be reported at all.

Vandalism of Palestinian property is a story. Neo-Nazi rallies in Palestinian universities or in Palestinian cities are not – I saw images of such rallies suppressed on more than one occasion.

Jewish hatred of Arabs is a story. Arab hatred of Jews is not. Our policy, for example, was not to mention the assertion in the Hamas founding charter that Jews were responsible for engineering both world wars and the Russian and French revolutions, despite the obvious insight that this provides into the thinking of one of the most influential actors in the conflict.

100 houses in a West Bank settlement are a story. 100 rockets smuggled into Gaza are not. The Hamas military build-up amid and under the civilian population in Gaza is not a story. But the Israeli military action in response to that threat – that is a story as we saw last summer. Israel's responsibility for the deaths of civilians as a result – that's a story. Hamas responsibility for those deaths is not. Any reporter from the international press corps in Israel, whether he or she works for AP, Reuters, CNN, the BBC, or elsewhere, will recognize the examples I have cited here of what is newsworthy and what is not as standard operating procedure.

In my time in the press corps I saw, from the inside, how Israel's flaws were dissected and magnified, while the flaws of its enemies were purposefully erased. I saw how the threats facing Israel were disregarded or even mocked as figments of the Israeli imagination, even as these threats repeatedly materialized. I saw how a fictional image of Israel and of its enemies was manufactured, polished, and propagated to devastating effect by inflating certain details, ignoring others, and presenting the result as an accurate picture of reality.

Lest we think this is something that has never happened before, we might remember Orwell's observation about journalism from the Spanish civil war;

"Early in life," he wrote, *"I has noticed that no event is ever correctly reported in a newspaper, but in Spain, for the first time, I saw newspapers report which do not bear any relation to the facts, not even the relationship which is implied in an ordinary lie...I saw, in fact, history being written not in terms of what had happened but of what ought to have happened according to the various 'party lines.'"* That was in 1942.

Over time, I came to understand that the malfunctions I was witnessing, and in which I was playing a part, were not limited to the AP. I saw they were part of a broader problem in the way the press functioned, and in how it saw its job.

The international press in Israel had become less of an observer than a player in it. It had moved away from careful explanation and toward a kind of political character assassination on behalf of the side it identified as being right. It valued a kind of ideological uniformity from which you were not allowed to stray. So having begun with limited criticism of certain editorial decisions, I now found myself with a broad critique of the press.

Eventually, however, I realized that even the press wasn't the whole story. The press was playing a key role in an intellectual phenomenon taking root in the West, but it wasn't the cause, or not the only cause. It was blown on a certain course by the prevailing ideological winds, and causing those winds to blow with greater force.

Many journalists would like you to believe that the news is created by a kind of algorithm – that it's a mechanical, even scientific process in which events are inserted, processed, and presented. But, of course, the news is an imperfect and entirely human affair, the result of interactions between sources, reporters, and editors, all of whom bear the baggage of their background and who reflect, as we all do to some extent, the prejudices of their peers.

In the aftermath of last summer's Gaza war, and in the light of events in Europe more recently, it should be clear that something deep and toxic is going on. Understanding what that is, it seems to me, will help us understand something important not only about journalism but also about the Western mind and the way it sees the world.

What presents itself as political criticism, as analysis, or as journalism, is coming to sound more and more like a new version of a much older complaint – that Jews are troublemakers, a negative force in world events, and that if these people, as a collective, could somehow be made to vanish, we would all be better off.

This is, or should be, a cause for alarm, and not only people sympathetic to Israel or concerned with Jewish affairs. What is in play right now has less to do with the world of politics than the world of psychology and religion, and less to do with Israel than with those condemning Israel.

The occupation of the West Bank, with which I opened, would seem to be at the heart of the story, the root cause, as it were, of the conflict portrayed as the most important on earth. A few words, then, about this occupation.

The occupation was created in the 1967 Middle East war. The occupation is not the conflict, which of course predates the occupation. It is a symptom of the conflict, a conflict that would remain even if the symptom were somehow solved. If we look at the West Bank, the only Palestinian area currently occupied by Israel, and if we include Jerusalem, we see that the conflict in these areas claimed sixty lives last year – Palestinian and Israeli.

An end to this occupation would free Palestinians from Israeli rule, and free Israelis from ruling people who do not want to be ruled. Observers of the Middle East in 2015 understand, too, that an end to the occupation will create a power vacuum that will be filled, as in all power vacuums in the region have been, not by the forces of democracy and moderation, which in our region range from weak to negligible, but by the powerful and ruthless, by the extremists. This is what we have learned from the unravelling of the Middle East in recent years. This is what happened in Iraq, Syria, Libya, Yemen and Egypt and before that in Gaza and southern Lebanon. My home in Jerusalem is within an easy day's drive of both Aleppo and Baghdad. Creating a new playground for these forces will bring the black-masked soldiers of radical Islam within yards of Israeli homes with mortars, rockets, and tunneling implements. Many thousands will die.

Beyond the obvious threat to Palestinian Christians, women, gays, and liberals, who will be the first to suffer, this threatens to render much or all of Israel unlivable, ending the only safe progressive space in the Middle East, the only secure minority refuge in the Middle East, and the only Jewish country on earth.

No international investment or guarantees, no Western-backed government or Western-trained military will be able to keep that from happening, as we have just seen in Iraq.

The world will greet this outcome with sincere expressions of sympathy. Only several years ago I, like many of the left, might have dismissed this as an apocalyptic scenario. It isn't. It's the most likely scenario.

People observing this conflict from afar have been led to believe that Israel faces a simple choice between occupation and peace. That choice is fiction. The Palestinian choice, it is said, is between Israeli occupation and an independent democracy. That choice, too, is fiction.

Neither side faces a clear choice, or clear outcomes. Here we have a conflict in a region of conflicts, with no clear villain, no clear victim, and no clear solution, one of many hundreds or thousands of ethnic, national and religious disputes on earth.

The only group of people subject to a systematic boycott at present in the world is Jews, appearing now under the convenient euphemism *"Israelis."* The only country that has its own *"Apartheid Week"* on campuses is the Jewish one. Protesters have interfered with the unloading of Israeli shipping on the West coast of America, and there are regular calls for boycotts of anything produced in the Jewish state.

No similar tactics are employed against any other ethnic group or nationality, no matter how egregious the human rights violation attributed to that group's country of origin.

Anyone questioning why this is so will be greeted with shout of *"the occupation"* as if this were explanation enough. It's not. Many who would like to question these phenomena don't dare, for fear that they will somehow be expressing support for the occupation, which has been inflated from a geopolitical dilemma of modest scope by global standards into the world's premier violation of human rights.

The human costs of the Middle East adventures of American and Britain in this century have been far higher, and far harder to explain, than anything Israel has ever done. They have involved occupations, and the violence they have unleashed continues. No one boycotts American and British professors. Turkey is a democracy, and a NATO member, and yet its occupation of northern Cyprus and long conflict with stateless Kurds – many of whom see themselves as occupied – are viewed with a yawn. There is no *"Turkish Apartheid Week."* The world is full of injustice. Billions of people are oppressed. In Congo, five million people are dead. The time has come for everyone to admit that the fashionable disgust for Israel among many in the West is not liberal but is selective, disproportionate, and discriminatory.

There are simply too many voices coming from too many places, expressing themselves in too poisonous a way, for us to conclude that this is a narrow criticism of the occupation. It is time for the people making these charges to look closely at themselves, and for us to look closely at them.

Naming and understanding this sentiment is important, as it is becoming one of the key intellectual trends of our time. We may think of it as the *"Cult of the Occupation."* This belief system, for that's what it is, uses the occupation as a way to talk about other things.

As usual with Western religions, the center of this one is in the Holy Land. The dogma posits that the occupation is not a conflict like any other, but that it is the very symbol of conflict; that the minute state inhabited by a persecuted minority in the Middle East is in fact a symbol of the ills of the West – colonialism, nationalism, militarism, and racism. In the riots in Ferguson, Missouri, for example, a sign hoisted by the marchers linked the unrest between African Americans and the police to Israeli rule over Palestinians.

The cult's priesthood can be found among the activists, NGO experts, and ideological journalists who have turned coverage of this conflict into a catalog of Jewish moral failings, as if Israeli society were different to any other group of people on earth, as if Jews deserve to be mocked for having suffered and failed to be perfect as a result.

Most of my former colleagues in the press corps aren't fully fledged members of this group. They aren't true believers. But boycotts of Israel, and only of Israel, which is one of the cult's most important practices, have significant support in the press, including among editors who were my superiors.

Sympathy for Israel's predicament is highly unpopular in the relevant social circles, and is something to be avoided by anyone wishing to be invited to the dinner parties, or to be promoted.

The cult and its belief system are in control of the narrative, just as the popular kids in a school and those who decide what clothes and music are acceptable. In the social milieu of the reporters, NGO workers, and activists, which is the same social world, these are the correct opinions. This guides the coverage. This explains why the events in Gaza were portrayed not as a complicated war like many others fought in this century, but as a massacre of innocents. And it explains much else.

So prevalent has this kind of thinking become that participating in liberal intellectual life in the West increasingly requires you to subscribe at least outwardly to this dogma, particularly if you are a Jew and thus suspected of the wrong sympathies. If you're a Jew from Israel, your participation is increasingly conditioned on an abject and public display of self-flagellation. Your participation, indeed, is increasingly unwelcome.

What, exactly, is going on?

Observers of Western history understand that at times of confusion and unhappiness, and of great ideological ferment, negative sentiments tend to coagulate around Jews. Discussions of the great topics of the time often end up as discussions about Jews.

In the late 1800's, for example, French society was riven by the clash between old France, the church and army, and the new France of liberalism and the rule of law. The French were preoccupied with the question who is French, and who is not. They were smarting from their military defeat by the Prussians. All of this sentiment erupted around the figure of a Jew, Alfred Dreyfus, accused of betraying France as a spy for Germany. His accusers knew he was innocent, but that didn't matter; he was a symbol of everything they wanted to condemn.

To give another example, Germans in the 1920's and 30's were preoccupied with their humiliation in the Great War. This became a discussion of Jewish traitors who had stabbed Germany in the back. Germany was preoccupied also with the woes of their economy. This became a discussion on Jewish wealth, and Jewish bankers.

In the years of the rise of Communism and the Cold War, communists concerned with their ideological opponents talked about Jewish capitalists and cosmopolitans, or Jewish doctors plotting against the state. At the very same time, in capitalist societies threatened by communism, people condemned Jewish Bolsheviks.

This is the face of this recurring obsession. As the journalist, Charles Maurras, wrote approvingly in 1911, *"Everything seems impossible, or frighteningly difficult, without the providential arrival of anti-Semitism, through which all things fall into place and are simplified."*

The West today is preoccupied with a feeling of guilt about the use of power. That's why the Jews, in their state, are now held up in the press and elsewhere as the prime example of the abuse of power. That's why, for so many, the global villain, as portrayed in the newspapers and on television, is none other than the Jewish soldier, or the Jewish settler. This is not because the Jewish soldier or settler is responsible for more harm than anyone else on earth. No sane person would make that claim. It is because they are the heirs to the Jewish banker or the Jewish commissar of the past. It is because when moral failure raises its head in the Western imagination, the head tends to wear a skullcap.

One would expect the growing scale and complexity of the conflict in the Middle East over the past decade to have eclipsed the fixation on Israel in the eyes of the press and other observers. Israel is, after all, a side show. The death toll in Syria in less than four years far exceeds the toll of the Arab-Israeli conflict in a century. The annual death toll in the West Bank and Jerusalem is a morning in Iraq.

And yet it is precisely in these years that the obsession has grown worse.

This makes little sense, unless we understand that people aren't fixated on Israel despite everything else going on, but rather because of everything else that is going on. As Maurras wrote, when you use the Jew as the symbol of what is wrong, *"all things fall into place and are simplified."*

The last few decades have brought the West into conflict with the Islamic world. Terrorists have attacked New York, Washington, London, Madrid, and now Paris. America and Britain caused the unravelling of Iraq, and hundreds of thousands of people are dead there. Afghanistan was occupied and thousands of Western soldiers were killed there, along with countless civilians, but the Taliban are alive and well, and undeterred. Gadhafi was removed, and Libya is no better off. All of this is confusing and discouraging. It causes people to search for answers and explanations, and these are hard to come by. It is in this context that the *"Cult of the Occupation"* has caught on. The idea is that the problems in the Middle East have something to do with Jewish arrogance and perfidy, that the sins of one's own country can be projected on to the West's old blank screen. This is the idea increasingly reflected on campuses, in labor unions, and in the media fixation on Israel. It's a projection, one whose chief instrument is the press.

As one BBC reporter informed a Jewish interviewee on camera, after a Muslim terrorist murdered four Jewish shoppers at a Paris kosher supermarket, *"Many critics of Israel's policy would suggest that the Palestinians suffered hugely at Jewish hands as well."*

Everything, it seems, can be linked to the occupation, and Jews can be blamed even for attacks against them. This isn't the voice of the perpetrators, but of the enablers. The voice of the enablers is less honest than that of the perpetrators, and more dangerous for being disguised in respectable English. The voice is confident and growing in volume. That is why the year 2015 finds many Jews in Western Europe eyeing their suitcases again.

The Jews of the Middle East are outnumbered by the Arabs of the Middle East by sixty to one, and by the world's Muslims by two hundred to one. Half of the Jews in Israel are there because their families were forced from their homes in the 20th Century, not by Christians in Europe but by Muslims in the Middle East. Israel currently has Hezbollah on its northern border, Islamic State on its north eastern border, Al-Qaida on its southern border, and Hamas in Gaza. None of these groups seeks an end to the occupation, but rather openly wish to destroy Israel. But it is naïve to point out these facts. The facts don't matter. We are in the world of symbols. In this world, Israel has become a symbol of what is wrong - not Hamas, not Hezbollah, not Britain, not America, not Russia.

I believe it's important to recognize the pathologies at play in order to make sense of things. In this context it's worth pointing out that I'm hardly the first to identify a problem. Jewish communities like the one in Britain identified a problem long ago, and have been expending immense efforts to correct it. I wish it wasn't necessary, it shouldn't be necessary, but it undoubtedly is, and becoming more so, and I have great respect for these efforts. Many people, especially young people, are having trouble maintaining their balance amid this ideological onslaught, which is successfully disguised as journalism or analysis, and is phrased in the language of progressive politics. I would like to help them keep their bearings.

I don't believe, however, that anyone should make a feeling of persecution the center of their identity, of their Judaism, or of their relationship with Israel. The obsession is a fact, but it isn't a new fact, and it shouldn't immobilize us in anger, or force us into a defensive crouch. It shouldn't make us less willing to seek to improve our situation, to behave with compassion to our neighbors, or to continue building the model society that Israel's founders had in mind.

I was in Tel Aviv not long ago, on Rothschild Boulevard. The city was humming with life. Signs of prosperity were everywhere, in the renovated Bauhaus buildings, in the clothes, the stores. I watched people go by; kids with bikes and tattoos, business people, men and women, all speaking the language of the Bible and Jewish prayer. The summer's Hamas rockets were already a memory, just a few months old but subsumed in the frantic, irrepressible life of the country. There were cranes everywhere, raising new buildings. There were schoolchildren with oversized knapsacks, and parents with strollers. I heard Arabic, Russian and French, and the country went about its business with a potent cheer and determination that you miss if all you see are threats and hatred. There have always been threats and hatred and it hasn't stopped us. We have enemies and we have friends. The dog barks, as the saying goes, and the convoy rolls by.

One of the questions presented to us by the wars of the modern age is what now constitutes victory. In the 21st Century, when a battlefield is no longer conquered or lost, when land isn't changing hands and no one ever surrenders, what does it mean to win?

The answer is that victory is no longer determined on the battlefield. It's determined in the center, in the society itself. Who has built a better society? Who has provided better lives for the people? Where is there the most optimism? Where can the happiest people be found? One report on world happiness ranked Israel as the 11th happiest nation on earth. Britain was ranked 22nd.

Israel's intellectual opponents can rant about the moral failings of the Jews, obscuring their obsession in whatever sophisticated way they choose. The gunmen of Hamas and their allies can stand on heaps of rubble and declare victory. They can fire rockets, and shoot up supermarkets. But, if you look at Tel Aviv, or at any thriving neighborhood in Jerusalem, Netanya, Haifa, Rishon leZion, you can understand that this is victory.

This is where we won, and where we win every day!

Matti Friedman's work as a reporter has taken him to Lebanon, Morocco, Egypt, Moscow, and Washington, DC, and to conflicts in Israel and the Caucasus. He is the author of 'The Aleppo Codex.'

FIGHTING BDS.

A short history of anti-Israel boycotts.

Arab and state-sponsored boycotts of Israel have been in existence longer than has the State of Israel.

Arab grievances against Jews expressed themselves as early as 1922 when they targeted Jewish-owned businesses in British Mandated Palestine. Arabs who did not support this boycott threat were physically attacked by fellow-Arabs and had their merchandise destroyed when Arabs rioted violently in Jerusalem and Hebron in 1929. The riots called on all Arabs in the region to apply harsher and more official boycotts on Jewish businesses. The Arab Executive Committee of the Syrian-Palestinian Congress called for a boycott of Jewish businesses in 1933 and in 1934.

The terms of the League of Nations Mandate for Palestine allowed for the Zionist enterprise to develop Palestine economically. In reaction to this, on December 2, 1945, the newly formed Arab League Council declared a formal boycott: *"Jewish products and manufactured [goods] in Palestine shall be [considered] undesirable in the Arab countries; to permit them to enter the Arab countries would lead to the realization of the Zionist political objectives. ... every State of the League should, before January 1, 1946, take measures which they consider fit and which will be in conformity with the principles of administration and legislation therein, such as making use of import balances in this respect in order to prevent these products and manufactured [goods] from entering [these] countries regardless of whether they have come from Palestine or by any other route."*

The Arab League boycott planned to envelope the nascent Jewish state with different levels of sanctions. Products and services originating in Israel was the *"primary boycott."* To a great extent, this is still in force by many Arab nations. Then there was the *"secondary boycott"* to which the Arab League swerved companies in non-Arab countries that did business with Israel. The *"tertiary boycott"* threatened businesses that shipped or flew goods to Israel.

Boycotts and sanctions are effective when universally adopted by a unified block of nations. Multi-national boycotts and sanctions were effective in setting back the white regime in South Africa. It badly weakened Communist Cuba. It brought Iran to slow their nuclear program and back to the negotiating table. And it isolated nuclear North Korea. It has never proven effective without a global reach of national consensus. This is the target of the BDS movement. Without it, the disparate efforts of local radical groups are little more than a temporary nuisance, although the elements are there for them to be more effective if inroads are made to network their activities.

A major factor why BDS hasn't succeeded with both general public opinion and national leaders is their dishonesty of purpose. BDS has never been honest about the aim of their protest. It somehow slides between removing the purported *"Israeli occupation"* to the elimination of Israel itself. It is not a global human rights organization as it concentrates of supporting the Palestinian cause while totally ignoring the hideous human rights crimes and abuses that have shook other people with terrible regimes that make the Palestinian issue pale into insignificance in proportion. That is one factor why BDS is not popular. BDS uses disproportionate force against Israel in comparison to other genuine cases of genocide and ethnic cleansing, which they ignore.

BDS was developed by a person called Omar Barghouti whose ambition, from the beginning, was to create a movement that would do away with the Zionist state. Boycotts and sanctions were to be the weapons to be used in this aim. He decided to build a global organization fashioned on the model of thousands of groups that worked and lobbied to bring down the white regime in South Africa in support of the black majority. The part played by BDS in the fall of the South African government was minimal. They were running a minor campaign in the shadow of a growing international diplomatic effort and it was this, and not Barghouti's BDS, that pushed Frederik De Klerk and Nelson Mandela together to negotiate and bring about change.

It must be stated that, although there are one or two Palestinian leaders who foster the boycott campaign, the official Palestinian voice opposes boycotts as it is damaging to the peace process that they hope will ease their progress into statehood and a better life for their people. They need the close cooperation and normalization with Israel to reach that goal.

During Nelson Mandela's funeral, it couldn't have been plainer: Mahmoud Abbas, the Palestinian president, told reporters: *"No, we do not support the boycott of Israel."*

Majdi Khaldi, one of his senior advisers, was even more explicit: *"We are neighbors with Israel, we have agreements with Israel. We recognize Israel. We are not asking anyone to boycott products of Israel."*

The Palestinian leadership views BDS activists as little more than embarrassing troublemakers, and wishes to suppress them.

Omar Barghouti responded by releasing an almost comically petulant statement: *"we should prosecute the Palestinian Authority for serving the Israeli occupation's project."*

In truth, however, it has long been clear that many Palestinian officials believe that the BDS movement does not serve the interests of the Palestinian people.

Barghouti behaves like a petulant child. He calls to boycott the university that gave him his higher education. Tel Aviv University is a thriving liberal democratic seat of learning that is open to all views. It is one of the academic centers in Israel that fosters a peaceful two-state solution. Yet Barghouti promotes the closing of academic minds, even against open campuses that support and are active in achieving a peaceful end to the Israeli-Palestinian conflict.

Barghouti has claimed that Palestinian Arabs have the *"right to resistance by any means, including armed resistance."* This clearly promotes and encourages acts of terror for the Palestinian form of *"resistance"* is not defensive, but offensive, violence.

Barghouti decides for Jews and Israelis that they are not a people and have no connection to the land of Israel. Barghouti's campaign is to ally with a Palestinian movement to eventually destroy Israel. This was confirmed by an ardent is a supporter of BDS, Lebanese-American Asad Abu Khalil, who has said that "*the real aim of BDS is to bring down the state of Israel...Justice and freedom for the Palestinians are incompatible with the existence of the state of Israel"* That, in a nutshell, is the core belief of the BDS Movement. It was also confirmed by a one-time advocate of BDS, leftist professor, Norman Finkelstein.

BDS claims are shot through with ridiculous lies. The idea that BDS can liberate Palestine is divorced from reality. BDS calls itself the largest civil society movement within Palestinian society is patently untrue. It spends ninety percent of its time trying to run an anti-apartheid regime campaign where the basic premise that Israel is at all an apartheid state is preposterous.

The big problem for BDS fanatics is their disloyalty to the creed they claim to represent. Campuses, for example, are places where you ought to question. BDS comes from as far left political position. Karl Marx credo was to doubt and question everything, but BDS was a dogma where doubt about their aims and cause id considered treason and anyone doing it becomes *"enemies of the state"* so to speak. Just ask anyone on any campus who disagree and expose the falsehood of BDS claims. On campuses, when it comes to offering an opposing view, they close down the debate, often with violence.

The biggest fallacy of BDS is their oft-quoted three point plan which, they claim, is based on international law which includes Palestinian self-determination and the *"end of occupation,"* the right of return for Arab refugees, and full equality of Palestinians in Israel. They know that the last two items would demographically destroy the concept of Israel as the Jewish state. That is why they remain as pillars of their agenda. But, putting that aside, if BDS is so morally right about upholding international law, then the same law, which is the source of their important plan, namely the UN General Assembly and the UN Court of Justice, also clearly designates and recognizes Israel as a state. When you press BDS on this point they say they don't take a position on it. I'm sorry! That is hypocrisy! If you make your case quoting international law you have to stand by all the rights and obligations of that law. You cannot cherry-pick the parts you like and dismiss the part that doesn't fit your argument. You cannot assert your right and dismiss others under the law. That just doesn't make sense. Neither is it just. BDS champions the rights of Palestinians, but if Palestinians have the right to self-determination and statehood then Israel also has the same right to self-determination and statehood. You can't say, *"to hell with the law"* and then claim your principles are anchored in international law but you have no position on Israel. It doesn't make any sense.

When you question BDS on this you can never get a sensible answer and, when that happens, in the words of Finkelstein, who has become disillusioned with the aims and tactics of BDS and has now turned his back on them, it becomes a cult of absolute beliefs where nothing central can be questioned. Followers in cults don't question. They just nod their heads and say, *"Amen!"*

Individually, a number of BDS followers believe in a one-state solution, which has no legitimacy under international law. But these pro-Palestinian one-staters are appalled when some Israelis say, *"OK! Bring it on!"* A one-state solution, from an Israeli perspective starts with the dismantling on the Palestinian Authority infrastructure and annexation of all the land under Israeli sovereignty. After all, one-state can only have one governing body, not two. By annexing all the land under one-state and encompassing all the population living inside that territory it would still leave Jewish Israelis as the majority. Therefore, in a one-state solution under these terms, Israel would remain as a Jewish democratic state, albeit with a larger possibly hostile minority, but this minority would have democratic representation within the Israeli

Knesset, thereby upholding the democratic nature of the state. This is something that would be denied to Jews under a Palestinian state.

*

BDS quotes;

"We oppose a Jewish State." Omar Barghouti, founder of the BDS Movement.

"The real aim of BDs is to bring down the state of Israel." Assad Abu Khalil, leading BDS activist.

"BDS does mean the end of the Jewish state." Ahmed Moor, leading BDS activist.

"BDS will help bring about the defeat of Zionist Israel and a victory for Palestine." Ronnie Kasrils.

*

BDS lies, but facts are stubborn things.

What I find objectionable about any BDS campus debate, if it is at all possible to have an even-handed debate about BDS, is that they inevitably take the form, not of examining the real motives and ultimate aim of BDS but, instead, turn solely to the *"merits"* of its perceived mission.

These forums include BDS activists and delegitimizers of Israel with rarely an opposing voice, in the name of *"balanced debate."* Any Israeli voice is a person carefully selected for their outspoken opposition to Israel.

Sadly, we increasingly see this bent growing in Jewish *"intellectual"* and academic circles.

Empty emotion-filled epithets such as *"ethnic cleansing"* and *"apartheid"* are tossed around in place of reasoned discourse.

These insults intimidate anyone who comes with a contrary argument. They are designed to put such a person on the defensive, to explain how and why Israel is not an apartheid state and that it is the Palestinian side, BDS and Free Palestine movements with their "From the River to the Sea Palestine will be Free" slogan that are inciting ethnic cleansing, an ethnic cleansing of the right of Jews to their state on their ancient land. Not that these provocateurs are listening to any rebuttal. The words are meant to be an insult to the pro-Israel side to close down debate.

It is, therefore, staggering how many revered institutions find these arguments so persuasive as to warrant preferred expression and campus activism.

Even in its simplest form the BDS apologists have the wrong end of the stick. The core of their soft-sell appeal goes like this;

The Israeli Palestinian conflict has been going on for far too long. It has caused too much suffering to the poor Palestinians. It has to end.

Israel is guilty for prolonging the conflict

Boycott is a non-violent way of pressuring Israel to stop oppressing the Palestinians.

Simply put, the pro-Israeli argument goes like this;

Everyone agrees that the Middle East conflict has inflicted much suffering on both Palestinians and Israelis. It must end through some sort of agreement between the parties.

Note the fundamental differences between the BDS position and their pro-Israel opponents;

BDS sees one side as suffering. The pro-Israel sees suffering on both sides. This is just one example of the profound asymmetry of BDS.

It can rightly be claimed that consecutive Israeli governments for decades have reached out with generous concessions in pursuit of a solution that would satisfy both Palestinian and Israeli needs. All have been rejected by the Palestinian side. The Palestinians have never come to the Israelis with any pragmatic and flexible terms that would lead to peace.

Needless to say, it is the Palestinians who are the plaintiffs for a state, and for that they need Israel's acquiescence. Surely that should make them the more flexible party if they really do want a place of their own alongside the Jewish state of Israel? Yet, they are the side that has always refused to accept a negotiated state while crying how much they want one. It is this significant point that is the rub concerning both Palestinian and BDS intent.

Based on this indisputable fact is it not more reasonable for the international community and BDS to put pressure on the Palestinian leadership to accept a solution that Israel can live with, if this really is their aim? This line of thought, however, only brings us to one conclusion. This is NOT their aim.

BDS advocates can translate into horror selected versions of the 1948 war, a war that Arab nations inflicted on the nascent State of Israel, in an effort to twist responsibility for an on-going Palestinian refugee crisis onto the Jewish state.

Prior to this war, and as a result of Arab riots and killing of Jews, the British government blocked Jewish refugees trying to flee Nazi persecution from entering the territory designated in international treaties to be the National Home of the Jewish People.

After the British reneged on their responsibilities under the Mandate by pulling out of Palestine, five Arab armies attacked Israel in a genocidal war against the Jews. Instead of another Holocaust, so soon after the European one, the tiny outgunned Jewish state miraculously survived. The land, now known as the West Bank, however was occupied by Jordan from 1948 to 1967 by virtue of their army's territorial gains. These gains included parts of Jerusalem including all of the Old City where they desecrated Jewish holy sites and destroyed synagogues. Yet, nobody made claims against Jordan of *"illegally occupying Palestinian land."* Palestinian claims to nationhood simply did not exist at that time. Strange!

The fury in the surrounding Arab nations from losing this war and bringing shame upon themselves was taken out against their beleaguered and threatened Jews. Those that weren't killed were summarily expelled, forcing them to leave their properties and assets behind with no compensation.

If there were 500,000 Arab refugees that left Israel, there were almost one million Jewish refugees thrown out of Arab lands. This fact never comes up for discussion in BDS circles, even if the topic is human rights.

Their biased narrative concentrates on the Arab Nakba (disaster), not the Jewish one.

The BDS bias is seen in its one-sided argument for *"self-determination."* It is a right not given by them to the Jewish state. This exclusivity is awarded to the Arabs who became lumped into a *"Palestinian"* identity around 1967.

Prior to 1948 a *"Palestinian"* was a Jew as proven by the results of the Zionist enterprise in the National Home of the Jewish People.

One of the many Arab statements prior to 1948 was made by Auni Bey Abdul-Hadi, Syrian Arab leader to British Peel Commission in 1937;

"There is no such country as Palestine. 'Palestine' is a term the Zionists invented. There is no Palestine in the Bible. Our country was for centuries part of Syria. 'Palestine' is alien to us. It is the Zionists who introduced it."

There were many such Arab statements at the time. They were right.

The first Palestinian flag had the Star of David in its center. It also had the two blue horizontal stripes that were replicated into the current Israeli national flag.

This Zionist enterprise before, during and after the Mandate for Palestine gave birth to the Anglo-Palestine Bank that later became Bank Leumi, the Palestine Post newspaper that became the Jerusalem Post, the Palestine Electric Company originally founded by Pinhas Rutenberg became the Israel Electric Company.

Walid Shoebat, a former PLO terrorist and now a fighter for truth, posed this question;

"Why is it that on June 4th 1967 I was a Jordanian and overnight I became a Palestinian?"

While BDS activists push the *"self-determination"* button in favor of the *"Palestinians"* they deny the legal, moral right of the Jews to develop the sovereignty granted to them not only in a tow thousand year heritage and legacy but also solidly founded on unanimous international treaties that precede, and have not been revoked by, any resolution or vote since.

BDS love to through around expressions like *"occupation"* in a derogatory manner and it is true that Israel has been battered ceaselessly with this word as if it alone is the culprit for an ongoing *"occupation"* even if you accept the notion of that word. But I claim that the Palestinian Arabs equally share a responsibility and the blame for maintaining this status due to their refusal to accept the offers made to them by Israel but also by their adamant rejection of ever agreeing to live alongside the Jewish State of Israel in permanent peace and security.

They do so by promoting a domestic culture of *"resistance"* inciting a futile dream that, with force, Israel will disappear. The Ramallah leadership refuses to accept the presence of the Jews, and Hamas goes much further in steadfastly announcing and attempting to destroy Israel and kill Jews.

Is it any wonder that Israel holds firm to its lines of security until these people can find their way out of this dark and dangerous cul-de-sac of hatred?

The BDS may put forward campaigns based on *"human rights"* and *"social justice,"* but these noble goals are not at the heart of what they stand for.

They use these expressions while putting forward the *"criminality"* of Israel by championing Palestinian human rights and social justice. If BDS really were concerned about human rights and social justice for the Palestinian Arabs they would be there assisting the human rights activists in Gaza and under the thumb of the Palestinian Authority who are putting themselves at risk by exposing the numerous human rights abuses being executed by Palestinian authorities in both camps. Opposition voices are silenced by threats, imprisonment, violence and murder. Journalists and human rights activists with the courage to reveal cruelties, corruption and lawlessness of their leaders are imprisoned and sometimes tortured. Neither BDS nor the Free Palestine campaigners demonstrate about the oppression and persecution of minorities in Palestinian-controlled area. Christians have fled Bethlehem and Gaza. Bethlehem was once a thriving town. When under Israeli rule 80% of the population was Christian. Today, under the oppressive control of the Palestinian Authority, and with a bullying Muslim population, they are down to below 10%. Gays and lesbians in support of BDS hit on Israel, but if you are a gay in Gaza you either stay in the closet, or escape to Tel Aviv.

BDS and Free Palestine fail to support the human and social rights of Arabs living under Palestinian control. Instead, they spend their money and efforts promoting propaganda circuses like *"Israel Apartheid*

Week," an annual pantomime of farce and lies that fail to address the harsh human rights abuses Arabs suffer under the corrupt regimes in Gaza and Ramallah. This is how *"human rights"* and *"social justice"* are used hypocritically by anti-Israel fanatics.

The boycott campaigns are, for BDS, a flexible weapon that can be maneuvered to where they can gain best advantage. It began as a total attack against the existence of Israel attempting to use political, cultural, scientific, academic and economic boycotts. Basically it failed dismally. It then shifted to a partial campaign concentrating on what they call *"the settlements,"* but they make no bones about refusing to accept a Jewish state standing anywhere.

They bully against normalization and co-existence even when this results in unemployment and poverty for Palestinian bread-winners who are gainfully employed and even promoted in Israeli industry and commerce.

Just ask 25 year old Basel Ja'afar. He was one of the five hundred Palestinian workers that got fired from the Soda Stream factory in Mishor Adumim that is repositioning to the Negev. He used to receive six thousand shekels a month salary. Under the Palestinian Authority he'll draw a salary of 1,450 shekels. Another four hundred Palestinians, working happily alongside their Jewish co-workers, will be fired when this factory closes its doors and moves. Palestinians will lose, the Negev Bedouin will gain.

So much for the BDS claims of supporting improved conditions for Palestinian Arabs.

Notice how evidence of Jewish heritage, belonging, and development in the land of Israel is tippexed out of the BDS narrative, replaced by the accusation that Israelis are latter-day *"white settlers"* and *"colonizers."* Were the nearly one million Jewish refugees from Arab lands white settlers and colonizers? I don't think so.

They fail to explain that colonizers are people who set out from foreign lands to claim other territory for their sovereign country. This clearly is not the case with Zionists exercising their multiple rights to settle in the land bequeathed to them as a historic and legal right.

As Judea Pearl asks in his *"BDS, Racism, and the new McCarthyism,"* BDS advocates would be hard-pressed to give one case of white settlers moving into a country they deemed to be the birthplace of their history and heritage. Even more tellingly, could they offer one case of settlers reviving the language that was spoken in that land by their predecessors? Or, one case of settlers adopting national and religious holidays commemorating historic events that took place in that land, and not the land these *"settlers"* came from.

Try as they may, neither the Palestinians nor the Free Palestine campaigners can manufacture a Palestinian history and identity as a timeless nation in a sovereign land that matches the Jewish narrative.

Hamas can scream "Islam!" as loudly and as bloodily as they like. Jewish heritage goes back a thousand years and more before the dawn of Islam.

Elsewhere in this book I talk about the Malmo Symptom, a new strain of anti-Semitism I discovered as part of my research for this book. Briefly, it is the growing demand that Jews must divorce themselves from Israel or face punishment or excoriation. My first evidence of this appeared in Malmo, Sweden. It has since gone viral and has made its way to South Africa.

The Students Representative Council of Durban University of Technology (DUT) demanded in February, 2015, that Jewish students who support the State of Israel should be kicked out of the Union.

The Secretary of the SRC, Mqondisi Duma, said: *"As the SRC, we had a meeting and analyzed international politics. We took the decision that Jewish students, especially those who do not support the Palestinian struggle, should deregister."*

Natan Pollack – the national chairman of the South African Union of Jewish Students - said the suggestion was *"deplorable."*

"To discriminate against people because of their religious and political standpoint goes against freedom of speech," Pollack said.

It's more than that. It's anti-Semitism.

*

BDS recruits Palestinian terrorists.

Nowhere could the convergence of BDS and Palestinian terrorism have been starker than the invitation by the South Africa branch of the BDS Movement for Leila Khaled to visit South Africa for a series of fundraising events in February 2015.

On August 29, 1969, Khaled was part of a team that hijacked TWA Flight 840 on its way from Rome to Athens, diverting the Boeing

707 to **Damascus**. No one was injured, but the aircraft was blown up after hostages had disembarked.

On September 6, 1970, Khaled and **Patrick Argüello**, a Nicaraguan-American, attempted the hijack of El Al Flight 219 from **Amsterdam** to **New York City** as part of the **Dawson's Field hijackings**, a series of almost simultaneous hijackings carried out by the PFLP. The attack was foiled when **Israeli sky marshals** killed Argüello after he shot a member of the air crew before eventually overpowering Khaled. She was carrying two hand grenades. The pilot diverted the aircraft to Heathrow airport in **London**, where Khaled was delivered to **Ealing** police station. On October 1, the British government released her as part of a prisoner exchange.

Dawson's Field was a remote desert airstrip in Jordan to where the hostages on four hijacked planes were taken before the planes were blown up by Palestinian terrorists. While the majority of the 310 hostages were taken to Amman, Jordan, the crew of the planes and 56 Jewish hostages were segregated.

This incident of Palestinian terrorism of Jordanian soil led King Hussein to banish Arafat's PLO from his kingdom in a bloody exchange of what became known as *"Black September."*

More recently, South Africa, a hub of the delegitimization campaign against Israel, adopted radical actions to demonize the Jewish state including the ridiculous campus-based *Israel Apartheid Week*. No other political or human rights cause warrants a whole week of colleague action. This is exclusively dedicated to the brainwashing of students to present Israel is the most heinous terms.

The extent of BDS desperation is seen in the recruitment of Palestinian terrorists to make their case. The hijacking incident involving Khaled which included the targeting and selection of Jewish passengers and the link between BDS and a Palestinian terrorist shows us clearly the intricate web between BDS, Palestinian terrorism, and the ever-present anti-Semitism at the heart of their cause.

The promotion material of the South African branch of BDS showed this terrorist wearing a keffiyah and carrying a machine gun.

You know BDS is morally bankrupt when they have to recruit a terrorist to help their cause.

*

In the 30s, 40s, and even 50s, European anti-Semites told the Jews to *"go to Palestine where you belong!"* I personally experienced this in Britain. Now in the 21st Century, BDS and other anti-Semites are shouting, *"Jews, get out of Palestine. You don't belong there!"*

*

The implied anti-Semitism of Western politicians and diplomats supporting BDS.

When an Australian politician makes a speech in the Federal Parliament endorsing BDS as a *"perfectly acceptable form of protest"* against Israel one wonders why this left wing politician failed to apply that yardstick to countries with openly blatant acts of illegal occupation by force, terrible human and civil rights records.

Melissa Parke, from the Labour Party, publicly supported boycotting the Jewish state. Not the *"occupied"* part of Israel, but the whole of

Israel. Parke worked in Gaza with the Union Nations Relief and Works Agency, a body that is infected with *"Stockholm Syndrome"* in that they employ Hamas members as salaried members of staff, they have been caught allowing rabid anti-Israel propaganda material in the textbooks of schools under their supervision, and were caught red-handed having their facilities used as weapon store houses only to foolishly return rickets back into the hands of Hamas operatives. This, for Mrs. Parke, goes unpunished and unspoken. It's only Israel that gets her back up.

This lady may dress up her attacks on Israel in a moral superiority quoting the Socialist language of *"international justice"* and *"non-violence"* to cover up her biased and barbed attacks on Israel. She carefully distinguished between Jews as a people and displeasure of Jews as a people with connection to a national home, even if that is enshrined, as I will repeat throughout this book, in charters and treaties of international legitimization.

Parke quoted, of all people, the noxious Richard Falk, a former UN human rights rapporteur, to support her proposition that the BDS Movement is not anti-Semitic and not *"intent on the destruction of Israel."* This would be fine if it was true, but it isn't. This leaves us to ask if Mrs. Parke was ignorant of the aims of the BDS Movement, or is aware of them and covered this up in fine *"progressive"* language.

Her mentor Falk was rightly rebuked by many prominent politicians, including British Prime Minister, David Cameron, when he published a nasty anti-Semitic cartoon on his website, which he hastily removed under the withering criticism he received. He also met wide scale disapproval for giving an endorsement to a book by a self-described *"proud self-hating Jew,"* Gilad Azmon, which begged the question whether *"Hitler might have been right after all."*

Falk also blamed the Boston Marathon bombing on what he called *"the American global domination project"* and *"Tel Aviv"* begging the question, putting two and two together, if Falk was more than hinting at a Jewish global conspiracy.

The British Government Equality and Non-Discrimination Team noted that Falk's writings *"resonate of the longstanding anti-Semitic practice of blaming the Jews for all that is wrong in the world."*

To further promote BDS, MP Parke often quoted Peter Slezak. Slezak is a Sydney-based academic and an executive member of Australia Palestine Advocacy Network (APAN). There was a terrible anti-Semitic incident in Sydney when a bus full of Jewish school children were threatened with having their *"throats cut"* and subjected to shouts of *"Heil Hitler"* and *"all Jews must die."* This didn't embarrass Slezak into silence. On the contrary, Slezak announced that *"all Jews are fair game because of their influence and militant support for crimes of the Jewish state."* Faced with an outburst of criticism Slezak squirmed an excuse that he only meant that Jews were fair game for criticism, though what *"criticism"* had to do with an anti-Semitic attack on young Jewish kids is anyone's guess.

People like Melissa Parke place all the blame of the problems of the Middle East, and even beyond, on to the shoulders of Israel, accusing it of all the heinous crimes they can concoct. They then position divisive groups like BDS as the way forward to a better world, while ignoring the actual racist agenda of BDS and others. This is dishonest advocacy. Instead of praising and supporting the only liberal democracy in the Middle East as a virtue to be emulated, especially by the Palestinian Arabs, their intellectual dishonesty exposes them for the bigots they are.

Although the British Parliament, including both the House of Commons and the House of Lords, issued a cross-party report on UK Anti-Semitism, there is deep anti-Semitic sentiment oozing out of members of both chambers.

In June, 2013, MP Patrick Mercer, during a visit to Israel, was caught on camera calling a female Israeli soldier *"a bloody Jew."*

On entering an intelligence facility he was approached by a female security guard. Describing the soldier to a British reporter he called her *"an 18 year-old girl, wearing a uniform, with her sort of hair in plaits, and crazy jewelry and open-toed sandals, with a rifle up my nose."*

He told the reporter how he responded to the girl by saying to her, *"Who the f—k are you?"* The girl replied that she was a soldier which was obvious due to her uniform. Mercer responded arrogantly, *"Are you? You don't look like a soldier to me. You look like a bloody Jew."*

Elsewhere in this book, the poisoned utterances of Lib Dem representative, Jenny Tonge, are highlighted. Another Lib Dem member with a history of anti-Semitic statements is David Ward. In 2013, He was temporarily suspended by his party for his comments about a *"losing Zionist battle"* calling Israel an *"apartheid state."*

On the eve of Holocaust Memorial Day, the MP for Bradford East wrote on his website that he *was "saddened that the Jews, who suffered unbelievable levels of persecution during the Holocaust, could within a few years of liberation from the death camps, be inflicting atrocities on Palestinians in the new State of Israel and continue to do so on a daily basis in the West Bank* [Judea and Samaria] *and Gaza."*

Paul Charney, Chairman of the Zionist Federation, welcomed the move against Ward's *"use of anti-Semitic language veiled in anti-Israel rhetoric."*

Comparing Ward's statements about Jews and the Jewish state to other minorities, a spokesperson for Stand for Peace - a British counter-extremism group - told Israel's Arutz Sheva that the decision to suspend Ward *"did not go far enough,"* noting that the period for which he will be *"suspended"* falls over the summer recess, when parliament is not in session.

"Time after time Anti-Semites are using anti-Israel sentiment as a means to further their agenda. It is with dismay that we note the withdrawing the whip is for the summer recess only.

"If David Ward had made these comments about any other minority, I suspect he would have been expelled from the party."

This unrelenting far-left MP continued his jaundiced comments against Israel during the Paris terror attacks, including the one that killed four Jews in the Jewish supermarket, by posting insensitive tweets saying *"Je suis #Palestinian"* and *"#Netanyahu is Paris march – What!!!! Makes me feel sick."*

Conservative MP, Andrew Bridgen, launched an unrepentant attack against *"the Jewish lobby"* in a Parliamentary debate of Palestinian statehood on October 13, 2014.

Britain's Jewish Leadership Council chief executive, Simon Johnson, said in response: *"It is scarcely credible for an MP with one breath to* claim that he is not anti-Semitic and with the next breath make reference to Jewish lobbying power based on unattributed comments by persons unknown on a trip to Washington."

The Anti-Defamation League (ADL) condemned anti-Semitic remarks, on February 15, 2015, made by Andre Louis, an extreme-right member of the Belgian Parliament, who said that *"pioneers of Zionism had organized and financed the Holocaust"* thereby echoing the anti-Semitic doctorate of Mahmoud Abbas, referred to elsewhere in this book.

*

A Dutch university that cancelled a panel discussion on boycotting Israel due to the Paris terrorist attacks was accused by a radical anti-Israel student group of violating academic freedom and free thought.

Students for Justice in Palestine at the VU University in Amsterdam seem to know something about academic freedom and free thought. They posted on their Facebook page, *"Free Palestine. Vrije Universiteit Israel-free!"* So much for SJP free thought. The intimidation on this campus took a turn for the worse. A Facebook user with the name Muhammad Seher commented on the SJP page, *"Free Palestine. Vrije Universiteit Jew-free!"* after a Jewish student referred to as Sonja reported to the Dutch-Jewish broadcast *Joodse Omroep* that she was afraid to return to that university. *"I don't want to come back, and in fact I think it's a bit scary,"* referring to the harassment of pro-Israel students and Jews.

*

Manchester's Jewish community came out to counter abusive demonstrations that congregated outside the Kings Street *Kedem* store selling Israeli Dead Sea products. They experienced the venom of protesters that lapsed into anti-Semitic rhetoric of *"loving Hitler,"* Nazi salutes and claims that Jews killed Jesus. They were also subjected to chants of *"Death to Jews!"*

Complaints to the police resulted in the anti-Israel, anti-Semitic demonstrators being restricted in size and location for their protests and subject to immediate arrest if conditions were breached, in order to prevent intimidation and harassment.

Raphi Bloom, one of the organizers of the Jewish counter-rally said, *"A lot of hard work went into removing the hate-mongers."* He added that the Manchester grassroots Jewish community could be proud of the way it had *"fought back and stood up to people peddling lies about the Jewish-run shop and about Israel."*

Bloom and Manchester Jews did, indeed, point the way to counter an anti-Semitism dressed up as pro-Palestinian protest.

*

When BDS demonstrators burst in to a Sainsbury supermarket in Birmingham, England, in August 2014 they damaged a range of kosher products. This store decided to remove their kosher items from their shelves.

Just what supporting a free Gaza has to do with pickled gherkins and matzo ball soup mix is anyone's guess. Except, of course, that Israel is Jewish and therefore all Jews are fair game for demonization and destruction. This is how the BDS Movement triumphs. By forcing

Sainsbury's to remove all their kosher products from the shelves of their store, as happened in their Birmingham establishment.

When the axis of anti-Israel, anti-Semitic hatred hits out against kosher food you know this blind hostility. When BDS hurls hate slogans against Israel yet boycotts Jewish food is when you see the dogmatic anti-Semitism behind their anti-Israel façade.

This is how the twisted web of supporting a violent Palestinian cause becomes inexorably linked to violence and lies. Anti-Israel thought and action so easily warps in to anti-Jewish thought and action. Actually, my premise is the opposite. It is all too often the anti-Jewish thought that motivates the anti-Israel action.

As Oren Segal, the director of the Anti-Defamation League's Center on Extremism said in the Jerusalem Post on August 18, 2014, *"it is one thing to express your criticism, your anger, of Israeli military operations or of Israeli policies. But, when trying to that, you interchange Israelis and Jews; it then becomes a different narrative."*

*

If one needs to know who, politically, are driving local boycott actions one need look no further than the city council of Leicester in the UK. In December 2014, this Midlands town decided on a motion to boycott Israeli goods from Judea and Samaria (the West Bank).

It is illuminating to study the statistics and trends of this English town. According to census figures, the ethnic composition of Leicester in 2001 was 80.5% White UK residents. By 2011 it was down to 45.1%, less than 50%, and falling. Parts of the north-west of Leicester are more than 70% Asian.

It was the Muslim members from the Labour Party that proposed the boycott resolution. In Leicester, 51 of the 55 council members are from the Labour Party, and they all voted for the boycott.

As Britain's UKIP leader, Nigel Farage said, *"What is fueling the rise of anti-Semitism in the UK and across the EU, is that there are many more Muslim voices, some of them are deeply critical of Israel, some of them question Israel's right to exist."*

The vast majority of physical attacks on local Jews in Europe are carried out by violent Muslims.

This is the factual heart of the problem of a Europe containing a turbulent and unhappy immigrant population hate Jews and Israel.

*

Supporting Zionism and a national homeland for the Jewish people is not some racist, bigoted, fascist, or extremist point of view. Zionism is the idea that the Jewish people should, by right, have a state in their historic homeland.

Monitoring NGOs.

Examining European human rights funding exposes an alarming discrepancy that targets Israel instead of other regional actors who are regularly guilty of serious human rights abuses. The European Instrument for Democracy and Human Rights (EIDHR) is supposed to promote *"democracy and human rights in non-EU countries."* It has an annual budget of 160 million Euros. According to NGO Monitor, between the period of 2007-10 EIDHR issues of Israel and the *"Occupied Palestinian Territories"* received over eleven million Euros in funding and the bulk of that money went into examining Israel while ignoring much of the human rights and anti-democratic abuses that took place in territories under the control of the Palestinian Authority and Hamas.

When NGO Monitor issued a report entitled *"Evaluating Funding for Political Advocacy NGOs in the Arab-Israeli conflict"* which analyzed EU funding, a Dutch member of the European Parliament, Bastiaan Belder, said that he regretted *"to see that 57% of EIDHR funding was given to Israel and the Palestinian 'occupied' territories while Israel is regarded by Freedom House as the only 'free' country in the Middle East."* He went on, *"While other countries, scoring much lower and classified as 'unfree' (such as the Palestinian Authority administered territories, Saudi Arabia and Iran) receive much less or even no funding under EIDHR. This is illogical and funding allocations to Human rights priorities in the region should be reconsidered."*

Belder finished his comments with a warning. *"I am deeply concerned about the findings of the report and I call upon the European Commission and the EU Delegation in Israel to stop the funding to NGOs that undermine Israel's legitimacy and the Middle East peace process."*

Belder's concerns were amplified by Sarah Ludsford, a British member of the European Parliament who told the Jerusalem Post back in February 2014 that the report *"raises serious concerns which the European Commission needs to answer in a very detailed, open and forensic manner, which it has not so far done...Grants to NGOs working in the context of the Israel-Palestinian conflict are bound to be somewhat controversial, but it is not acceptable to European taxpayers money to fund political activities which are in basic contradiction to EU goals."*

Ludsford emphasized that not only was EIDHR funding designed to advance democracy, non-violence and the rule of law, but that it was meant to advance trade and economic partnership with Israel based on the association agreement. *"To have EU money support the BDS agenda is shooting ourselves in the foot."*

The NGO Monitor report highlighted other EU sponsored NGOs that engage in biased political adventurism without any commitment to balance or neutrality. They quoted the 169,661 Euros that the *Israeli Committee against House Demolitions* received from the EU. This political NGO uses irrational expressions such as *"ethnic cleansing," "genocide,"* and *"apartheid"* to describe Israel while saying little about illegal building by Palestinian Arabs.

The *Holy Land Trust*, another recipient of EIDHR funding, supports the Kairos Palestine Document which rejects the Jewish historical connections to Israel in theological terms and calls for BDS against Israel.

While calling for transparency and condemning fund-receiving NGOs for their lack of neutrality, the EU itself has been guilty of both these transgressions when it comes to Israel. Verbally, and with their funding, they continue to advance a biased approach to the Israel-Palestinian issue that increasingly causes friction, and encourages the Palestinian leadership into a bolder rejection not only of peace but of Israel as it feels it has the EU, via the NGOs it supports, advocating its agenda.

*

Anti-Semitism and Israel hating.

"Anti-Semitism has become a unifying global ideology of the totalitarian Left. An intense propaganda campaign, begun in the Soviet Union in the 1970s was designed to undermine the legitimacy of the State of Israel by explicitly comparing Zionism to Nazism."

This was not some recent political observer. This was Daniel Patrick Moynihan, former US Ambassador to the UN, decades ago.

He acknowledged that bigots hide behind criticism of Israeli policy. *"The anti-Israel, anti-Zionist campaign is not uninformed bigotry, it is conscious politics. We are dealing here not with the primitive but with the sophisticated. It is not merely that our adversaries have commenced an effort to destroy the legitimacy of a kindred democracy through the incessant repetition of the Zionist-racist lie, it is that others believe it also."*

In anti-Israel societies and groups Jews feel forced to take a position. They feel exposed as Jews on this issue. They have to decide either to be a Jew for the anti-Zionist movement, or to be a Jew for themselves, namely to support the premise of the Jewish state. Sadly, too many Jews either take the anti-Israel position, or they openly criticize Israel to appease their anti-Israel neighbor.

Left-wing film-maker, Ken Loach, an avid Israel boycotter, once said about the rise of anti-Semitism, *"It's perfectly understandable because Israel feeds feelings of anti-Semitism."* What this arrogant cameraman was really saying was that he is an anti-Semite and Israel gives him the legitimacy to express his Jew-hatred and get away with it.

He's the type that, if Israel didn't exist, he'd have to take his loathing out of Mike Leigh, the Jewish film-maker that I went to cheder with in north Manchester. He would probably describe Leigh as that *"shitty little film-maker"* under his breath because Leigh, being a Jew, makes better movies than he does.

*

Notes about academic boycotts.

One place where movements and boycotts are troubling is on the campus. Faculties that specialize in humanities, languages, and social themes have been infiltrated by left-wing, often extremist, professors and lecturers that inculcate a leftist, often radical, interpretation of facts into their students. They shape students who enter the world and become the influence and opinion makers. This has the effect of shaping future generations and the way they view things. In their doing they seditiously reshape the founding principles of academia itself.

Academia is supposed to be the heart of open-minded discourse, the crucible of thought and debate. It is increasingly becoming the hard-core center of dogma when it comes to issues concerning Israel. When it comes to Israel we increasingly see the closing of the academic mind and, when the academic mind closes, it is no longer academia. It becomes something dangerous to an open, free thinking, society.

In their book, *"The Case against Academic Boycotts",* the authors Cary Nelson and Gabriel Noah Brahm, claim that left unchallenged, the academic spread of anti-Israel activity could lead to a strategic threat to Israel's security. I highly recommend their detailed research into BDS in academia.

Their claims are made by understanding the nature of the anti-Israel student body. It goes beyond the brainwashing by their radical professors and the biased direction of their educational courses on topics affecting opinion about Israel. It has the potential to become a political movement beyond the hallowed chambers of academia. Students share a social life that creates inter-relationships that go beyond their college lives. There is a bonding that creates a network of personal and professional connections that go with them into their careers and life ambitions. If a cause and philosophy is rooted in dislike, hatred even, of Israel and deepened by anti-Israel activity during their campus days, it is likely to carry with them into what they do in later life.

Brahms thinks that BDS is threatening to become the catalyst, a fashionable cause that links the lives of impressionable students during their formative years and leads them into their professional careers. If students get their thrills by characterizing Israel as a racist, colonizing, illegitimate regime guilty of ethnic cleansing, they are likely to carry this distorted opinion into everything they do as they further their career advancement in positions of power and influence. They sense of righteousness and political virtue which they shared with their college friends and masters and became the basis of meetings, activities, social get-togethers that later will crisscross their personal, political, and professional lives is likely to affect Israel in anything it may do in the future.

The struggle for Israel's and Jewish souls in America is being waged on the campus and in the faculties of foolish progressivism. Students who may be shallow-minded if not blindingly ignorant on world affairs are dogmatically certain that anti-Israelism is their life's passion.

The enormous ignorance was amply displayed when Jewish media activist, Avi Horowitz, went to Berkley, a campus that holds the ridiculous but poisonous Israel Apartheid Week and which passed an anti-Israel divestment resolution in 2013, and unfurled the flag of ISIS (the Islamic State terrorist organization) students walked by without even one making any protest. One person even wished him *"good luck!"* The only criticism he received was a friendly warning from one student who told him politely that he couldn't smoke on campus. No problem about someone waving the flag of Islamic State at Berkley. But when Horowitz stood on the campus steps waving the Israeli flag he became subject to repeated abuse. Responses included *"F—k Israel!" "Israel is a thief in the night," "Hamas is the greatest!" "All of Israel are killers."* Such is the intellectual depth of Berkley students when it comes to defining Israel and Islamic State.

Students, usually in the humanities and social science classes are taught a fiction for fact, hysteria for history. They go out from the lecture halls to join the campaigns that form their lives. They are active in the questionable pantomimes that turn Israel into an evil like no other. They bond and break bread together. They demonstrate and drink together. They form a fraternity and friend together, each giving the other the confidence that only a close comradeship can create.

The danger of this determined dogma is that these students graduate and take that bonding into their professional lives and careers whether it be teaching, the media, business or politics. They become the future influence makers who will eventually insert their school of thought into policy and public opinion.

As Professor Russell Berman of Stanford University's faculty of comparative literature told the Jerusalem Post in January 2015, *"There* is a radical fringe promoting BDS that wants to manipulate the structures of professional associations in order to generate anti-Israel statements."

Anti-Israel boycott resolutions were passed in 2014 by the American Studies Association but BDS was unsuccessful both with the American Historical Association and the Modern Languages Association. There has been blowback against BDS and the American Studies Association with legal challenges as to the nature of their discriminatory actions. The most radical BDS group on American campuses appears to be Students for Justice in Palestine (SJP) who have been known to use coercive and intimidating tactics in closing down Israeli opinion.

The starkness of pro-Palestinian activism linked to hatred of Jewish and pro-Israel campus support was radically expressed at UC Davis in late January 2015 when students pressing for a divestment resolution against the Jewish state jeered the minority Jewish students with shouts of *"Allah Akbar!"* as the Muslim member of the student senate, Azka Fayyaz, triumphantly bragged about how *"Hamas and Sharia law has taken over UC Davis,"* according to student Daniel Mael in *Truth Revolt*.

The Davis decision was overturned when it was exposed that the boycott resolution violated the senate constitution.

These actions illustrates the religious hate against anything Jewish, be in personal or collective, that lies within the BDS Movement.

It is increasingly common to witness the closing down of debate on campus. This point is made elsewhere in this book. But the actions of the BDS radicals are seen to be more anti-Jewish state and person than pro-anything. They deprive Jews and Israel supporters of their dignity. They behave with a sense of disrespect for other people's presence or position. This degradation is a crucial element of the demonization process so familiar to students of Jewish history. As we have seen in the past, the perpetrators, by dehumanizing their Jews, lose their own humanity.

The battle is raging around the concerns and questions of what danger academic boycotts, threats, and lack of freedom of speech and opinion pose to academic values. Certain academics, with or without opinions about Israel, are gravely concerned about the ongoing campaigns to subvert traditional open and free debate on campus.

As Booker Prize winner Howard Jacobson once called it, the dogma that closes down the academic mind troubles right-minded intellectuals. When bias and discrimination takes over teaching, when professors, lecturers and students are not prepared to listen to alternative or contrary thought or expression, when hatred blocks Israeli or pro-Israeli academics with valuable and original research and scientific information to contribute to higher education, it is no longer academia. It becomes the gloomy totalitarian corridors of Nuremburg. It is the closing of the academic mind.

The fact that Israel offers an academic life that is open to both Arab and Jew, where Israel is an open society in which an Arab can, and does, reach the highest echelon of society, and where Arabs have proper political representation in the Israeli parliament, will not soften the jaundiced aversion of students being produced in an academic industry of bias.

The jaundiced poison of academic disinformation will take some challenging in the years to come.

*

Attempts to apply BDS by, or to, the Palestinians has largely failed. This was confirmed by Professor Gabriel Brahm in his seminal article, *"The Disappearing BDS: From Anti-Zionism to Anti-Semitism."* BDS has failed to put a dent in Israel's economic and global development. In mid-December, a Palestinian official admitted as such. Mustafa Barghouti is an advocate of BDS. He is also a PLO Executive Committee member. He told Media Line that the self-imposed boycott of Israel products peaked during the 2014 Gaza conflict but has lapsed since then. This was confirmed by a Palestinian Birzeit University professor, Nasr Abdelkarim;

"If the boycott of Israeli goods reached its peak during the war on Gaza, and was eighty percent, now it is no more than twenty percent."

He admitted that items such as water, electricity, oil, and gas were impossible to boycott. When one looks at imports from Israel to the Palestinian Authority controlled West Bank we see that only $1 billion of the annual $4.5 billion total imports are Israeli products and not items like electricity and water that are essential and impossible to boycott. Even here, Israeli products are preferred for their quality and there is cooperation for Israeli entrepreneurs to provide improved water production including recycling and alternative energy sources to the Palestinians.

When activists try to close Israeli industry in the areas legally controlled by Israel, but where Palestinian workers are employed in large numbers, the effect of closure directly impacts on the fate of the Palestinians they claim to be helping.

*

The drip drip drip of Jewish anti-Israel, pro-BDS activism promoted as Zionism.

The Zionist Organization of America is engaged in a battle to prevent the infiltration into their body of groups whose main activity is to undercut the security of Israel and the safety of its people.

It has accused several candidates of pressing for membership into the American Zionist Congress while supporting the platform of BDS.

While most of these candidates vehemently protest that they do not promote boycotts against Israel and object to BDS, they have been found with their fingers in the cookie-jar.

Americans for Peace Now, for example, protests that they oppose the BDS Movement calling them *"misguided and counterproductive"* but they *"protest against the occupation and the settlements by boycotting products made in West Bank settlements."*

This is how two-faced (dare we call them liars) these activists can be even as they pose as being loyal Zionists.

Theodore Bikel, who is the chairman of Partners for Progressive Israel, also tries to define what Israel is and what it isn't. He hasn't got time, and cannot give Israel credit, for waiting for an end-of-conflict resolution. Instead, he pronounces that Israel's legitimacy *"does not extend to the settlements created in occupied territories."* His arrogance overrides his knowledge of the wording of the Oslo Accords signed between Israel and the Palestinians.

Other campaigners in support of an Israeli surrender from territory, fail to take into consideration the dangerous agenda of the Palestinians that would jeopardize the Jewish State post-withdrawal, as they come out with pious tones of purity that lack responsibility for their weakening and exposing Israel to legitimacy-threatening pressures. All of them want to infiltrate an affirmative Zionist Congress to impose their will on this body.

We have seen the outcome of such left-wing Jewish activities in Britain. Where JStreet failed to be accepted into the main Jewish organization in America, their UK equivalent, Yachad, was voted into the Board of Deputies of British Jews, much to the alarm and concern of grassroots Jews who do not want this fringe group to speak in their strongly pro-Israel name.

When Jews and Israelis were commemorating the fallen heroes of wars imposed on the Jewish state by invading Arab armies and Palestinian terrorists, Yachad was holding its own event on Israel's Independence Day which included a radical fringe group that accuses Israelis soldiers of *"war crimes."* Such is the level of their pro-Israelism.

In the name of nuance and pluralism, a break-away group from Hillel USA invites anti-Israel practitioners to speak. Open Hillel work with anti-Zionists as part of their *"pro-Israel, pro-peace"* platform.

Jewish Voice for Peace has been named among the top ten Anti-Israel groups by the Anti-Defamation League in America.

Anti-Israel activity has dramatically increased on campuses across North America and the work of these Jewish group engender and aid the spread by slandering the image of the Jewish state.

*

40 pro-Palestinian, anti-Israel protesters were evicted from the NYC Council Chamber in January 2015 after shouting abuse at the members during a meeting commemorating the 1.1 million people killed at Auschwitz.

This drew the following response from Councilman, David G. Greenfield;

"I have to tell you I am still shaken to my core. I'm upset and angry, but I tell you honestly, I am actually somewhat pleased what we saw here today.

If you are wondering why I am saying that is because for the last few weeks we have heard from people who have said, 'We don't dislike Jews, we only dislike the State of Israel. We have no problem with you. We only don't want you to go to Israel,' but we know that is not what is at the core of what they were saying and today they proved it.

While we were discussing the resolution regarding the murder of 1.1 million human beings – I will point out that 90% of them were Jewish but the other ten percent were political dissidents, they were Jehovah Witnesses, they were gays. These were the people who were being killed together in Auchwitz and Birkenau. While we were discussing that, they had the nerve, the chutzpah, the temerity, to unfurl a Palestinian flag and to yell at us while we were discussing that. So, the reason I am pleased is because we can stop pretending that this is about Israel when the reality is that every Middle Eastern country is not democratic and persecutes people of other faiths, and persecutes gays, and persecutes people that disagrees with them, and persecutes people on Twitter, and persecutes women who drive, except for one country which is the State of Israel.

And so, what you saw here today was naked, blind, anti-Semitism.

That's what you saw, and that's what you watched, and that's what you witnessed. People are upset for one reason. You want to know why they're angry. You want to know why they were unfurling that flag today. Because Hitler did not finish the job. He only wiped out half of my family, and only by the grace of God is the other half including me, the grandchild, still alive today. That's why those people are upset.

Shame on them! Shame of them for hating Jews! Shame on them for hating people! Shame on them for disrespecting this democratically elected body in America, and that's why we go to Israel. We go to Israel to take a message that is clear, that we will not be cowered by this fear and by this hatred that we have when these are people who would celebrate the deaths of Jews rather than mourn the deaths of innocents.

I am embarrassed at what happened here today, but I am pleased that we finally see what this is all about. Good old-fashioned anti-Semitism!"

*

Here is one example of the level of debate for campus activists. When the UCLA student council, led by the powerful and well organized Students for Justice for Palestine, voted for divestment from companies *"allegedly tied to violence against Palestinians"* an article appeared followed by a comment column.

In response the comments made by BigSticksWalkSoftly that spoke of the usual name calling *"illegal occupation, apartheid, ethnic cleansing, oppression and slow genocide,"* a student named Dan Spitzer wrote, *"Note that the pro-Israeli students, not wishing to dignify this patently biased kangaroo court, boycotted the meeting. They know it means nothing other than to slur the Middle East's sole democracy in an obvious manifestation of anti-Semitism aimed at the world's sole Jewish State. Meanwhile, no BDS vs Islamic societies which are butchering one another, relegating their women to second class citizenry, brutalizing gays, and suppressing dissidents. And, of course, no criticism of the Palestinian's favorite political party Hamas for openly calling for Jewish genocide.*

BTW, Soft Stick, since you champion the Palestinian 'cause,' it is reasonable to ask you if logically you also advocate Jewish genocide. Please respond to this question and come out of your closet."

Spitzer did get a reply from BSWS. This is part of it. *"Your juvenile name calling is highly representative of racist land thief illegal colonial olive tree burning settlers who are addicted to writing graffiti lie 'death to Arabs' all along Christian cemeteries.*

BDS was called by Palestinian civil society and does not answer to Abbas so what's your point.

The facts remain: Palestinians have a right to civil and human rights.

Criticizing the racist right wing policies of the terror Likud Israeli government does not make a person anti-Jewish.

Israel does not represent world Jewry (thankfully). In fact, Palestinians are real Semites and not fake imposters from another continent.

You and your racist brethren acknowledge that you are losing the advantage to silence Palestinians and their supporters and that is why you and your racist crew lacked the willpower to put up any defense, even when funded by pro-Israel groups.

Glad to see you are not so busy building apartheid walls and you have finally stopped being balls deep busy in your neighbor's goat you probably stole.

Brooklyn is your promised land, not Bethlehem.

Palestinians didn't do the holocaust. It is not Palestinian people's fault that Europeans can't get along and Americans don't want a boatload of Jewish immigration.

Go BDS go."

This gives you a nasty taste of the campus atmosphere for anyone who favors a reasoned debate. It is simply not possible. The hateful language does not allow space for dialogue.

A witness to the UCLA student divestment campaign who calls himself 'allone4World' added this comment, *"It's time for those of us who care deeply about Israel to organize and fight back hard against these actions. If it is fair for these students to vote to boycott and divest from companies that do business with Israel or West Bank Settlements then it is equally fair for us to boycott them. I am in a position to hire a fair amount of people and I check the resumes. When I see resumes from the BDS crowd and their supporters (and I check by going on line) the* resume gets tossed. No internships, no summer jobs, no permanent jobs, no exceptions. Donations I used to make to UCLA go to Friends of The Israel Defense Forces instead. Never again means taking action, not sitting idly by while our enemies organize and in spite of all of the moral outrages in the world choose to act against the one tiny Jewish state while the Arab states discriminate at will."

*

As January turned into February, two days after the student body passed a non-binding advisory resolution calling on the University of California to divest from Israel, swastikas were daubed on the frat house of Alpha Epsilon Pi proving, once again, that tainted anti-Israel actions are daubed with anti-Semitism.

Lawrence H. Summers, the Charles W. Eliot University Professor and president emeritus of Harvard University, and former Secretary of the treasury, delivered a lecture on *"Academic Freedom and Anti-Semitism"* at Columbia University at the end of January 2015.

He recalled that in 2002, when a petition circulated among the Harvard and MIT faculty and students, calling on universities to divest from companies doing business in Israel, he labeled the initiative "anti-Semitic in effect if not intent." Last week, he said his 2002 assertion *"seems to me to have stood up rather well,"* and warned that the situation has gotten even worse: *"It is my impression that there are more grounds for concern today than at any point since the Second World War."* Summers went on,

"We live in a world where there are nations in which the penalty for homosexuality is death, in which women are stoned for adultery, in

which torture is pervasive, in which governments are killing tens of thousands of their own people each year. But the proponents of Israeli boycotts, divestiture, and sanctions do not favor any form of pressure against countries other than Israel."

Summers asserted that a boycott of Israel vote by the American Studies Association (ASA) was "anti-Semitic in effect *and quite likely in intent"* since it applied only to Israel, sought to demonize the Jewish state, and was "unrelated to the expertise" of the ASA. By reaching out, beyond your area of competence, to delegitimize the Jewish state–and no other country–both the effect and intent of the action is crystal clear. As Summers states,

"The decision of the American Studies Association supported by a majority of its membership to single out Israeli institutions and Israeli scholars for selective boycott is abhorrent. The University believes it is very dangerous for scholarly associations to insert themselves into political issues outside of their range of competence. While individual members of the faculty are free to do as they wish, the University is withdrawing its institutional membership in the ASA. We will withdraw from any scholarly association that engages in similar boycotts with respect to Israel or any other country."

*

If you are a pro-Palestinian Jewish student on campus you have a charmed life. If you are a Jewish student on campus and are passionately pro-Israel, God help you!

For many Jewish students starting their academic life, Israel is not at the forefront of their minds until discovering the shock of anti-Israel hate and activism. Some keep their heads down, determined to progress in their higher education, while others take sides. For some Jewish students, taking the other side makes for an easier passage through to their graduation. For those dedicated to their pro-Israel position, life can be very challenging.

*

Using Zionism to beat BDS.

The way the world views Israel is so totally contradictory to the still-held vision of the Zionist, even Labour Zionist, household.

Compared to the original Zionist pioneers that led the early days on Israel with their Socialist ideology the current Labour Party have shifted even further left that many old-time Labourites such as like Hillel barely recognize the Labour of today. Halkin claims to have stood steadfast with those founding principles as he sees the current Labour Party as having moved further left when it comes to Zionism.

If anything characterizes Zionism in general it is the sheer conviction that it was, and is, proper to establish the national homeland for the Jewish people in the Land of Israel, that this right in enshrined in the ingathering of the Jewish people to their ancestral homeland as written in prayers and poems that have been uttered by Jews for a millennia, that history first inscribed in the Bible that is sanctified by both religious teaching and scholarly research proves beyond a shadow of doubt that the Jews are the true indigenous people of the land.

The rights and legitimacy of the Zionist enterprise was finally recognized and codified into law by several international treaties and documents going back a century and these legal commitments have yet to be rescinded or replaced by any legal remedy no matter how hard they try to concoct false descriptions of laws from resolutions, advisories, and false manipulation of texts.

If it is true that, according to Zionist principles it is important and matters what we do, the Zionist endeavor had produced the most remarkable achievements of the last one hundred years. From turning arid desert into fertile valleys, transforming malarial swamps into rich orchards and fishponds, and changing a barren land into the most productive, innovative hi-tech nation on earth. Detested refugees from the horrors of Nazi Europe and hateful Arab regimes have raised their heads, fought for their survival, freedom from persecution, and self-determination. They have become scientific, agricultural, medical, technological leaders while the languishing Arabs and others still detest us for what we are and continue to protest the presence of the Jew in their midst, as they did in the past.

They are unable to praise this shiny little country for all the good it does for mankind, but they are quick to condemn this *"shitty little country"* when it does things *"disproportionately."*

Let's see how this disproportionality stacks up, shall we.

Two thousand killed in Gaza as Israel defends its citizens attacked by noxious Hamas terrorists hiding behind its own citizens are a reason to drag Israel to the International Criminal Court on war crimes charges, but let's look at the ratio of less than one civilian killed for every terrorist, according to documented proof.

That's terrible, but not as terrible as the ratio of three civilians for every terrorist killed in Afghanistan, and a ratio of four civilians killed for every terrorist in the Iraq invasion, yet nobody dragged the US-British led coalition forces to the ICC.

Now that is disproportionate – and that is cynical bias.

And notice everyone applauding the US-led air force strikes against Islamic State where nobody is crying about civilians that have been killed in huge numbers. Here, nobody is counting dead civilians. We are all rooting for the coalition forces and hating the terrorists.

I guess it depends on whose terrorists are being fought against as to which garners public approval, or condemnation.

Now that really is disproportionate and biased.

So, getting back to my premise, it doesn't matter what we Zionists do or don't do. It's what we are that makes the difference.

Dr. Einat Wilf agrees with my premise. Born in Jerusalem, and after serving as an intelligence officer in the IDF, she received a BA I government and fine arts at Harvard before earning a PhD in political science at Cambridge University. She is a Senior Fellow with the Jewish People Policy Institute and an Adjunct Fellow at the Washington Institute for Near East Policy.

She was a member of the Foreign Affairs and Defense Committee of the 18th Knesset after serving as Foreign Affairs Advisor to Shimon Peres when he was the Deputy Prime Minister.

Dr. Wilf is widely travelled and has had years of close contact with the international diplomatic and academic communities and, like me, has seen a disturbing change in attitude toward Israel that troubles her.

This has been a transformative experience for her. In her words she explains things from her perspective.

"I think that in general every person wants to believe that it matters what we do. But, in recent years as I go around the world, I've had to question that premise — that it's all about what we do. If we only end the occupation, if we only stop building settlements, the world would treat us differently.

The reason I started questioning that assumption is that in many of my talks abroad, where I generally expressed the left-wing Zionist position of two states for two peoples, I began to sense that when people spoke against Israel, I sensed a passion, emotion, and hatred that could not be accounted for by people simply disagreeing with Israeli government policies. I had to admit that this was not about what we do. It is very much about who we are.

I often wonder what Theodor Herzl would have thought if he were told that establishing a state for the Jewish people would do nothing to solve anti-Semitism, to solve the Jewish question.

He thought he had an analysis of the problem: the Jews are hated because they are homeless among the nations — they do not have the dignity and freedom, they would be able to walk with their heads high among the nations.

What would he have thought if he were told that as soon as the Jewish people would have a state, the hatred toward the Jews would merely mutate itself into hatred toward the state, and that nothing fundamentally would change?"

Einat Wilf agrees that what she calls the *"current tsunami"* of BDS, criticism from the EU, anti-Israel resolutions in many of the UN bodies, are not about settlements, occupation or even the Gaza conflict. They are excuses for something else.

"There is the analysis that if Israel merely changes its policies, or simply negotiates in good faith, much of this would disappear. But I believe that there's something far deeper going on. I believe that this is essentially a war waged by different means.

Ever since Israel was established, it has had to face warfare: initially by gangs, then by military invasion, then terror, then state-based economic boycott. It took a while from 1948 to 1973, to get them to realize that they have failed. It took around twenty five years to get Arab armies to finally give up on the possibility of getting Israel to surrender by the use of military force. Then it took a few more decades to get terrorism to no longer be considered a primary strategy. The Arab boycott still lives, but by and large we have been able to build a thriving export economy. But every time we pull through, the other side doesn't give up. They just look for other means. And that is what we are seeing right now.

This is the same war against Israel and Zionism, but through other means. What are these means? Words, images, idea, arguments. And this is a real strategic danger. The world's greatest atrocities, historically, were preceded by preparing people's minds for the belief that what they are about to commit is not an atrocity.

Even when people do some of the worst things possible, they have in their minds a mental set that tells them that what they are doing is good. Even people who committed the world's greatest atrocity, the mass-murder of six million Jews in Europe, had been led to believe that they were ridding the world of evil.

Today, people are being prepared by what I call the placard strategy. People hold placards – both physically in demonstrations and in things people say on panels, on television, at every opportunity. The placards don't say 'Zionism equals the liberation movement of the Jewish people for their self-determination in their homeland.' They say that 'Zionism equals racism, colonialism, imperialism, apartheid, ethnic cleansing,' and now, after last summer, 'genocide.'

These words are chosen not because they reflect reality but because they all have something in common: they are all internationally accepted as evil. So putting them next to 'Zionism' or 'Israel' is basically a way of repeating the message that Zionism and Israel are the ultimate evil.

Therefore, as a citizen of the world, as someone who cares about justice and human rights, your responsibility is to ensure that ultimate evil is erased from the world, by any means possible.

It is a non-violent strategy that has been chosen because violent strategies have failed, but the sinister purpose remains the same: the end of Zionism and the destruction of the State of Israel.

People are being prepared that if Israel is somehow made to disappear, not only would that not be a tragedy, but would be desirable. The world would rid itself of a sickness, a disease, of an evil. That is exactly how minds are being prepared for the carrying out of an atrocity.

We need to fight head-on this sinister battle that is taking place against Israel and ultimately defeat it.

Our winning this war would mean the day that those who hold anti-Zionist views would have the legitimacy of neo-Nazis have today. It means to reverse the social acceptability of anti-Zionism that we have today. How? We need to mobilize – people, resources, leadership.

Our military gets sixty billion shekels a year. Our Foreign Ministry gets 1.6 billion shekels a year. We still don't understand that this is a war for which we need to mobilize the same way we did for all our other struggles, challenges and wars.

When Zionism knew that in order to get a state we needed to gain world legitimacy, we sent our best people to 'the front.' These were people who told our story and inspired people. Then we sent our best people to the military.

I think we need to send some of our best people to the legitimacy front. We need to create what I would call an 'IIDF,' an Intellectual Israel Defense Force. We need to understand that this must be a world-wide effort, and we need to understand that this will take time."

*

Using lawfare to defeat BDS. The UK Lawyers for Israel example.

Much of the actions of anti-Israel provocateurs go unchallenged in many Western countries. There is a dire need for lawyers of conscience to create civil rights groups in support of those seeking justice for Israel and to protect individuals and groups defending Israel from intimidation and abuse. In many cases this has not happened because people have been cowed into silence and inactivity by powerful threatening and organized forces.

Things began to change in Britain after a couple of conversations I had on this issue with London barrister, Jonathan Turner, previously a lone battler against BBC misreporting. Jonathan held talks with Andrew Balcombe, former Chairman of the UK Zionist Federation, Jon Goldberg Q.C., and others.

UK Lawyers for Israel was formed by amalgamating a group of lawyers established by the UK ZF and a group of lawyers who attended a 2010 conference in Israel. This band of volunteer lawyers have grown and are dedicated to examine cases, incidents and issues where anti-Israel campaigns infringe British laws and regulations and cause damage to individuals and pro-Israel groups.

Within a very few years, the successful intervention of UK Lawyers for Israel in issues where legal red lines were crossed attracted other like-minded lawyers to their cause and their membership has grown. Their efforts for justice attracted the attention of lawyers in other countries and a network of similar legal groups is expanding globally in the fight against dishonest and dubious deeds of damage-causing practitioners.

An early, and major, success was in stopping the 2011 Gaza flotilla. Their request to a leading Athens lawyer led to the Greek Coast Guard impounding the ships and preventing them from sailing in a provocative act in support of Hamas.

The London-based UK Lawyers for Israel disrupted the transmission of funds by Viva Palestina to Hamas in Gaza by informing the Serious Organized Crime Agency that its bank account held money that might be used for terrorism. Following this action, a Viva Palestina convoy was aborted.

UK Lawyers for Israel have helped students to prevent the implementation of anti-Israel student union resolution on various British campuses on the grounds that they fell outside the unions' charitable objects, thereby setting a precedent that has helped turned the tide of many campus boycott campaigns.

They have also defended Israeli supporters against false accusations and threats of libel proceedings by their opponents. One such action allowed a student to attend a meeting at the University of Middlesex where his recording of a speech made by Jenny Tonge resulted in her removal from the Liberal Democratic Party.

Importantly, UK Lawyers for Israel have prevented the passage of anti-Israel resolutions by many UK local authorities by citing the public sector equality obligations, public procurement laws, and other legal requirements.

Their actions seek justice and rights for people threatened by Palestinian and other sources. One such action helped a young Palestinian Christian woman, threatened with death by the Palestinian Authority secret police after she spoke out in support of Israel, to obtain asylum in the UK, after several law firms declined to accept her case.

They obtained compensation and an apology for an Israeli student at Warwick University, whose MA dissertation had been marked down by a BDS-supporting lecturer.

UK Lawyers for Israel prevented advertising by the Palestinian Authority on the public transport system that claimed Haifa, Jaffa and Jerusalem were Palestinian cities.

They defeated a call by the Royal Institute of British Architects (RIBA) to have the Israeli Association of United Architects suspended from the international body of architects after establishing that such a decision was outside RIBA's charitable objects and, therefore, contrary to the UK charity law.

UK Lawyers for Israel could do a lot more but they are restricted because their growing team of lawyers act voluntarily and do not, as yet, receive funding for their valiant efforts to obtain justice and fairness against the powerful and blatantly anti-Israel campaigning that often have no legitimacy under domestic laws and regulations.

They are an example to lawyers in other countries to replicate their successes.

ADDITIONAL INSIGHTS INTO FIGHTING BDS.

To the Students for Justice in Palestine, a Letter from an Angry Black Woman
'You do not have the right to invoke my people's struggle for your shoddy purposes'

Fighting words from Chloe Valdary.

The student organization Students for Justice in Palestine (SJP) is prominent on many college campuses, preaching a mantra of *"Freeing Palestine."* It masquerades as though it were a civil rights group when it is not. Indeed, as an African-American, I am highly insulted that my people's legacy is being pilfered for such a repugnant agenda. It is thus high time to expose its agenda and lay bare some of the fallacies they peddle.

• If you seek to promulgate the legacy of early Islamic colonialists who raped and pillaged the Middle East, subjugated the indigenous peoples living in the region, and foisted upon them a life of persecution and degradation—you do not get to claim the title of *"Freedom Fighter."*

• If you support a racist doctrine of Arab supremacism and wish (as a corollary of that doctrine) to destroy the Jewish state, you do not get to claim that the prejudices you peddle are forms of legitimate *"resistance."*

- If your heroes are clerics who sit in Gaza plotting the genocide of a people; who place their children on rooftops in the hopes they will get blown to bits; who heap praises upon their fellow gang members when they succeed in murdering Jewish school boys and bombing places of activity where Jews congregate—you do not get to claim that you are some Apollonian advocate of human virtue. You are not.

- If your activities include grieving over the woefully incompetent performance by Hamas rocketeers and the subsequent millions of Jewish souls who are still alive—whose children were not murdered by their rockets; whose limbs were not torn from them; and whose disembowelment did not come into fruition—you do not get to claim that you stand for justice. You profess to be irreproachable. You are categorically not.

- If your idea of a righteous cause entails targeting and intimidating Jewish students on campus, arrogating their history of exile-and-return and fashioning it in your own likeness you do not get to claim that you do so in the name of civil liberty and freedom of expression.

- You do not get to champion regimes that murder, torture, and persecute their own people, deliberately keep them impoverished, and embezzle billions of dollar from them—and claim you are "pro-Arab." You are not.

- You do not get to champion a system wherein Jews are barred from purchasing land, traveling in certain areas, and living out such an existence merely because they are Jews—and claim that you are promoting equality for all. You do not get to enable that system by pushing a boycott of Jewish owned businesses, shops, and entities—and then claim that you are *"against apartheid."* That is evil.

- You do not get to justify the calculated and deliberate bombings, beatings, and lynching of Jewish men, women, and children by referring to such heinous occurrences as part of a noble *"uprising"* of the oppressed—that is racism. It is evil.

- You do not get to pretend as though you and Rosa Parks would have been great buddies in the 1960s. Rosa Parks *was* a real Freedom Fighter. Rosa Parks *was* a Zionist.

Coretta Scott King was a Zionist.

A. Phillip Randolph was a Zionist.

Bayard Rustin was a Zionist.

Count Basie was a Zionist.

Dr. Martin Luther King Sr. was a Zionist.

Indeed, they and many more men and women signed a letter in 1975 that stated: *"We condemn the anti-Jewish blacklist. We have fought too long and too hard to root out discrimination from our land to sit idly while foreign interests import bigotry to America. Having suffered so greatly from such prejudice, we consider most repugnant the efforts by Arab states to use the economic power of their newly-acquired oil wealth to boycott business firms that deal with Israel or that have Jewish owners, directors, or executives, and to impose anti-Jewish preconditions for investments in this country."*

You see, *my* people have always been Zionists because *my* people have always stood for the freedom of the oppressed. So, you most certainly do not get to culturally appropriate *my* people's history for your own.

You do not have the right to invoke *my* people's struggle for your shoddy purposes and you do not get to feign victimhood in our name. You do not have the right to slander *my* people's good name and link your cause to that of Dr. King's. Our two causes are diametrically opposed to each other.

Your cause is the antithesis of freedom. It has cost hundreds of thousands of lives of both Arabs and Jews. It has separated these peoples, and has fomented animosity between them. It has led to heartache, torment, death and destruction.

It is of course your prerogative to continue to utilize platitudes for your cause. You are entirely within your rights to chant words like *"equality" "justice"* and *"freedom fighter."*

You can keep using those words for as long as you like. But I do not think you know what they mean.

Chloe Valdary founded a pro-Israel student group, Allies of Israel, while a student at the University of New Orleans. She is a Consultant at Committee for Accuracy in Middle East Reporting (CAMERA) and the recipient of the David Bar Ilan Award for outstanding student leadership. Chloe is also the author of 'Reclaim the Zionist Dream.'

How to fight the academic boycott more effectively.

How can the academic boycott of Israel be fought more effectively? This question becomes increasingly relevant as anti-Israeli forces, whether on various campuses or within professional associations, push for actions against Israel.

The anti-Israeli boycott campaign among academics started in April 2002, with an open letter in the Guardian from scholars of various countries. It called for a moratorium on all cultural links with Israel at European and national levels. In recent years, the main growth of anti-Israel boycott activities has occurred in the United States. One has to differentiate, however, between boycotts originating from student organizations and those coming from the academic faculty. Students will leave campus after a few years, but academics stay on and their boycott decisions are therefore more dangerous.

The boycott is yet another derivative of the successful Arab propaganda to push the Palestinian-Israeli conflict to the center of the international stage. This debate distracts attention from the huge and ever-increasing criminality in many parts of the Arab world.

Arab academics may play a role in the anti-Israeli boycott on some campuses, but it is the Left, however – including sometimes Jews or Israelis – who provide its main power. There are other factors at play, though. This was explained by Curtis Marez, the former president of the American Studies Association (ASA), which supports the anti-Israel boycott. He was reported to have said that many other countries, including some in the Middle East, have a human rights record comparable or worse than that of Israel. Marez added that, *"One has to start somewhere."* He mentioned that Palestinian civil-society groups had asked his organization to boycott Israel and no similar requests had been made by groups in other countries.

So far, the boycott battle has been run according to classic lines. The anti-Israeli boycotters attack, and afterward, some pro-Israeli professors oppose the move.

Depending on the local situation and on the support often given by Jewish grassroots bodies, one of the sides wins. The majority of scholars often do not participate in the vote. This was the case with the ASA boycott vote.

One of the most complex battles took place in 2009, concerning an anti-Israeli boycott proposal by a number of professors to the board of The Norwegian University of Science and Technology (NTNU) in Trondheim. Many major Jewish organizations, including The American Jewish Committee, The Anti-Defamation League and The Simon Wiesenthal Center were involved in the battle. A key role was played by Scholars for Peace in the Middle East, who mobilized thousands of scholars, including a number of Nobel Prize winners, who requested that they be included in the boycott if Israeli academia were to be boycotted.

The Norwegian Jewish community, the Israeli embassy and the American ambassador also intervened. Finally, when the Norwegian government realized that this was becoming a potentially major international issue, it told the state university that it had no business making foreign policy. Ultimately, the entire NTNU board voted against the boycott.

Yet there is one less conventional, potentially successful avenue to fight the academic boycott which has not yet been attempted.

The inspiration for such a method can be taken from events that have occurred within several European countries, and are far from being theoretical.

In 2011, the popular German defense minister, Karl-Theodor du Guttenberg, was forced to resign after his doctoral thesis was found to contain substantial plagiarism.

His doctorate was also taken away. Annette Schavan, the German Minister of Education and Research, had to resign in 2013 following the revocation of her doctorate due to plagiarism.

These are the best known such cases, but the German Guttenplag Wiki site gives a list of many other dubious researchers at various German universities that have been exposed over the years. In Poland there is such a plagiarism-checking site, as well.

Several Dutch professors, too, have had to give up their positions due to falsification of data or sloppy work. The best known among them is Diederik Stapel, a former professor of social psychology. An investigation found that 55 of his papers contained fraudulent material.

One does not have to limit one's investigations to plagiarism or fraud. A number of scholars are also sloppy with their footnotes and may quote from incorrect or poor sources. If a scholar has many footnotes as references, the risk of a significant number of mistakes increases.

Once one has a list of those university lecturers who support the boycott of Israel, one can select targets among them for investigation. It is likely that if one chooses one's targets intelligently, one would find a few who plagiarize, publish using incorrect sources or are guilty of academic fraud. It is also likely that some of their colleagues would gladly provide the names of those to be investigated. The lecturers that do not meet academic standards would then be exposed within their universities and among their professional colleagues. One only has to find a few such cases in order to greatly diminish the threat of boycotts.

Much like the general population, most academics are cowards. Many of those who enjoy the free anti-Semitic boycott lunches today may think twice before joining any boycotts in the future if it could means their careers would be at risk.

There would be nothing wrong with the Israeli government partly financing such investigations, in addition to private funding.

The boycotters are hostile elements and might even be called Israel's enemies.

There is also a potential side benefit from such activities: exposing negligent and fraudulent academics is of benefit to academia at large.

Manfred Gerstenfeld's upcoming book "The War of a Million Cuts" analyzes how Israel and Jews are delegitimized and how to fight it. He is a former chairman (2000-2012) of the Jerusalem Center for Public Affairs.

Hashtag Maccabees

Hour by hour and day by day, the world's only Jewish country is being slandered.

Whether by misleading graphic posts on Facebook, via lies told in a stream of tweets or through vicious propaganda videos on YouTube, there is a drip-drip of defamation aimed at the State of Israel. In this campaign of misinformation, no lie is too big, no accusation too inflammatory. Far too frequently, baseless charges and twisted accounts of history intertwine to paint a picture that is the polar opposite of what is true. In the reputational war being waged against Israel, all too often the heat is generated on the online frontline.

Israel's supporters can and must utilize social media to redress the balance. We need to expose the lies and, at the same time, reach out to people about the real Israel – democratic, diverse and sizzling with creative energy, showing the world the truth about the ancient nation-state of the Jewish people that was reborn and became the modern, dynamic, start-up nation.

Back in 2009, following the first air strikes on Gaza, which were in response to a huge escalation in Hamas rocket fire onto Israel, StandWithUs set up the first Israel advocacy Social Media Situation Room, in partnership with the IDC Herzliya.

At that time, in an interview with Reuters, I called Operation Cast Lead the *"first social media war."* Indeed, it was the first campaign in which online activists acting on behalf of Israel energetically fought back against the steady stream of misinformation flowing from Hamas and its global supporters. Likewise, in the 2012 Pillar of Defense conflict, multiple social media rooms emerged, manned by devoted activists. It was then that the hashtag *#IsraelUnderFire* was coined and this has been utilized ever since to underline the perils that Israel faces from Hamas rockets.

Most recently during Operation Protective Edge in 2014, we saw a large spike in social media response by Israel's supporters. In the David vs. Goliath of the Middle East, Israel still is the David, surrounded by numerous terrorist organizations which include Hezbollah, Hamas, Islamic Jihad, and strong nations calling for Israel's destruction, such as Iran. This David/Goliath dichotomy plays out online too. It's hard to assign winners and losers to social media battles, but the fact that Time magazine cited *#IsraelUnderFire* as well as *#GazaUnderAttack* as some of the most-utilized hashtags of 2014 should be seen as positive, especially given that on the web as in real life, Israel is numerically the David facing a Goliath.

Via the Internet, organizations and even individuals can have a greater impact than that of a country, and Israel's enemies have long known this. In a perceptive article in *The Washington Post* shortly after the terrorist attacks on 9/11, the late US diplomat Richard Holbrooke asked of Osama bin-Laden, *"How could a mass murderer who publicly praised the terrorists of Sept. 11 be winning the hearts and minds of anyone? How can a man in a cave out-communicate the world's leading communications society?"* The terrorist adversaries of Israel and of Western society know that as well as being a fertile recruiting ground for extremists, the Internet and social media are the central battleground for their PR.

That's the challenge – now we must counter it. This month, the Israeli Prime Minister's Office chose StandWithUs, based on our experience and expertise, to deliver a program – *"Social Media Ambassadors"* – aimed at training Israeli students, as well as some of their peers abroad, to use the Internet to better share the reality of Israel. The Prime Minister's Office has rightly identified that the reality of Israel is best portrayed through the eyes of citizens and those who visit Israel, as was particularly borne out during last summer's campaign against Hamas in Gaza.

StandWithUs has pioneered social media outreach for many years and achieved much success doing so. Our Twitter following reaches over a million people. Our YouTube videos have been viewed well over two million times. Our peak weekly Facebook posts reach is 30 million and we operate on multiple platforms in over a dozen languages. While leading this new program, StandWithUs will continue to fashion its own messaging and material as it has done for the 13 years since its inception. More importantly, program participants will use the training to tell Israel's story from their own points of view.

Who is our audience? The vast swathes of the world who are susceptible to anti-Israel propaganda; those who simply do not know enough about Israel to challenge the lies peddled to them by extremist groups. It is high time to call out the slander, to fill that knowledge vacuum with a true depiction of who Israelis are and what Israel is.

Most importantly, as cliché as it may sound, the truth is on our side.

Churchill reminded us that *"The truth is incontrovertible. Malice may attack it, ignorance may deride it, but in the end, there it is."* There it is, indeed. Our challenge is to show it.

This new program aims to empower people to utilize social media to take a stand, to act as a force multiplier and to engage more and more people to fight back against the misinformation; showing people the real Israel. It is time for the Hashtag Maccabees to stand up for Israel and help more people educate themselves and others.

Michael Dickson is the Israel director for StandWithUs.

FIGHTING ANTISEMITISM.

"Western Europe is undergoing a wave of Islamization, anti-Semitism and anti-Zionism."
Israel's Prime Minister, Benjamin Netanyahu. January 18, 2015.

"Anti-Zionism became a magical formula enabling one to be 'democratically anti-Semitic.'"
French philosopher, Vladimir Jankelevitch. 1978.

"They couldn't destroy Israel, so they attack Judaism."

When attacked, the European Jewish targets are inevitably synagogues, Jewish schools and where people eat kosher, the heart of affirmative Judaism and Zionism.

Anti-Semitism can no longer hide behind a facade of legitimate criticism of Israel.

Anti-Semitism is a disease that cannot be cured. Sometimes it's hidden and sometimes it's seen. Not everyone is infected by it, but once you've got the virus it's difficult to erase.

One thing that Jews have learnt over the centuries is that when people say they want to kill you they really mean they want to kill you. Jews, therefore, cannot be blamed for taking such threats seriously, and taking every conceivable step to prevent the slaughter. Such steps may be defensive. They may be offensive. But both steps are legitimate because Jews have the longest history of being the world's victim. It's only recently that they have learnt to fight back.

At the 2014 UN General Assembly an ambassador from one of the Latin American countries approached Israel's Ambassador to the US, Ron Dermer, and talked to him about the situation in the region, saying, *"You know what the word Israel means? It means 'to deceive.'"*

He was wrong. Although the name *"Jacob"* had a connotation of struggle, following the biblical Jacob's struggle with the angel, Jacob's name was changed. We are told in Genesis 32:29 that *"No longer will it be said that your name is Jacob, but Israel, for you have striven with the Divine and with men, and you prevailed."*

That is the fate of Israel and the Jewish people, to strive and struggle against mankind until we prevail.

Truth be told, the Latin ambassador, thinking he was biblically clever, displayed an arrogant anti-Semitism by trying to disparage Israel by hiding behind a high theological perspective. In fact, the truth comes back to haunt him because a correct reading of Genesis shows the real character of the Jewish people and Israel. It is one of centuries of spiritual and physical struggle from which the State of Israel shines like a statement in overcoming overwhelming adversary and firmly staking its place in its God-given land.

On January 16, 2014, Laurent Louis of the center-right People's Party in Belgium said in their parliament that *"The Holocaust was set up and financed by the pioneers of Zionism."* What clearer link can you find between an anti-Semite hatred of Jews and modern-day Israel? This comment was condemned by the president of the Belgium parliament. His party disowned him but he remained in the legislative body as a non-partisan politician. More recently, he accused Israel of Nazi crimes against Palestinians, an oft quoted aspersion that turns Jews into Nazis. To complete the picture of an anti-Semitism posed as contempt for Israel, he was photographed outside the Belgium parliament while standing on an Israeli flag. How these people get their jollies!

In July, 2014, during the Gaza conflict, French Prime Minister, Manual Valls, warned of a *"new form of Anti-Semitism"* following the Paris anti-Israel protest riots that were rife with anti-Semitic slogans and anti-Jewish action.

The Paris suburb of Sarcelles has a large Sephardic Jewish population. It is also home to a growing Muslim population. Dozens of youths, some masked, looted and damaged Jewish owned shops and businesses. They wrecked a funeral home shouting *"Fuck Israel!"* A drugstore was set on fire as young girls looted baby formula and other products off the shelves.

Valls was correct. This new form of anti-Semitism erupted into deadly reality in the Hyper Casher Jewish supermarket in Paris on January 9, 2015.

Holland saw an up kick in anti-Semitism even as Israel was being bombarded by Palestinian rockets. Esther Voet, the director of the Center of Information and Documentation on Israel in the Netherlands said that *"we are very aware that it's not about if something will happen in our country, but when."*

Benjamin Albalas, the president of the Greek Jewish community, speaking of the fate of European Jews with the attacks on Israel, said that the delegitimization of the State of Israel was *"a first step toward the intimidation of the Jews' right to live in their own home countries."*

In a dire warning, Nathan Norman Gelbart, the head of Germany's Keren Hayesod (United Jewish Appeal) spoke of Germany's Jewish community as being frightened *"because there are things that have not occurred since 1933."*

In September 2014, the Simon Wiesenthal Center called on the German government to take steps against growing anti-Semitism in that country. In the statement, Rabbi Abraham Cooper, requested that the German Justice Ministry issue an arrest warrant for Sheikh Abu Bilal Ismail. He is a Danish imam who called for the extermination of the Jews while visiting Berlin's al-Nur mosque in July. In his flagrant speech Ismail called to *"Destroy the Zionist Jews"* and to *"Count them and kill them to the very last one. Don't spare a single one of them…Make them suffer terribly."* One wonders what this imam is preaching back home in Denmark.

Cooper claimed that, at a meeting with the German Justice Minister, the minister *"had not heard of this incident at all"* and the state secretary told him he had *"read about the incident but not known the details."* How easily such hate speech and incitement to anti-Semitic violence flies under the radar in European countries that should be more sensitive to the dangers of radical violence and terrorism. The line between psychological and physical radicalization, when it morphs from thought to action, is crossed so easily. Yet people are shocked when it expresses itself on the streets of Europe.

The large street demonstrations against Israel were not spontaneous. They were the result of planned, well-coordinated mobilization of the radical left and the local Muslim immigrant communities employing anti-Semitic motifs and slogans, some deriving from the Koran, to delegitimize and demonize Israel and the Jewish people as a single identifiable entity.

The Simon Wiesenthal Center's Dr. Shimon Samuels, asserted that he had *"never seen the coming together of so many anti-Semitic and anti-Israel groups, coupled with the one-sided media hostility in effect demonizing Jews, Israel, and their supporters. I am seeing an unprecedented explosion across Europe of thousands of young Muslims, turned on by the call to jihad. Many of these young men have been fighting in Syria, and return to their home countries poisoned even further and ready to take out their hostilities on the Jews of Europe."*

Dr. Mordechai Kedar of Bar Ilan University positioned the significant role of young Muslims in Europe this way, *"they live in the social, economic and political margins, and their grievances against the system are too often conflated with grievances against the Jews."*

The American Agudath Israel organization summarized the summer attacks in Europe and America thus, *"The pretense that these attacks are not anti-Semitic, but merely a reaction to current events in the Middle East, is cynical and decidedly false. When a Paris mob besieges and throws bricks at a synagogue with two hundred congregants inside, it is anti-Semitism."*

A 2103 study showed that a third of European Jews refrained from wearing religious apparel or Jewish symbols out of fear. 23% avoided attending Jewish events or going to Jewish venues for the same reason.

These numbers inevitably grew in 2014 as Israel was forced to defend itself from Hamas terror and rocket onslaught. The 2103 report quoted a third of Jews polled seriously considering emigration as a response to rising anti-Jewish and anti-Israel hatred. This statistic began to express itself during and after the summer of 2014.

One response to this wave of anti-Semitic sentiment sweeping Europe was a marked increase in immigration of European Jews to Israel, even as their governments pointedly rebuked Israel for the Palestinian-inspired terrorism of the summer.

A European parliamentarian did speak up at the Go4Israel conference in Tel Aviv in late October, 2014. Bastien Belder, a Dutch member of the European parliament, admitted that *"all debates on the Middle East are very one-sided, badly informed, and ideological."* He called on the Israeli adversaries to drop their *"hypocrisy"* and embrace a fair, two-sided debate about the Arab-Israel conflict. Despite the mounting hate against Jews in Europe, Belder said that *"we in the European Parliament didn't have any debate on the anti-Semitic tide in Europe."*

In July, 2014, at the United Nations Human Rights Council, member nations were asked to vote on a one-sided motion condemning *"in the strongest terms the widespread, systematic, and gross violations of international human rights and fundamental freedoms from the Israeli military operations."* Notice no mention of Palestinian terror, or their human rights crimes. It was specific in detailing *"Israel military operations"* as the root cause of everything that followed in their condemnatory resolution. Instead of taking a principled stand over this perverse contrivance, instead of demanding a reading that would have included Hamas aggression and mention of Israel's right to defend itself, every EU country decided to abstain in an outright display of moral weakness. Only the United States voted against this heinous resolution.

Linking the abase actions of street demonstrators to the moral vacuum of European politicians, a Jerusalem Post editorial pointed out, *"By abstaining, EU leaders remained silent in the face of the UNHRC drawing a moral equivalence between a terrorist organization motivated by a violent reactionary interpretation of Islam and a liberal, democratic state. If European leaders are unable to make this distinction, why should we expect more of European masses?"*

*

Intolerant Europe.

Speaking at the organization's annual meeting in Tel Aviv, in January 2015, the heads of the WIZO branches in France, Belgium, Germany and Sweden described the difficulties facing their constituents in a Europe in which Jewish nationalism is increasingly unacceptable.

The president of WIZO France, Joelle Lezmi stated, *"There is a very bad atmosphere around Jewish people. People do not have the right to wear kippot; Jewish people are afraid to put on their Star of David; Jewish people have no place to say I am Jewish… If you are to say 'I am a Zionist' it's quite a revolution."*

Susanne Sznajderman, Lezmi's Swedish counterpart stated, *"A similar situation exists in Sweden. People self-censor themselves. They hear anti-Semitism, but do not act, because they don't feel safe in reacting,"* she said, condemning her government's *"very weak leadership"* on this issue. She went on to state that Sweden's recognition of a Palestinian state outside of the framework of a negotiated solution gave *"courage* to the Palestinians and to those who are violent and to the Muslims in our country to act. That strategy is extremely dangerous."*

Something is happening in Europe and it's not very pleasant, especially if you are a Jew.

Surveys have pointed to a rapidly increasing assimilation among European and American Jews. The assimilation process drags them away from their religion and their identity with the Jewish community. It also drags them away from a love, interest, or support for Israel. This assimilation process leads to the death of Judaism. Polls have shown that, especially for non-Orthodox Jews, Judaism cannot survive without a positive connection with Israel. In fact, a secular liberal European world, in which too many of these assimilated Jews live, is becoming intolerant and antagonistic toward Israel.

Israel as a rare liberal democratic state in a dangerous region should, one would assume, attract them. On the contrary, and against all their principles, Israel infuriates them. It is strangely easy to persuade them to support the Palestinian cause with shallow slogans and false narratives that position Israel as a party worthy of reprobation. One would assume that Jews would see Israel as a tiny island in a sea of radical terrorism and corrupt regimes guilty of human rights abuses that would offend any liberal, Jewish or not. And yet this patently obvious equation is lost on them. The derision of Israel is so mainstream that liberal *"progressive"* Jews are discomforted by the noise that they find themselves turning their backs on the Jewish state. They don't like being associated, in their faith, with a country that is accused of being a *"racist"* or *"fascist"* state. They lack the knowledge or the courage to counter the common argument against Israel. Instead, they adopt a *"who needs it!"* attitude, and get on with their secular lives. Added to this is a leadership that fails to take a stand against anti-Israel activism. This increases the isolationism they feel and wish to escape from.

The result of this increasing trend is that European Jews, both secular and religious, are suffering from increased anti-Semitism and a growing sense of insecurity.

"It's not only a question for Jews, it's also a question for Europe," says Natan Sharansky. *"Jews are always the first litmus test. The fact that Jews feel that liberal society is not ready to protect them can be a sign that liberal society is not ready to protect itself against external threats."*

I would add that European liberal societies have failed to adequately protect themselves and their Jews from internal threats, the very threats that affect Jewish attitudes. It is this domestic pressure, not Israeli policy or actions, which affect too many Jews in Europe.

It was a post-World War Two Europe that decided to do away with border policy between their countries to ensure European peace. They called themselves post-nationalists and multi-cultural. Among the baggage this tolerance brought them was an unbridled immigration. Many came from the Middle East and northern Africa. They did not leave those regions; they brought the thought-process, the political and religious biases of undemocratic and intolerant societies with them.

As they failed to integrate, they added their traditional distaste for Western values, European multiculturalism and the Jewish national state, to an already existing baggage they imported into Europe, and began demanding that Europe transform to meet their cultural and political needs. To a great degree, European nations bent to accommodate them, particularly as they grew in numbers. But the more their received, the more affirmative they became, staying apart yet asserting themselves onto an indigenous populations in ways that became too demanding, too foreign, and too objectionable to them. Hence, the developing polarization we are seeing throughout Europe.

One of the phenomenon that has sprung out of the friction caused by a rejectionist but affirmative minority has been the awakening of a new brand of anti-Semitism, one built around ancient Jew-hatred of Middle East and Muslim political and religious incitement.

In modern liberal Europe, rabbis are telling Jews not to be seen in public places wearing kippot or distinctive Jewish wear. You cannot be seen in public as a proud Jew, or as a Jew that is proud of Israel.

I have been instrumental is setting up support groups for Israel in various countries. One of the most effect type of groups have been lawyers who challenge and counter anti-Israel and anti-Semitic actions that cross the line into the illegitimate, actions such as criminal trespass into stores for noisy and disruptive demonstrations or the trashing of food shelves, intimidation, prevention of free speech and violence on campuses, threats, damage to property or person, all criminal actions according to laws and regulations that govern personal and institutional behavior. The application of law practiced by UK Lawyers for Israel, South African Lawyers for Israel, Australian Lawyers for Israel and the Lawfare Project based in New York have prevented many criminal actions.

Such has been the increase in such anti-Israel, anti-Jewish activity that these groups will be needed in even greater force in the future.

But in mainland Europe it has been extremely difficult to persuade lawyers to forge similar action NGOs. They are afraid. They are fearful of bring stigmatized, of being seen openly standing for Israel, or for Jews. They fear it may adversely affect their professional standing in countries such as Holland, Sweden, Denmark, and Belgium. To me, this feels like Germany in the early 30s where Jews thought it advisable to keep their heads down, not to announce their Jewishness publicly, not to challenge the growing anti-Semitism in the vain hope that it is a passing phenomenon, because it may not help their careers or their personal lives, because of fear. The lack of courage and commitment to stand for what is right and just is all too prevalent in parts of Europe.

The Simon Wiesenthal Center published their Top Ten worst outbreaks of anti-Semitism in 2014. Europe ranked in six of the ten incidents. Topping the list went to a Belgian doctor who refused to provide medical care to a 90 year old Jewish woman with a fractured rib. The doctor told her son, who had requested the care, *"Send her to Gaza for a few hours, then she will get rid of the pain. I'm not coming."* The son filed a formal discrimination complaint on behalf of his mother, Bertha Klein. According to the *Joods Actueel* paper, he said, *"I never thought those days would be repeated."* They have! No Jews died in this incident, but it highlighted the poisoned atmosphere of Europe for Jews as 2014 lapsed into a depressing 2015.

*

Europe today is Berlin 1930. First they banned the books. Then they banned the Jewish academics and teachers. Then they boycotted the

Jewish shops. Then the doctors fail to treat elderly Jews. Then came the shouting mobs and the violence, and then......

*

Europe is lost in a self-made Gordian knot of political incorrectness.

If European nations want to keep their Jews they have to improve their relations with Israel. To understand the fears of their Jews they need to understand the reluctance of Jews to forego their inherent love for the Jewish State, and they need to understand the reluctance of Israel to take dangerous steps for peace when faced with the hateful language and deeds of the Palestinians.

They have underestimated, or closed their eyes, to the danger of a minority of their Muslim population who are radicalized and anti-Semitic, just as they close their eyes to the dangers of a minority of the Palestinian population who are radicalized and anti-Semitic, including their leaders.

To save their Jews and understand the concerns of Israel they need to reform their political thinking.

*

Norway reported that 5,198 foreign citizens were expelled from the country in 2013, an increase of 31 percent since 2012, when 3,958 people were deported. *"It is the highest number we've had ever,"* Frode Forfang, head of the Directorate of Immigration (UDI), told NRK. *"We believe that one reason for the increase is that the police have become more conscious of using deportation as a tool to fight crime."*

Denmark deported a record number of foreign criminals. Trine Bramsen, the judicial spokesperson for Socialdemokraterne, told Metroxpress newspaper. *"Convicted foreigners do not belong in Denmark."* Britain also deports foreign criminals, and the Home Office wants to deport more.

Which begs the question, why can't people be deported for the crime of anti-Semitism, especially when such crime is linked to violence?

*

Myopic Europe is lost in a world of denial.

There is a cultural disposition going back to Mohammed for Muslims to target and wreak violence against Jews. This will become apparent in this book if it is not already self-evident by the statistics of the identities of the perpetrators of attacks against Jews in recent times in Europe.

Rationally, it is not possible to assess particular cultural structures and influences if, under the adoption of a multiculturism, a country surrenders the ability to define its own individual identity and culture due to altering, changing it, and immersing it under a blanket of pluralism. This vacuum disables Western countries of the ability to properly assess the positives and negatives of their own cultures as these are non-existent, a thing of the past. They have been abandoned to the new value system of tolerance to the stranger within its midst as the core value system of many European countries.

This would be fine if the stranger would be properly integrated into the society but, in too many cases, this has failed. The Socialist altruism, offering the multiple benefits and welfare of their social system has not prevented much of their Muslim population from retreating into ghetto areas of high unemployment, high grievances, rising crime and rising intolerance.

In increasing numbers, second generation Muslim immigrants find little of value in the secular blandness of the country of their birth. They are filling this cultural void by affirmatively adopting the faith traditions and cultural habits of their religion. Yet, when incidents occur in out in the name of a radical form of Islam, the secular authorities, who have in the main discarded their own cultural and religious value system, plead that these incidents have nothing to do with that religion.

How can they possibly claim to know the various interpretations of Islam better than the perpetrators themselves? They can't. It is a knee-jerk reaction in order to keep the growing number of immigrants from joining the extremists by rebelling, in large numbers, against the social breakdown of a badly conceived immigration policy whose failure began by a desertion of everything that kept a country cemented in cultural-based national values that included loyalty, patriotism and integration. By jettisoning these essential elements of national pride, they have nothing to teach the immigrants that have poured into their midst, immigrants who are reverting to their own ancient values in countries that are still myopically in denial.

*

European Jews have to hide their Jewish identity.

According to reports about forty percent of European Jews feel they have to hide their Jewish identity. While fewer Jews attend synagogue, there has been an increase in demand from parents wanting to enroll their children in Jewish schools. How do we explain this paradox? In both cases, it reflects the growth of anti-Semitism. Jews refrain from wearing outwardly visible Jewish symbols out of fear. The same fear factor applies to parents preferring to have their children educated in the more secure facilities provided by the Jewish schools, rather than have them intimidated as minorities in an open school atmosphere. The evidence of this intimidation against Jewish students is painfully evident on the campus of higher education.

There is another explanation in the distancing of Jews to their Judaism. For every Jew that makes Aliyah to Israel as a result of European anti-Semitism, many others cut their ties and distance themselves to Judaism and, with it, a Jewish way of life. They favor assimilation rather than strengthen their identity. It was claimed that anti-Semitic incidents increased by 500% in one month in England during the 2014 Gaza conflict started by Hamas. European Jews are feeling the hate from both right and left wing political factions, and also from Muslim immigrants. It is in such an atmosphere that Moshe Kantor, the president of the European Jewish Congress said that *"normative Jewish life is unsustainable"* in Europe without decreased *"fear and insecurity."*

*

FRANCE.

When examining the twisted web of pro-Palestinian anti-Semitism that is haunting much of Europe today it is useful to begin in France.

France has the largest Jewish population in Europe. It also has the largest Muslim population. This makes France an interesting case study.

Throughout history it has been shown that Jews are the perennial canaries in the mineshaft. In the early mining day, miners took canaries down into the dark shafts were dangerous gasses lurked. The birds were more susceptible to the noxious fumes than humans. Their sweet chirping changed into streaks of alarm as the gasses reached and eventually killed them, if the miners did not take them with as they escaped the deadly threat.

So it has been with Jews under intolerant and totalitarian regimes. Under Communism, it was the Jews that were among the first to be dragged off to gulags or murdered. Under Hitler, Jews were the first and greatest victims as the poison of Nazism seeped into the world in the early 1930s.

France is a case study in political breakdown, radicalism, terrorism, and anti-Semitism, and it can be done with a Jewish perspective.

Leon Blum was a former Prime Minister of France but who, nevertheless, was transported to Dachau by the Nazis. In poor health, he was transferred with other prominent death camp prisoners to a camp in the Austrian Alps to keep them away from the advancing Allied forces as World War Two approached its end.

At the age of seventy one, Blum was liberated and returned to France where, as an emblem of French resilience, he was briefly reinstated as France's Prime Minister. As a figurehead, he attracted the immigration of North African Jews into France. The Jewish population grew, prospered and contributed greatly to French society.

21st Century France demonstrated that anti-Semitism was re-emerging, that there was a new toxic strain of anti-Semitism that migrated into Europe from Arab and Muslim countries, a migration that failed to integrate and found its frustrations expressed in rebellion, crime, and anti-Jewish slogans and violence.

Jews are often the first victim. They are rarely the last. They are a warning sign of worse to come.

It began with the brutal torture and gruesome murder of Ilan Halimi. Halimi was targeted and kidnapped in Paris in 2006 simply because he was a Jew.

During a three week period he was beaten all over his body. His head was completely wrapped in duct-tape except for his mouth through which they forced fed him. They stabbed him, burnt his body with cigarettes and lighters.

He was found naked, handcuffed and bound to a tree with a nylon rope. More than 80% of his body had been burnt with acid, as well as gasoline, to the point where he was difficult to recognize. He had multiple broken bones; one ear and one big toe were missing. Most of his penis had been burnt off, and his tentacles were described as *"like blackened oranges."*

Incredibly, he was still alive when found but died on the way to hospital.

The people who did this to him were not radical Islamic extremists. They were a local Arab Muslim gang who called themselves *"les barbares,"* the barbarians, who got their kicks out of torturing to death a young man because he was a Jew.

One of the many disturbing elements of this most awful acts of lethal anti-Semitism was the information received that the perpetrators, and there were twenty nine of them, had gone is search of their Jewish victim for weeks. They targeted both prominent Jews, including lawyers, doctors, and TV personalities as well as non-descript Jews, before picking on Halimi.

Another worrying aspect was the knowledge that, according to one reporter on this case, there must have been at least fifty other people associated with these barbarians that knew of it, even during the twenty four days of Halimi's prolonged torture, and none of them felt moved to inform the authorities.

In a triple terror attack similar in character to the 2015 Paris incidents, in March 2012 Mohammed Merah killed four French soldiers in two separate incidents before turning his gun on Jewish targets in Toulouse. His first victims symbolized French authority before he turned his intentions to his anti-Semitic hatred that found expression in his targeting of a Jewish school. The description of Merah's bloodfest was almost as barbaric as the killing of Ilan Halimi. Merah drove to the school on his motorbike. On arrival in the early morning of March 19 at the Ozer HaTorah children's school he opened fire immediately killing the Rabbi and teacher and one of his sons outside the school gates.

Merah then shot dead one of the rabbi's sons who was trying to crawl away. He then walked into the schoolyard as people ran into the school for shelter. He chased an eight year old girl and caught her by her hair and raised his gun to shoot her. The gun jammed so he reached for a second weapon and shot the girl in her head at point blank range before making his get-away.

The reason given by Merah for his slaughter of Jewish schoolchildren in Toulouse was because *"the Jews killed our brothers and sisters in Palestine."*

Notice the confusion between Jews and Israel, and the excuse to murder Jews in the higher cause of *"Palestine."* Anti-Semitic murders can always be placed in a high moral tone, as have the slaughter of Jews down the centuries.

In a book written by Abdelghani, the brother of Mohammed Merah, the author explained how his family of Algerian descent had been raised in an *"atmosphere of racism and hatred"* brought on by the teachings of extremist and anti-Semitic Islam. He even secretly filmed his sister, Souad, proclaiming her pride in her brother and talking about her hatred of Jews. Abdelghani wrote that his brother had stabbed him seven times because he refused to give up a relationship he had with a girl of Jewish origins.

What was particularly disturbing about the Toulouse incident was the removal and denial of the anti-Semitic nature of Merah's murderous assault on Jewish schoolchildren by the media and political pundits, some of whom had a left-wing or anti-Israel bias.

One of the worst pieces of twisting the truth was written by Oxford Professor and Islamic thinker Tariq Ramadan, who declared that Merah was a young man, *"imbued neither with the values of Islam, or driven by racism and anti-Semitism."* He was merely attacking symbols, *"the army and Jews."*

France 24 put down the murder of Jews in Toulouse as being a young man's frustration at being unemployed, while The Guardian was more concerned about any politicization of the incident and the general threat to society of extremisms without mentioning Merah's obvious anti-Semitism.

In an article, written in the Israeli Ha'aretz newspaper on March 29, 2012, Joel Braunold wrote that the dissipation of France's Jewish community to a mere symbol of Western European society demonstrated a dehumanization of the Jewish victims of Merah's anti-Semitic attack.

Braunold asks these pertinent questions, *"How does the slaughter of a religious leader and three small children of a particular minority community merely become a symbol of attacking society in general? Do the victims' identities mean nothing to these analysts except to demonstrate this was another disaffected immigrant angry at the West and demonstrating that anger in just any way he knew how?"*

During the 2014 Gaza conflict these were many anti-Semitic incidents in France.

On the streets of Paris they were not screaming *"Death to Israel!"* They were screaming *"Death to the Jews!"*

On July 20, French riot police prevented about 150 demonstrators at an unauthorized protest by the Bastille from reaching the synagogue of Rue de la Roquette where about two hundred Jews had barricaded themselves inside to escape the mob. Demonstrators were heard chanting, *"Death to Jews."*

Rioters burned a store, smashed windows in another seven shops, and hit another synagogue in Sarcelle with firebombs. Sarcelles is known as *Little Jerusalem* because it is the home of many Jews.

In September, the Correctional Tribunal of Strasbourg sentenced a woman to three months in jail for insulting a Jew she saw on a bus, calling him *"a dirty Jew,"* removing his kippa. She even assaulted the bus driver as he attempted to remove her from his bus.

In September, a 15 year-old girl was arrested after her parents reported to the police she tried to join jihadists in Syria. One of her handlers told her she had to carry out an attack against Jews in France in revenge for Palestine. According to her testimony, she was under pressure to commit a suicide attacks against Jewish targets or, alternatively, an attack similar to the one committed by Mohamed Merah, the Algerian Muslim who murdered three Jewish children and a rabbi in Toulouse in 2012.

In October, the prosecutor of the Paris suburb of Sarcelles ordered a criminal investigation into the televised interview of a man who spoke of killing Jews. Standing with friends on a street he said to the camera, *"I have rage against the Jews. What they are doing over there in Palestine, we are doing here to the Jews. And if we get really angry we might just kill them. If I get angry I will light up all of them, all the Jews."* This is incitement to hate and violence.

Sarcelles is a poor neighborhood in which 60,000 Jews live amidst a dominantly Muslim population.

The congregation of the Brith Chalom Synagogue on Rue Saint-Lazare is mostly Jews who fled the anti-Semitic violence of Algiers in the 1960s. Rabbi Malka has been rabbi here for 25 years. In a *New York Times* article written by Celestine Bohlen, he asked *"Those who demonstrate against Jews, what is their feeling towards France? That's the question: Do they feel French or Muslim? The problem is not well understood, and we're afraid to look at it in its face."*

In Rabbi Malka's view, the Israeli assault in Gaza, with its mounting toll of Palestinian civilian deaths, has given an anti-Zionist cover to attacks against Jews, spread on the streets and on the Internet by an angry fringe of France's Muslim population. *"Why bring a war to a country that is not at war?"* he asked. *"This conflict has nothing to do with the Jews and Arabs of France."*

He noted that the most deadly attacks in the region — against a Jewish school in Toulouse in 2012, and a Jewish museum this year in Brussels, both committed by French-born Muslims — came about when there was no shooting war between the Israelis and the Palestinians. *"Anti-Semitism today is hiding behind anti-Zionism,"* he said, *"and hate speech has become uninhibited."*

Once again, the link between Palestinian support and anti-Semitism was expressed in hate-filled calls for death to Jews. It dares us to ask of the Palestinian cause to destroy the Jewish state is a metaphor for a desire to kill Jews.

Anti-Israel and anti-Jewish attitudes are not confined to the left wing. In France David Rachline was elected to the French senate as a member of the far-right National Front party. He was born to a Socialist, non-practicing Jew who died when he was just sixteen years old. Rachline downplays his Jewish roots claiming he was never circumcised, did not have a barmitzvah, and was not Jewish as he says *"according to the books."* Rachline says he does not practice any religion but, given the choice, would choose to be Catholic. What is more troubling with Rachline is his admission that he is attracted to the '*Equality and Reconciliation*' movement of the far-right Holocaust-denier and anti-Israel activist (another example of how they go together), Alain Soral. In a hypocritical statement, Rachline said in a *Rue89* interview, *"What I like about Soral is his criticism of liberalism. Besides, you can oppose Israel's policies without being anti-Semitic."*

Yes, you can, but, in Rachline's case, it's a tall reach of imagination to accept that anti-Semitism is not lurking in there somewhere.

It is unacceptable for a city to name a street in honor of a terrorist convicted of murder, but this is what happened in the French town of Valenton, near Paris, who named a street after Marwan Barghouti who is serving five life sentences for five murders and forty years for attempted murders as part of his role as a Palestinian terrorist commander who killed Israeli civilians. Francois Baud, the Communist mayor of Valenton, called Barghouti *"the face of unwavering Palestinian resistance."* To complete the whitewash, he described the Israeli government as being guilty of "occupation, crimes, destruction, apartheid," and *"colonization."* No truth about why Barghouti sits in an Israeli jail.

This scene of far left hypocrisy was repeated in December 2014, when the Parisian suburb of Aubersville rewarded the Muslim Paris rioters of that summer by naming Barghouti with an honorary citizenship. Once again, the mayor is a representative of the Communist Party of France. Pascal Beaudet claimed the award was partly out of his concerns for political prisoners comparing Barghouti to Nelson Mandela.. Roger Cukierman, the President of CRIF, the umbrella organization of the French Jewish community, protested in these words, *"Nelson Mandela, whom you have the audacity of referencing, was indeed a political activist sentenced to prison but for his opinions – not his actions."*

Such is the perversion of narrative in many parts of Europe. The effect of honoring terrorists emboldens the extremists. What further proof can we have than the horrific terror attacks in Paris in early January 2015?

In Israel, there was a feeling of horror and familiarity when watching the terror attack on the offices of Charlie Hebdo unfolding on our TV screens. Israelis are well versed in such lethal assaults against our citizens. Our hearts went out to the journalists going about their daily business who were confronted by Islamic terrorists who gunned them down in cold blood.

Yet, there was another underlying thought among Israelis. That was a silent prayer of thanks that these murderers had not, this time, targeted, once again, French Jews. How wrong we were.

Stand-up Muslim comedian, Dieudonné M'bala M'bala was amusing French audiences with his anti-Jewish hatred. It is important to stress that this obnoxious, not-very-funny, comic was not spouting satirical material a la Charlie Hebdo. He was spouting hateful anti-Semitism that included making fun of Jews in gas chambers and concentration camps.

Dieudonne initiated the infamous neo-Nazi arm salute that became all the rage, especially among European immigrants from Muslim countries. In December 2014, CRIF, the umbrella organization of French Jews, strongly objected to the fact that twenty French theaters planned to host this anti-Semites one-man show.

Despite being condemned by French law-makers, this heinous character still had the gall to poke fun of Jews being slaughtered by one of his own in a Jewish supermarket. Dieudonne identified himself with the terrorist murderer of four French Jews by declaring on his Facebook page, *"Tonight, as far as I'm concerned, I feel like Charlie Coulibaly,"* paraphrasing the hashtag popularity of *"Je suis Charlie"* and replacing sympathy for the murdered staff of the satirical Charlie Hebdo magazine with sympathy for the killer of Parisian Jews.

Muslim hatred of Jews in France was made evident by one honest imam, Kamel Kabtane of Lyon's Badr Eddine Mosque who acknowledged ignorance of French Muslims in how they perceive Jews. Asked on French radio is anti-Jewish sentiments exist among the Muslim population, he answered, *"It is true there's a lack of knowledge, yes. It is bad."*

To his credit he is working towards a better understanding between young members of both faiths by coordinating cultural exchanges with Lyon's liberal Jewish community with young local Muslims. This, at least, is a start.

Half of the hate crimes in France are against Jews, who make up less than one percent of the population, according to a Guardian newspaper report.

The airbrushing out of the anti-Semitic nature of attacks against Jews and Israelis has allowed, in France in particular, the twisted perversion of honoring murderous terrorists by French mayors. As Irwin Cotler, the renowned international jurist and expert of global anti-Semitism put it, *"if people sanitize anti-Semitism, then they'll be sanitizing terrorism."* This is precisely what French and Sweden mayors are doing.

Cotler describes *"genocidal anti-Semitism"* and terrorism as being two sides of the same coin.

And so we come to the prolonged Parisian terror attacks of January that captured world attention. The French Muslim terrorists could not complete their murderous rampage without turning their rage on to Jewish targets. It was almost inevitable.

At the Jerusalem funeral of the four Jewish victims of the Hyper Casher outrage in Paris. Member of the Knesset, Eli Yishai, summed up the feelings of Israeli Jews. *"Millions of people in the State of Israel went into last Shabbat with fear and worry for the fate of those caught up in the terror attack on the Jewish store in Paris. This is what it is to be Jewish, one nation, one blood, one fate."*

Referring to the French penchant, detailed elsewhere in this book, for naming streets and squares after Palestinian terrorists, Alain Azria, a Jewish photojournalist who specializes in documenting France's anti-Semitism problem, said of Aubervilliers, a poor and heavily-Muslim suburb of Paris where the mayor had honored Marwan Barghouti, a

Palestinian terror commander serving multiple-life sentences in Israel for murderous terrorist attacks against Israeli civilians;

"Hollande can speak against anti-Semitism as much as he likes, but when public officials hold up Barghouti as an example, we see the result in blood on our streets, which are emptying of Jews."

In an interview with *Le Figaro,* Roger Cukierman, the head of CRIF, said French Jews *"feel like the nation's pariah."*

In this, they share the fate of Israel, the Jewish State that is constantly being treated as if it was the world's pariah.

Meanwhile, Eli Ringer, former president of Belgium's Jewish community, spoke of a Europe that grants recognition of a Palestinian state with a terror organization as a unity member.

"The authorities did not want to be woken up. Recognizing a Palestinian state whose leaders signed a unity agreement with Hamas sends a strong signal to all those extremist organizations that we are weak and frightened and giving them a free hand to do whatever they want."

He went on, *"By always blaming Israel unilaterally and by amalgam the Jews, we Jews become the scapegoat for all the problems in the world. Europe claims high moral ground for itself and pretends to be the moral judge of Israel."*

Ringer suggested establishing a pan-European Jewish body, divorced from day-to-day community politics, to focus exclusively on anti-Semitism. He said that only Jewish unity could bring security for European Jews. As did Professor Cotler, Ringer pointed to the failure of the European Parliament to establish a task force on anti-Semitism as showing a lack of understanding of the severity of the issue of anti-Semitism. Neither did the Europeans understand the importance of the threat of radical Islam as a growing ideology. These two issues go hand in hand.

It is hoped, albeit with low expectations that, following the Paris attacks, European politicians will be stimulated to rethink their incorrect perspective of what is driving attacks against Jews and Israel and readjust their political thinking and policies.

When governments are fearful of a Muslim population that puts the smaller Jewish community under threat and at risk it is a basic breakdown of values in liberal democratic Europe.

In the meantime Jewish children are afraid to go to school. Parents have a dilemma about where to place their children. As Avi Zana of the Israeli-based *Ami Israel* group that assists French Jews immigrating to Israel sees Jewish parents are apprehensive today about enrolling their children in French public schools because of the rampant anti-Semitism there. *"On the other hand,"* he says, *"they are afraid to put them in Jewish schools because they are targets for attack."*

With the doubling of Jew felling France for Israel certain areas are feeling the depletion. Bernard Mouchi, the president of the Jewish community of Courneuvre, a poor and heavily Muslim suburb of Paris, complained that *"fifteen years ago this was a large Jewish community of over a thousand families. Now we are barely a hundred families. Actually, we are a community of pensioners."*

The accumulation of French-speaking immigrants already in Israel paves the way for those contemplating escape. Newcomers join family and friends who preceded them and help in their absorption into Israeli society by giving advice and sharing their knowledge that softens the landing in a new country. This snowball effect adds momentum to the Aliya process.

We can feel comforted, maybe even assured, that the French government have said they will take all measures to attempt to prevent anti-Semitism in their country, but will the Muslim community do their part to eradicate anti-Semitism from within their midst?

With Marseilles touted to be the first European city with a Muslim majority, this is a highly relevant question.

*

French Prime Minister, Manuel Valls, in his speech to Parliament on Tuesday, January 13, 2015, said that France was engaged in a war against radical Islam and that such a war had to be fought and won first and foremost within Islam itself. He said it was as much a fight for French Jews not to feel scared of living in France, as it was a struggle for French Muslims never again to be ashamed of being Muslims in France.

Some points need to be expressed. Many French Jews arrived back to France after World War Two with nothing following the most harrowing experiences in Nazi concentration camps.

Many others arrived in France following anti-Semitic pogroms in which they fled Arabs lands with nothing, leaving all their properties and possessions behind with no compensation. They were genuine refugees from hate and oppression. Yet, they never turned to the blame-game, never turned to violence, never developed a chip on their shoulder, never cut themselves off from the society of their host country. On the contrary, they educated themselves, worked hard to improve their lot, and integrated into the society, eventually contributing their talents to the benefit of the population in all fields. This makes the grudge and alienation of European Muslim populations all the more unacceptable.

The immigrant Jews should be their example to emulate, not hate. In this, Muslims in European societies have a responsibility to themselves as much as to society, to integrate and self-improve. They should head out with a determination to succeed and create, not to fail and destroy. They should adopt the Jewish character that swerves the negatives in religion and politics for the positives of resourcefulness, education, and initiative. With success come prosperity and a sense of contributing to society. This encourages integration not alienation.

This applies in all societies, not just in France.

*

BELGIUM.

Belgian schools have become Jew-free zones. This is the opinion of Joel Rubinfeld, president of the Belgian League Against Anti-Semitism. He made this statement after the only Jewish student at the Emile Bockstael high School left it after she endured a series of harassment and threats from classmates after she posted a picture of an Israeli flag on her Facebook page.

"The school has become 'Judenfrei,' there are no more Jewish students there," pronounced Rubinfeld, using a term the Nazis applied to locations that had been cleared of Jews by them.

Despite the fact that this Jewish girl moved to a Jewish school for protection the abuse followed her. One of the pupils at the school she was forced to leave sent her a photo performing the Nazi salute.

On 24 May, 2014, four Jews were killed at the Brussels Jewish Museum. The killer was a French Arab.

In November 2014, an Orthodox Jew in Antwerp was stabbed as he made his way to synagogue.

*

GERMANY.

German Chancellor, Angela Merkl, stood by Berlin's Brandenburg Gate, under which Hitler rode in triumph, to denounce the rise of anti-Semitism in Germany following a surge of abuse against Jews and spreading anti-Israeli sentiment aroused by the Gaza conflict. Anti-Semitic incidents have been a constant, though it peaked with the outbreak of the conflict.

In 2012, a 53-year-old rabbi, David Alter, was attacked in Berlin as he was walking down the street with his six-year-old daughter. The rabbi was wearing a yarmulke at the time. He was approached by a group of young Arab men who asked if he was Jewish. One then screamed at him, in the presence of his small daughter, *"I will f--- you! I will f--- your wife! I will f--- your daughter!"* Then they attacked him breaking his cheekbone and hitting him over the head before they ran away.

Walter Rothschild, a rabbi in Berlin, told RBB news radio that the attack represented a *"new dimension."* But it is not a *"new dimension"* in Berlin. It is the reawakening of an old dimension. He also has been attacked and has received abusive emails. He no longer wears yarmulkes in public.

In April, 2014, a young Israeli living in the German capital was beaten outside his apartment in broad daylight by six young men who identified themselves as Palestinians.

There is little doubt that Middle East immigrants have brought their anti-Semitism with them into Europe and express it under the guise of grievances against Israel, often at the cost of injury and insult to local Jews.

In late January, 2015, a judge in Essen ruled that an anti-Israel activist incited hatred against Jews through his calls to kill Zionists.

Judge Gauri Sastry said in a groundbreaking legal decision, *"'Zionist' is the language of anti-Semites is a code for Jew."*

A German of Turkish extraction, Taylan Can, yelled *"death and hate to Zionists"* at an anti-Israel rally in Essen during the Gaza conflict on 2014. A video showed Can inciting the crowd by shouting for Zionists to be killed. The *Die Welt* newspaper reported that the Left Party organized the rally in July and *"an anti-Semitic mob"* marched through the streets of Essen. After this protest rally, anti-Israel demonstrators attacked pro-Israel supporters in the main train station. Here there were shouts of *"shitty Jews"* and Hitler salutes.

At another anti-Israel rally in Hagen, Taylan Can was allowed by the police to use their megaphone to chant, *"Child killer Israel!"* According to media reports, at this rally the crowd shouted, *"Hamas, Hamas – Jews to the gas!"*

Can's defense was that because there is no group in Germany called Zionists, he had done no wrong. He told Judge Sastry that he hates Zionists and wished them dead but that is only a punishment of God.

"We can agree that is a punishment of God, right," Can asked the judge. The judge replied, *"No! When in the past year you called for the death of, and hate of Zionists, you mean the State of Israel and Jews. It was the State of Israel that found itself at war."*

In July 2014, a 67 year old man, wearing a Star of David pendant, was attacked while sitting on a bench in Tiergarten Park in Berlin. Two men harassed and then repeatedly punched him. He was treated in a hospital for multiple lacerations to the head. The assailants fled.

The Israeli ambassador to Germany, Yakov Hadas-Handelsman, said: "They pursue the Jews in the streets of Berlin... as if we were in 1938."

Murderous slogans dating back to the days of Hitler have been chanted at pro-Palestinian rallies in Germany. Posters depicting Israeli Prime Minister, Benjamin Netanyahu, with a blue Star of David painted in his forehead and red blood oozing from his mouth as he devours a crying Palestinian child appeared at one such event. Protesters chanted *"Jews to the gas chambers"* were heard in Germany.

Police officers had to protect an Israeli tourist after protesters spotted his yarmulke and reportedly charged towards him shouting *"Jew! We'll get you."*

Fourteen people were arrested in the western city of Essen on suspicion of planning an attack on a synagogue. The imam of a Berlin mosque is under investigation after allegedly calling on Muslims to murder *"Zionist Jews"*.

Dieter Graumann, president of the Central Council of Jews in Germany, said the rise in attacks was a terrifying reminder of an era that was thought to be in the distant past.
He said: *"We are currently experiencing in this country an explosion of evil and violent hatred of Jews, which shocks and dismays all of us.*
'We would never in our lives have thought it possible any more that anti-Semitic views of the nastiest and most primitive kind can be chanted on German streets.'"

The violence may have ebbed with the cessation of the Gaza conflict but the hatred and anti-Semitism still simmers awaiting the next outbreak of violence. It is being stoked by radicals who have entered politics and other influential circles and are continuing their anti-Israel campaign.

Germany's second largest political party, the Social Democrats (SPD), designated the Palestinian Fatah party as its sister party. In September, the Bundestag deputy, Rainer Arnold, the SPD's defense spokesman, compared Israel to Hamas. This party reeks of anti-Semitism even as it attacks Israel.

In response to widespread criticism, Sabine Wolfle, a German Social Democrat politician, was forced to close down her Facebook page after she posted a crude anti-Semitic conspiracy video alleging that the Jewish Rothschild family controlled the finances of the world. Wolfle served as a parliamentary member in the government of the state of Baden-Wurttemberg. Her video echoed the 1940 Nazi propaganda movie *"The Rothschilds."* In a similar vein, her video was called *"The Power of the Rothschilds."* In a blood libel, the narrator accused the Rothschilds of being responsible for the *"mass murders of millions."* Like a number of *"enlightened"* left-wing politicians, Wolfle indignantly denied being anti-Semitic but, like all Anti-Semites, she plays on Jewish characters, and the Jewish State, as being guilty of horrible and gross crimes that any decent person must deplore and condemn, even if those crimes do not exist except in the fevered mind and rabid tongue of the accuser.

Another chapter of the SPD, in the city of Hagen, accused *"Zionists"* of controlling the German media.

The SDP Foreign Minister, Frank-Walter Steinmeister, wrote in the German Jewish weekly *'Judische Allgemeine'* that *"We are shocked by the anti-Semitic agitation and attacks"* in Germany. Sadly for him a large proportion emanate from his own party, but his party's anti-Jewish attitude reflects several other Social Democrat parties in Europe.

"Anti-Semitism was limited to the Nazi period." This appalling remark was made by a German judge in a civil case brought to the Munich regional courtroom of Petra Gronke-Muller on October 8, 2014. The case was brought against a co-founder of the German Green party, Jutta Ditfurth, who called Jurgen Elsasser, an extreme right-wing journalist, *"a fiery anti-Semite."* Ditfurth accused Elsasser of working together with anti-Semites and actively participating in anti-Semitic demonstrations and organizations.

Whatever the merits of the case, it was shocking that a German judge legally restricts anti-Semitism to the limited Third Reich period. This was done shortly after Muslims at a German anti-Israel demonstration were heard shouting *"Gas the Jews!"*

This is not an isolated incident. Nathan Belbart, a leading Berlin attorney won another case in which a judge attempted to strictly limit the definition of anti-Semitism.

Max Moses Bonifer resigned his post as the student spokesman for the Offenbach city's school system after Arab and Turkish students attacked him and threatened to kill him. He used to wear a kippa with a Star of David. They shouted at him, *"We spit on your people. We'll find you and kill you!"*

He told the German weekly Jewish paper *Judische Allgemeine* that *"since the Gaza conflict in the summer, youths of Arab and Turkish origin have regularly insulted me, spat at me and attacked me."* Bonifer said he could no longer represent students who want him and Jewish people dead.

Dr. Elvira Grozinger, of the German branch of Scholars for Peace in the Middle East, told the Jerusalem Post that *"the anti-Semitism, especially by Muslim students at German schools, is becoming a very serious problem also for the teachers and school directors who have to deal with it daily."*

*

AUSTRIA.

The purpose of this chapter is to show the Gordian knot that binds one aspect of anti-Semitism with *"criticism"* of Israel.

The case of a Turkish man who, in December 2014, posted on his Facebook page *"I could have annihilated all the Jews in the world, but I left some of them alive so you will know why I was killing them"* as if it was a quote from Adolf Hitler.

The man, given the name of Ibrahim by the Austrian prosecutor's office in Linz, had posted Hitler's picture on his Facebook page and his Nazi-type quotation was part of his criticism of Israel's counter offensive in the Gaza conflict.

Philip Chritl, representing the Austrian state prosecutor, said that the statement was simply expressing *"displeasure toward Israel"* and was not anti-Semitic. Ibrahim also called on Allah to annihilate the Jewish state, according to the *Oberosterreichische Nachrichten* newspaper.

Stefan Schaden, a member of the advisory board of the Austrian-Israel Society, told the *Jerusalem Post* that *"Everything passes as so-called criticism of Israel. Anti-Semitism seems to have been officially abolished."*

The Austrian-Israel Society protested the decision of the state prosecutor, saying that it *"legitimizes anti-Semitic agitation through Austria's judiciary."*

Richard Schmitz, the president of the Society called on politicians and authorities to do more to stop undermining such anti-Semitic displays.

"It is troubling when the most disgusting agitation against Jews, as well as against the State of Israel, takes place without consequences."

The editor of the Vienna-based Jewish news website, *Die Juedische*, said the prosecutor's decision was *"shocking."* He pointed to demonstrations against Israel under the slogan of *"Zionists are fascists"* and comparing the swastika with the Star of David that had gone unpunished.

Apparently, in Austria, the call to kill Jews is legal criticism of Israel.

*

SWEDEN.

The Swedish brethren of the German Social Democrats raced into a firmly anti-Israel mode within three days of assuming power in 2014 with a shockingly unilateral announcement that *"Sweden will recognize the state of Palestine."*

One would think that a liberal country such as Sweden would bring such a motion to a democratic vote, but no. The minority government got together with the Environment Party, well known for its anti-Israel pronouncements, and slammed through a law that would have failed had it gone to the Sweden parliament.

What this Sweden government also failed to do was to condition it to the outcome of peace talks thereby giving the Palestinians the incentive to negotiate in good faith.

It was only after their attention was drawn to the fact that the wording of their motion undercut the peace process and was in breach of the

Oslo Accords that the new Prime Minister, Stefan Lofven, was forced to back down by tacking a continuum to his government's public statement that such recognition would only come after a negotiated settlement between Israel and the Palestinians.

This government was new, fresh into power, but its attitude followed in the footsteps of Olof Palme who was an admirer of Yasser Arafat and supporter of the PLO who killed thousands of civilians during their reign of terror. During Palme's leadership, his friend Arafat perpetrated the 1972 Munich Olympic Games massacre in which eleven Israeli sportsmen were murdered, the 1974 killing of twenty one Israeli schoolchildren at Ma'alot by Arafat's terrorists, as well as many other terrorist incursions and artillery attacks by Arafat's PLO.

Yet, part of Palme's support for Arafat was to overlook these heinous international crimes and, instead, to compare Israel to Nazi Germany and to cut diplomatic ties with Israel during his years in office.

This hypocrisy continues today.

It is hardly surprising that the new Socialist government in Stockholm followed Palme's biased example by coming out so quickly in support of a Palestine that included the terrorist Hamas who barely had time to hide their remaining stockpile of rockets after a fifty day bombardment of Israel, linked to a partner that rejects any notion of peace with the Jewish state. After all, Sweden's left-wing politicians have never seriously questioned what sort of Palestine they are creating. They were, after all, representing the demands of a large minority of their electorate which had swept them into power.

Visitors to Stockholm should visit the Vasa Museum. It contains the wreck of a Swedish warship, built in 1626, that sank on its maiden voyage. No sooner had it been launched than it sank immediately after leaving the harbor. This is an apt metaphor for the newly launched Swedish government which sank almost as soon as it took office.

In no way can Stefan Lofven be called an anti-Semite. It is fair to assume that he based his action on an altruistic sense of justice and a mistaken optimism, so prevalent among politicians and diplomats that all Israel has to do is withdraw from much of its land and peace will break out like sunshine after rain.

Politicians like Lofven are in reality denial, and that is dangerous for Israel. Influential people such as Lofven need to adapt and adopt a worldview based on reality, not on empty optimism.

The international community has wasted decades encouraging and promoting Palestinian demands at the expense of Israel to the extent that the Palestinians have become entrenched in their exaggerated demands, and have even radicalized them in trenchant rhetoric and incitement. All creative thinking about alternative solutions has been locked down to maintain an unworkable dogma, unworkable in the face of the reality of an uncompromising Palestinian leadership.

The Palestinian Authority, the PLO and Hamas, are light years away from genuinely accepting Israel in peace as the national homeland of the Jewish people. Anyone with eyes and ears can see this to be true. Reason and sense must appreciate that, without this, no peace agreement is possible. Unfortunately, reason and sense is lacking in European capitals.

As I said, Lofven is no anti-Semite, but his party has its fair share of anti-Israel, anti-Jewish, provocateurs. In 2011, Omar Mustafa, a Swedish Social Democratic politician tweeted that instead of targeting the regime of Muammar Gaddafi in Libya, that Sweden should send warplanes against Israel. It is noteworthy that Mustafa, was elected to the governing board of the Social Democratic party in 2013 after serving as chairman of the Swedish Islamic Association. After revelations that his organization rejected women as having equal rights to their male counterparts, and invited a speaker with hardcore anti-gay opinions, Mustafa resigned from his position.

Raoul Wallenberg was the Swedish diplomat who saved thousands of Jews from Nazi-controlled Hungary in the Second World War. Wallenberg's first sympathetic encounter with Jews was during his brief work stay in Haifa. Although coming from a wealthy banking family, he found work with a Hungarian Jew in his return to Stockholm in an import-export business. Raoul Wallenberg was arrested by the Russians in early 1945, taken to the infamous Lubyanka jail in Moscow where he disappeared with the Soviets giving no information of his fate.

During the war, Sweden used its neutrality to rescue desperate Jews in neighboring Norway and Denmark who were threatened by the Nazis. This is the reason that Sweden has the largest Jewish population of all the Scandinavian countries.

However, Sweden today seems to be a long way from the Sweden of Raoul Wallenberg. Their political attitude to the Jewish state and its own Jews is less than sterling. Today, Wallenberg seems to be a unique Righteous Gentile, a Swede of rare moral honesty and courage.

*

The Malmo Symptom.

The Swedes gave the world *The Stockholm Syndrome*. This is a psychological condition whereby a hostage begins to sympathize, even support, with his or her captor. It originated in 1973 when an escaped criminal, armed with a loaded machine-gun, held four hostages inside a Stockholm bank. By the end of the siege the hostages ended up supporting the armed criminal rather than the police trying to rescue them.

There is now a new Swedish mental disorder. I call it *"The Malmo Symptom."* It's where left-wing radicals to a cause attempt to silence or neutralize opponents of their cause.

It finds an outlet in attempts to drive a wedge between an indigenous Jewish population and Israel for the sole purpose of advancing the Palestinian cause by isolating Israel even from its Jewish support.

The initial example is that of the mayor of the Swedish town of Malmo who laid down a decree to the Jews of his city that their support for Israel, which conflicted with his political anti-Israel views, had to side with him and be silent under threat of stigmatization.

Hence the name – *"the Malmo Symptom."*

Ilmar Reepalu was the Social Democratic mayor of Malmo, a Swedish town with a large and growing Muslim population who's Jews feel increasingly threatened. Reepalu demanded that his town's Jews would *"denounce Israeli violations against the civilian population in*

Gaza. Instead, it decides to hold a (pro-Israel) demonstration in the Grand Square, which could send the wrong signals."

The Malmo Symptom is not confined to Swedes. It has spread to other countries, blown by the winds of bias and hate, tainted further by this new strain of anti-Semitism.

The tactics of divide and rule in support of the Palestinians, that attempts to split Jews from Israel, will be referred to throughout this book with other examples of the Malmo Symptom.

*

During the 2014 Gaza conflict a Malmo city councilman, Adrian Kaba, also a Social Democrat, posted on his Facebook page in July that *"ISIS is being trained by the Israeli Mossad. Muslims are not waging war. They are being used as pawns by other peoples' game."* Here is yet another not-so-subtle anti-Semitic libel.

Following the vandalizing of Malmo's main synagogue on 30 July 2014, Malmos's Rabbi Shnuer Kesselman was attacked less than a week later when he and one of his congregants were walking away from the synagogue in the evening. Kesselman, who has experienced several previous attacks going back to 2009, was unharmed.

In December 2014, Bjorn Soder of the Swedish Democrats said that Jews must abandon their religious identities to become proper Swedes. He claimed that *"most people of Jewish origin who have become Swedes leave their Jewish identity"* and that, according to Soder, is important to distinguish between *"citizenship and nationhood."*

Soder, who is a deputy speaker in the Swedish parliament, was forced to backtrack following widespread condemnation of his remarks. He posted an article in the Jerusalem Post proclaiming his support for Israel and clarifying his view. Jews in Sweden must view him with a jaundiced eye, as must Israel.

In Sweden, anti-Israel accusations are not the exclusive reign of the SD party. Sweden's city planning and environment minister, Mehmet Kaplan, was on the infamous *Mavi Marmara* in 2010 which attempted to break Israel's legal naval blockade on the Hamas-controlled Gaza Strip. He was detained by Israel after the ship was intercepted and then released. According to some, Kaplan rejects the existence of the Jewish state. He spoke at a pro-Palestinian demonstration in Stockholm in July during the conflict. At this event is spoke of *"sixty six years of occupation"* which clearly indicates that, according to Kaplan, Israel has no right to exist because sixty six years would take us back to 1948, not 1967. This is the not so covert dogma of the BDS Movement, a total rejection of the existence of the Jewish state. As such, this is anti-Semitic.

Linking Jews to Israel is a disparaging anti-Semitic manner goes back a number of years.

In 2009, the Aftonbladet newspaper printed a stereotypical anti-Semitic article accusing Israeli soldiers of killing Palestinian teenagers to steal their organs. It also featured a cartoon showing two characters dressed in Jewish attire saying *"Hitler killed the wrong Jews."*

In January 2015, a non-Jewish reporter went to Malmo to test attitudes towards Jews. He walked around the town wearing a kippa and a Star of David pendant. Swedish TV aired secretly filmed footage of his visit.

Within hours he was hit and cursed by passersby before departing in shock and fear. One person called him *"Jewish shit"* while another told him to *"get out."*

In the heavily Muslim area of Rosengard the reporter, Petter Ljunggren, was surrounded by a dozen men shouting anti-Semitic slogans as eggs were hurled at him from an apartment building.

Fred Kahn of the Malmo Jewish community told the LTA media agency that most of the anti-Semitic incidents are perpetrated by Muslims or Arabs.

*

HOLLAND.

On the night of July 17, 2014, just over a week into the Hamas rocket barrage into Israel, four bricks were hurled through the window of a rabbi's home in Amersfoort in the Netherlands. This was the fifth time that his home was attacked.

65 year old Rabbi Binyamin Jacobs worked intensively to build bridges between non-Jews and the Dutch Jewish community of 40,000. Now he says, *"The fact that these attacks are recurrent shows the depth of hatred that exists against Jews."*

Anti-Semitism linked to Palestinian sympathies is only part of the problem in Holland. In 2011, the Dutch passed a law banning kosher slaughtering. This was later reversed by the Dutch Senate after much protest.

Rabbi Jacobs thinks that assimilation in a liberal society where many people have anti-religious sentiments has an influence on Dutch anti-Semitism. "It comes as part of a package," he said at the time.

A year before the July attack on his home, the rabbi spoke to the youth of Arnhem. This is where some Muslim youths expressed virulent anti-Semitism in interviews with a university researcher. Put on video, many people in Holland were shocked to hear these young men use expressions that included one youth who said that he was *"happy about what Hitler did to the Jews."* Note that this was a year before the 2014 Gaza conflict. One wonders what these youths would have said a year later.

*

UNITED KINGDOM.

According to the numbers, reaction in Britain to the Gaza conflict contributed to the record number of anti-Semitic incidents in the UK in 2014.

The Community Security Trust recorded 1,168 incidents in their annual report. This figure more than doubled the anti-Semitic events of the previous year and was the highest annual number ever recorded in Britain.

The report pointed to the Israeli-Palestinian conflict as being the "single biggest factor" in the rise of anti-Semitism. As further proof of this, the numbers spiked during July and August as the war raged in Israel and Gaza. Of the 542 incidents during these two months, 48% made specific references to events that were taking place in the Middle

East. Clearly people were taking sides in the conflict and taking their anger out on local British Jews.

A worrying aspect of the CST statistics is that violent assaults on Jews in the UK rose during 2014 by 17%.

Three quarters of the incidents against Jews were concentrated in London and Manchester where the two largest Jewish communities are found. Anti-Semitic incidents also occurred in eighty nine other locations around the UK, some of which have no or few Jews. Sixty nine incidents targeted synagogues, and 213 incidents targeted Jewish communal organizations as compared to fifty nine the previous year. Incidents on campuses also doubled.

Although a third were defined as perpetrated by members of the far right, anti-Israel activists, or people with Islamist beliefs, the majority of anti-Semitic assaults were caused by common garden local anti-Semites who took the Israeli-Arab conflict to express their Jew hatred.

One example of this was the victim Luciana Berger, the shadow health minister, who received a message on Twitter from a 21-year-old neo-Nazi, Garron Helm, which showed her with the Star of David on her head. It used the hashtag #Hitlerwasright and called her a *"communist Jewess"*. Helm was jailed for four weeks.

Berger was then bombarded with more than 2,500 hate messages tagged #filthyjewbitch. After Helm's release, more anti-Semitic tweets began to emerge from his Twitter account. When Ed Miliband tweeted a link to his article about Holocaust Memorial Day, the user of the account tweeted back *"Burrrn! Lol."*

The configuration of the Holocaust, the Israeli-Arab struggle and plain anti-Semitism was scrawled on a not received by a north London synagogue which said, *"You Jews are murderers. Shame on you! So many innocent people, children slaughtered! May God punish you for ever, may you all go to hell! Hitler was right."*

Visceral Jew-hatred latches on to anything that enables the anti-Semite to spill his bile.

The Gaza conflict may have ended in mid-August, but the anti-Semitic spin-off raged on into October.

Liverpool Football Club posted a tweet wishing their Jewish supporters a *"Happy New Year."* This drew a global wave of anti-Semitic abuse which caused the club to remove the tweet declaring, *due to the number of offensive comments that were attached to a tweet on the official LFC twitter account, the tweet and comments have since been removed from the account."* Questions arose asking why the Liverpool club removed the whole thread rather than just removing the abusive messages.

In September, a *Jewish Chronicle* reporter, Rosa Doherty, witnessed an anti-Semitic incident on a London bus as it passed through a predominantly Jewish suburb of Golders Green. The bus was full of Jewish schoolchildren as a man began shouting *"Get the Jews off the bus. All they do is f--- us."* Doherty complained to the driver who chose to deposit the man at the next bus stop. Having heard the man threaten to "burn the bus" and *"burn the Jews"* she was horrified when the driver allowed the man back on to the bus to continue his verbal abuse. With concern for the safety of the children, she called the police who told her that *"if the driver does not stop the bus, we cannot send police to you."* It was only after further complaints that the Metropolitan Police responded. After checking CCTV images of the suspect he was arrested and charged with a *"racially and religiously aggravated public order offence,"* and using *"threatening, abusive, or insulting words or behavior to cause harassment, alarm or distress."*

A coffee shop in London, Café Crema in New Cross, had a sign that read, *"Please boycott Israeli goods. Thank you."* It changed it to *"We do not use any Israeli products. We are not anti-Semitic, but anti-fascist. Jews are as welcome here as anyone else."* Israel was no longer bad, it was bad and fascist.

The owner claimed he was not anti-Semitic. That he is willing to take money from Jews. As an Israeli Jew, this poses a dilemma. Which part of me would he allow into his shop? I guess it's OK for me to enter as a Jew, but not as an Israeli. This is yet another example of the conditionality that is breaking out in Britain. You have to be a Jew on their terms. What is devious in this Palestinian support portrayed as *"we don't hate Jews, only fascists"* is the owner of Café Crema supports an entity that has openly announced itself to be fascist.

Mahmoud Abbas has declared that any Palestinian state will be Judenrein (free of Jews). Hamas, a partner in a Palestinian Unity government, has a Charter calling for the destruction of Israel and the killing of Jews.

This all leads me to the conclusion that, despite Café Crema's purported tolerance of Jews but hatred of Israelis, he is, at the end of the day, supporting the establishment of an anti-Semitic racist state that outlaws the notion of a Jewish state. Sorry Café Crema, you can't hide your anti-Semitism under the excuse that some of your paying customers are Jewish.

Café Crema's racist selection process of attempting to divide Jews from Israel is a further example of the Malmo Symptom. Here are some others;

The Malmo Symptom was played out at the Tricycle Theater in London. The Jewish organizers of the 2014 UK Jewish Film Festival were told they could not accept a funding donation from the Israeli Embassy.

Under the weight of protest the theater changed their decision, but other independent London theaters had offered to host the festival leaving Tricycle with even more egg on their face. But question remain. Why are displays taking place in Europe that try to drive a wedge between Jews and Israel?

In Ireland, the Holocaust Education Trust imposed a ruling that Israel was not to be mentioned at the 2015 ceremony marking the Nazi Holocaust of the Jews. This horrendous decision was given by the Irish board chairman, Peter Cassells, in an instruction which read, *"It was decided in future the MC of Holocaust Memorial Trust will not refer to the Jewish state or the State of Israel during any part of the ceremony."*

This led to a deserved outcry by, among others, Yad Vashem, the Simon Wiesenthal Center, the American Jewish Committee, the British Board of Deputies of British Jews, and the Holocaust Survivors Foundation-USA.

Yanky Fachler, who left his position as host of the event and to whom the instruction was sent, said, *"They came to an absolutely inacceptable decision and someone must be held accountable for it. "*

The frightening thing about the Tricycle Theater was that they couldn't see the anti-Semitism inherent in their act in that they would only accept Jews on their conditional terms. As with Café Crema, London Jews could only be accepted by the Tricycle Theatre if they renounced connections with the Jewish state. *(Malmo Symptom)* In their ignorance they completely failed to comprehend the place of Israel in Jewish identity. At the heart of this incident was the London Tricycle Theatre, via its artistic director, Indhu Rubasingham, who tried to lay down the boundaries on what would be acceptable or legitimate for Jews to believe.

As Danny Ben-Moshe, an associate professor on the Center for Citizenship and Globalization at Deakin University in Melbourne, Australia, wrote in an article printed in the Jerusalem Post, *"If people like this had their way Jews will be like modern day Marranos, watching Israeli films and discussing Israel in secret."* Ben-Moshe was referring the covert Jews of Spain who continued to practice their faith under pain of death during the Spanish Inquisition. Fixing the link between Jews anywhere and Israel he asked rhetorically, *"Maybe all Jews need to do is stop praying toward Jerusalem and then the way will be found [to accept them]?"*

The Malmo Symptom was clearly expressed during a debate in Britain's House of Lords on January 30, 2015 in which Baroness Jenny Tonge, the disgraced Liberal Democrat infamous for her inflammatory, often anti-Semitic, statements against Israel, made a parliamentary demand of pressuring British Jews to collectively condemn Israel.

Tonge tabled a written question in which she asked *"Her Majesty's Government whether they plan to encourage Jewish faith leaders in the*

United Kingdom publicly to condemn settlement building by Israel and to make clear their support for universal human rights."

Tonge called Israel *"a pariah state,"* and claimed that, *"because of its cruelty towards the Palestinians, the general public is conflating the Jewish State of Israel with Jewish people all over Europe"* before repeating her demand that British Jews must condemn Israel if they want to avoid increased expressions of anti-Semitism.

"When those of us who criticize the Government of Israel are accused of anti-Semitism by the Israel lobby, it further reinforces the view that Jewish people everywhere support the actions of the Israeli Government. Can the Jewish community not understand this?

This challenge to the Jewish community to divorce itself from Israel is a stark example of the Malmo Syndrome strain of anti-Semitism.

One year earlier Tonge used the platform that the House of Lords afforded her to disparage the Jewish state by saying, *"I have a dream of what a wonderful force for good Israel could have been, and I think still could be, if only it dropped its exclusivity of being a Jewish state."*

Apparently Tonge will not be able to see the remarkable ingenuity and innovation and the universal improvements to health, science, agriculture, and the amazing advances in technology that the Jewish state produces until it no longer calls itself the Jewish state.

In the past, Tonge has fallen foul of her party due to her anti-Israel remarks tipped with the old tropes of anti-Semitism.

At a fringe meeting of 2013 Liberal Democrat party conference she said, *"The pro-Israeli lobby has got its grips on the western world, its* financial grips. I think they have probably got a certain grip on our party."

In response, the party whip, Ming Campbell, said, *"I have written to Baroness Tonge dissociating myself and the party from her deeply offensive remarks and what I believe to be their clear anti-semitic connotations. I have asked for a review of the disciplinary powers available to the Liberal Democrat leaders in both the House of Lords and Commons."*

In the past Tonge accused Israel of *"organ harvesting"* when an IDF medical unit was the first humanitarian mission to arrive in the aftermath of a massively destructive earthquake that ravaged Haiti and set up a field hospital in 2010. For her sins the Lib Dem leader, Nick Clegg, sacked her from the front bench, but Tonge was not repentant blaming her punishment on *"the Israel lobby."*

The have been many other statements that dripped from the poison Tonge but I rest my case with these few examples.

In Britain, when a Member of Parliament receives death threats you know that not only that politician but the country has a problem.

Jewish MP, Lee Scott, disclosed that he had been threatened five times in the last few years. Scott, who represents the Ilford North constituency, recalled that during the 2010 general election campaign he was involved in a street confrontation with two men who called him *"a dirty Jew"* before threatening to kill him.

Scott says that his constituents have told him of their concerns about anti-Semitism. According to the Metropolitan Police's website, London has suffered a 92% increase in anti-Semitic incidents in 2014. Much of this increase can be ascribed to the Gaza conflict and Israeli-Palestinian tensions. This proves once again that, for many in Britain, Israel equates to British Jews when they look for a target to express their anger.

Vicki Kirby, a candidate of Britain's Labour Party for the contested Parliamentary seat of Woking, was quoted, in a 21 September 2014 edition of the Sunday Times, as posting on her Twitter account that, *"We invented Israel when saving them from Hitler, who now seems to be their teacher."* Israel wasn't saved by Hitler. Israel didn't exist. Neither, for that matter were Jews saved by Kirby. The war wasn't waged to save Jews. It was because Europe had fallen, Britain was in danger of Nazi invasion, and America had been attacked by the Japanese. The Jews, for people such as Kirby, could die in silence, totally ignored until the shame was exposed for all to see.

Beyond that piece of Kirby's ignorance and blatant anti-Semitism, we read further. According to this newspaper, Kirby claimed that Hitler might be *"the Zionist God."* See how easily anti-Semites turn their Jew-hatred into Zionist-hatred. Just change a word – job done! But then she exposes the hate that is perpetuated for generations with her horrendous statement, *"I will never forget and I will make sure my kids teach their children how evil Israel is."* That is how latent anti-Semitism is bred into children by the blind hate of mothers. Kirby, it needs to be said, was suspended by the Labour Party for her remarks.

*

Following the French terror outages of January 2015, particularly the attack of the Jewish store, British Jews began to feel more fearful.

Security at prominent Jewish cultural, educational, and religious centers was beefed up.

British police and security authorities thwarted an unprecedented number of 327 attacks in 2014, a 32% increase from the year before. Doubtless the 2015 figure will be even higher.

In Britain, the Community Security Trust provides protection for the UK Jewish community. Among the things they do are patrol key Jewish areas, coordinate security issues with the police and with community leaders. The CST has a series of threat levels according to the rise and fall of perceived danger.

A survey by the UK *Campaign against Anti-Semitism* showed that 25% of UK Jews were contemplating leaving Britain. Prior to this poll, the *Jewish Chronicle* newspaper on August 15, 2014, had the banner headline that *"63% say there may be no future for Jews in the UK,"* and this was before the 2015 terror targeting of Jews.

With the heightened tensions following the terror-related incidents in France and Belgium, British Home Secretary, Theresa May, said, *"I know that many Jewish people in this country are feeling vulnerable and fearful, and you are saying that you are anxious for your families, for your children, and for yourselves. I never thought I would see the day when members of the Jewish community in the UK would say that they are fearful of remaining here in the UK. That means we must all double our efforts to wipe out anti-Semitism here in the UK."*

A reformed David Cameron has stood squarely with Israel and with British Jews since he made a 2010 speech in Turkey in which he called Gaza *"a prison camp."* Years later, he stood up to criticism in championing Israel's right to self-defense, in opposing boycotts of Israel, and objecting to unilateral parliamentary moves to recognize a state of Palestine.

The British Prime Minister strongly deplored the rise of anti-Semitism in Britain. *"We are going to take the spirit of the march in Paris and we are going to fight anti-Semitism with everything we have. My policy is zero-tolerance. No disagreements on politics or policy will ever be allowed to justify racism, prejudice or extremism in our society."*

He went on, *"I want everyone in our Jewish community to know that if they want help or advice on security they should find an open door with the police."*

Fine words from the Prime Minister and the Home Secretary! The British government may indeed increase security and take steps to tackle the scourge of anti-Semitism, but there is little chance that Jewish fear will be assuaged in Britain, or anywhere else in Europe, until they see that the Muslim community double *their* efforts to wipe out anti-Semitism and reduce tension in their countries of residence.

The British Government should more closely supervise where their taxpayers' money goes to. In certain cases it goes to foster anti-Semitism.

In an All-Party Parliamentary Enquiry into Anti-Semitism report produced in February 2015, part of the assessment as to what is anti-Semitism was described as;

"Anti-Semitism is the scourge of civilized society and an indicator of societal problems. As the Community Security Trust explains, anti-Semitism at its heart is hostility, phobia or bias against Judaism or

individual Jews as a group. It should be of concern not just for the Jewish community but for all of us, when anti-Semitism is on the rise. Whilst overt anti-Semitism has become somewhat of a taboo since the Holocaust, it would be a mistake to consider the phenomenon inert. Anti-Semitism has mutated in form throughout time from religious to ethnic and racial-biological to nationalist.

Whenever racial abuse tends to be anchored in a perception of the victim as primitive, lowly, inhumane and worthless, anti-Jewish hatred conversely portrays the victims as all-powerful and duplicitous rulers. Therefore, historically, anti-Semitism has been rooted in allegations of Jewish cunning, conspiracy, immorality, wealth, power and hostility to others. It is that perspective which can still resonate within mainstream discourse about the Middle East conflict in relation to "Zionists" or "the Jewish Lobby" and is more difficult to divine than say attacks on a synagogue or visibly Jewish people. However, any theory which relies upon stereotypes of Jewish cunning or wealth and alleged control of the media or politicians is anti-Semitic. "

The report mentions Dr Brian Klug who defined anti-Semitism as *"a form of hostility to Jews as Jews where Jews are seen as something other than what they are. And so Jews are depicted not as they are, but as maligned stereotyped figures."* This aptly applies to Israel, the corporate Jew.

Figures from the report show that Jews, in comparison to Christians, are nearly eight times more likely to be the victim of religious hatred while British Muslims are nearly three times as likely to be such victims.

UK Anti-Semitism stems from Islamic extremists, far left and far right groups though the report notes a lessening of far right anti-Semitism.

The report confirmed that when trigger events relating to Israel occur the perpetrators of anti-Semitism tend to be Arab, South Asian and North African in increasing numbers. Although the religion of the perpetrators is not listed in the report it is certain that the vast majority of these politically-motivated incidents are Muslim.

There was a rise of 17% in British Jews moving to Israel in 2014.

Dr. Ben Gidley, Associate Professor and Senior Researcher COMPAS Oxford University, claimed that the media had a particular responsibility in handling the reporting of anti-Semitic incidents so as not to *"amplify insecurity."* Dr. Gidley had nothing to say about the distorted reporting by the media of events like the Gaza conflict that absolutely made British Jews feel totally insecure.

The proposal for city councils to raise the Palestinian flag is a further provocation to their local Jewish communities.

Jewish student life was also featured on the All-Party Parliamentary report. For Jewish students, *"there is nothing new about the new anti-Semitism. The notion that antagonism towards Jews may be expressed in some way through antagonism towards the State of Israel has been a constant theme of recent Jewish discourse. Whether or not they have witnessed or experienced it, Jewish students will almost certainly recognize the concept, and be alive to the possibility that anti-Semitism may surface in the guise of criticism of Israel."*

Academic boycotts were condemned in the 2006 parliamentary anti-Semitism report. The British coalition government, and the Labour government before it, set out clearly and repeatedly that it was fully supportive of academic freedom and firmly against academic boycotts of Israel or Israeli academics, and that academic boycotts of Israel would be unlawful and in contravention of equality legislation.

The report talks about leading figures and commentators in public life must be clear that it is inaccurate to use the term *"Jewish lobby"* which used in this context is anti-Semitic and that there is nothing disreputable about the existence of an Israel lobby. Sadly, anti-Semitic stereotypes of Jewish influence and dual loyalty, albeit not as prolific as in other periods of modern British history, were used during Operation Protective Edge and afterwards.

The report gives ample evidence that, in Britain, hate crimes against Jews doubled when Israel was defending itself from Palestinian terror and rocket attacks during the 2104 Gaza fighting.

*

In 2013, a charity called the Peace Giving Foundation received a lottery grant of £118,000 to run a program *"empowering ethnic minority women"*.
At the time, the Peace Giving Foundation shared directors with the Islamic Education and Research Academy (IERA), which sends extremist speakers to mosques and university societies.
Abdurraheem Green, the founder and head of IERA, once demanded that a Jewish man be removed from his sight when preaching at Speaker's Corner.
He has also said that the Jewish homeland is a *"myth"* and British public opinion is *"totally hostage to the Zionist-controlled media"*.
Other IERA speakers include Sheikh Abdullah Hakim Quick, who has called all Jews *"filth"*. Past members of the group's advisory board are

Hussain Yee, who blamed the Jews for 9/11, and Haitham al-Haddad, who described them as *"the descendants of apes and pigs"*.

In Britain, the Muslim Public Affair Committee (MPAC) boasts about its huge electoral influence. It may indeed have helped change the outcome in strongly Muslim Bradford East.
The incumbent, Labour's Terry Rooney (not Jewish, but pro-Israeli) lost by 365 votes in the 2010 general election after MPAC distributed thousands of leaflets calling him a Zionist Islamophobe and *"warmonger"* who could not represent Muslims.
The victor, Liberal Democrat David Ward, has fulfilled all MPAC's wildest hopes. In 2013, he was suspended from the Lib Dem parliamentary party after criticizing *"the Jews"* for inflicting atrocities on the Palestinians and questioning Israel's right to exist.
During the Gaza conflict last year he tweeted that, *"If I lived in Gaza, would I fire a rocket, probably yes."* His response to Paris: *"Je suis Palestinian."*
His party said they would take no disciplinary action against Ward suggesting he might be ready to fire rockets from Gaza into Israel because his words were not *"in any way anti-Semitic."*
In other words, a British Member of Parliament representing a strong Muslim constituency could say in 2014 that he would bomb the Jews of Israel and get away unpunished.
Jeremy Apfel, chairman of Barnet Synagogue, said, *"The immediate lesson from France is that failure to stamp out anti-Semitism and attacks on Jews inevitably lead to attacks on democracy itself; historically the Jews have merely served as the hors d'oeuvres".*

Daniel Cohen, the BBC Director of television, admitted, *"I've never felt so uncomfortable being a Jew in the UK as I've felt in the last 12* months. And it's made me think about, you know, is it our long-term home, actually? You feel it. I've felt it in a way I've never felt before."

Popular actress and comedienne, Maureen Lipman, is Jewish. She is considering leaving Britain due to the rising anti-Semitism.

"When the going gets tough, the Jews get packing," she said in a January 2015 interview with London Broadcasting Company. *"It's crossed my mind that it's time to have a look around for another place to live. I've thought about going to New York. I've thought about going to Israel."*

Describing the tentative situation of British Jews she said, *"We don't proselyte, we don't fly planes into buildings, we generally keep on the right side of the law. What is it, because I don't understand it at all? We give in science and in art, we give, we integrate, we help, we try, we are philanthropic, and still they start – it start's – and it's very, very depressing."*

British comedian and satirist, David Schneider said, *"I was thinking 'is this how the comfortable intellectual Jew of 1930s Germany felt?' That they don't mean us, they mean the Ostjuden* [impoverished Jews from Eastern Europe], *but us assimilated Jews, we're OK. Some of my parents' generation would say 'never be complacent, have your suitcase packed.'"* This expresses the panic of uncertainty felt by Jews in Britain, France, and other countries. Today the fear of the 30s is translated to *"Surely they don't mean us, they mean those eastern Jews in Israel, don't they? After all, we assimilated and integrated into our societies. So, they won't pick on us, will they?"*

Howard Jacobson, the Booker prize winning author, expressed his feelings to *The Guardian* newspaper, *"Any Jew who is not frightened is mad. What makes it particularly frightening at the moment is the conjunction of classic anti-Semitism, the idea the Jews have got too much money and want to rule the world, and contemporary Islamic anti-Semitism, and we haven't had that before. There is more anxiety around at the moment. Your heart races and you don't know whether you feel strong or weak. The main thing is you don't know what to do."*

*

Anti-Semitism hiding behind the specter of Nazism on the social media.

A useful research was undertaken by Lancaster University Law School in the UK and published on their LancsLaw blog.

They surveyed the use of the words *"Israel"* and *"Gaza"* accompanied with the words *"Jew," "Jews,"* or *"Jewish"* through the months of July and August 2014 during the Gaza conflict on Twitter. The results were very telling.

A keyword analysis showed the specter of Nazism with words such as *"Hitler," "Holocaust," "Nazi,"* and *"Nazis"* present in the top 35 keywords with Hitler mentioned 1114 times, Holocaust mentioned in 505 Tweets, and Nazi or Nazis listed 851 times. The Nazi theme was evident in hashtag links.

The negative sentiments were stark. Explicit anti-Semitic invective, if shouted out on the street, would clearly be racial or religiously aggravated public order offenses. Others wished violence on Jews as proxies for Israel, or simply foe being Jews. Some expressed a view that

"Hitler did not finish the job." In other tweets, the use of gas chambers for Jews was invoked. Others simply included Nazi-slogans.

As the LancsLaw blog states, *"Deep wounds are scratched when the Nazi-card is played in this way in discourse against Jews. Playing the Nazi-card is not simply abusive. It invokes painful collective memories for Jews and for many others. By using those memories against Jews it inflicts profound hurts. Those who play the Nazi-card know exactly what it means.*

Reaction to the military practices of the Israeli state can be expressed in a variety of forceful and trenchant ways – none of which would be anti-Semitic. The hurts inflicted against Jews when the Nazi card is played cannot be written-off as collateral damage in the protest against Israel."

The Lancaster University Law School recommends clear grounds for prosecution for such offenses. In the UK a sufficient statutory framework is arguably in place to prosecute against the types of anti-Jewish abuse we identified by proceedings under the Malicious Communications 1988 or the Communications Act 2003. In such proceedings courts can treat the anti-Jewish abuse as racial or religious aggravation according to the Criminal Justice Act 2003. The inquiry's recommendation therefore that the Crown Prosecution Service should give consideration *"to the suitability of existing guidance on communications sent via social media"* and *"that hate crime guidance material on grossly offensive speech be reviewed to clarify what amounts to 'criminal acts' that 'will be prosecuted'"* is opportune.

*

AUSTRALIA.

Danny Ben-Moshe highlighted a particular incident in which a respected veteran journalist, Mike Carlton, published a vitriolic article against Israel in the *Sydney Morning Herald* with allegations of genocide in Gaza. It is worth noting that this piece appeared after Hamas terrorists had murdered three Israeli teenagers and had been bombarding Israel with rocket fire from Gaza and prior to the ground invasion by Israeli troops. His advice was that Jews, who experienced the Holocaust, should know better. To further emphasize the anti-Semitism of his Gaza conflict article, it was accompanied by a controversial cartoon depicting a hooked-nose Jew setting off a remote-controlled bomb in Gaza.

Here was yet another example where Israeli criticism was couched in anti-Semitic language and illustration which informed the *Herald* readership of the worst stereotypical perceptions of Jews.

Under threat of legal action against this racial vilification, the editor apologized for the cartoon, but not Carlton's words. The fact that the editor and cartoonist didn't need to be rapid anti-Semites to permit this anti-Semitic trash and imagery is worrying but increasingly practiced. Carlton's anti-Jewish attitude that clearly reflects on his writings about Israel was exposed by the *Australian*, a rival of his *Sydney Morning Herald,* who informed their readers of an email that Carlton had sent to members of the Sydney Jewish community who had objected to his article. In it, Carlton is alleged to have written, *"You're the one full of hate and bile, sunshine. The classic example of the Jewish bigot. Now f--- off!"*

As Professor Ben-Moshe reminds us, it is disturbing that people such as Carlton are not members of the Socialist Left or neo-Nazi Right. He is far from being the only mainstream member of the media or public elite to have such Israel-related anti-Semitic prejudice. It confirms for us that the boycott campaign against Israel is, and always has been, about boycotting and insulting Jews.

Anti-Semitic flyers were dropped in the letterboxes of homes in the Jewish suburbs of Bondi Beach and Double Bay in Sydney, Australia. *"Wake up Australia!"* they warned. *"Jews have been kicked out of countries 109 times through history. Could it be that having then in a European country is harmful to the host?"*

The flyers included an invitation to join Squadron 88, a local white supremacist group which has a neo-Nazi website.

*

TURKEY.

Turkey's Prime Minister, Tayyip Erdogan, demanded that Turkish Jews denounce Israel. In an interview with the *Daily Sabah* newspaper he compared the Jewish state to Nazi Germany and accused it of perpetrating genocide against the Palestinian Arabs. In this interview he served a veiled threat against the Jewish community in his country by saying, *"I talked with our Jewish citizens' leaders…and I stated that they should adopt a firm stance and release a statement against the Israeli government."* In a rebuff to Erdogan, several prominent Turkish Jews issued a protest in the *Hurriyet Daily News* at the end of August 2014 in which they declared that they had no obligation to *"account for, interpret or comment on any event that takes place elsewhere in the world, and in which he/she has no involvement. There is no onus on the Jewish community of Turkey, therefore, to declare an opinion on any matter at all."*

Where support for the Palestinian cause and objection to any Israeli counter action reaches the depth of age-old anti-Semitism was displayed in an open letter in the pro-government Turkish daily *Yeni Atik*. It was addressed to the country's chief rabbi. It said, *"You came here after being banished from Spain. You have lived comfortably among us for five hundred years and gotten rich at our expense. Is this your gratitude –killing Muslims? Erdogan, demand that the community leader apologizes."*

In a study conducted by the Hrant Dink Foundation and released in January 2015, anti-Semitism was found to be the most common racial or religious prejudice in the Turkish media.

The study, which followed derogatory coverage of over thirty different groups in media reports between May and August 2014, found that Jews and Armenians were subjects of just over half of the recorded incidents in a media landscape filled with biased and discriminatory language. Jews led the prejudicial reporting with 130 incidents. The next highest were Armenians with less than half that number – 60. There were thirty Christian prejudicial reporting incidents, and there were twenty one discriminatory reports against Greeks.

It is worth highlighting that, during coverage of Operation Protective Edge in Gaza, some of the Turkish media failed to differentiate between Jews, Israelis and Zionists, using the word *"Jew"* to refer to all of them indiscriminately.

One example of the Malmo Symptom referred elsewhere in this book was an article written by journalist, Faruk Kose, in *Yeni Akit*, a pro-government newspaper, that called on Turkish Jews to issue a communal apology on behalf of Israel.

During the conflict, the head of *Insani Yardim Vakfi* (IHH), the Turkish group responsible for the 2010 Mavi Marmara incident, told a Turkish TV station that *"Turkish Jews will pay dearly"* for Operation Protective Edge.

In a late 2014 Anti-Defamation League global poll, 69% of Turks were found the hold anti-Semitic attitudes.

*

AMERICA.

Attacks against Jews continued in America long after the ending of the Gaza fighting. In October, dozens of teenagers were caught vandalizing a Hassidic-owned deli in the Crown Heights neighborhood of New York. Yanki Klein, the store owner, said that he is accustomed to teens stealing from his store and yelling *"Heil Hitler!"*

A week prior to that the executive director of the King's Bay Y, Leonard Petlakh, was assaulted by pro-Palestinian protesters at the end of an exhibition basketball game between the Brooklyn Nets and Israeli champions, Maccabi Tel Aviv, at the Barclays Center.

When New York's prestigious Metropolitan Opera stages a production of *'The Death of Kinghoffer'* you know that this American cultural icon has gone off the tracks. Or, to put it more aptly, it threw itself off the ship and into an ocean of bile, just as the infirm Jew, Leon Kinghoffer, was pitched off the deck of the Italian cruise ship, *Achille Lauro*, by Palestinian terrorists in 1985. These were the terrorists that the Met transformed into victims. The fraud of the opera is seen in its title. Klinghoffer did not die. He was killed by Palestinian murderers who hated Jews and the Jewish state. The opera sympathized with the terrorists in order to equate a false humanity between them and Israel. When you compare this grotesque opera to the reality of what happened aboard the ill-fated Achille Lauro we again see how Israel is replaced, this time by a disabled Jew, for victimization. The defenseless elderly Klinghoffer symbolizes the Jewish state. This opera was staged at the Lincoln Center, a cultural center that was mostly built by the patronage of Jews. The arrogance of bringing this anti-Semitic work to this place was a slap in the face of its founders.

What was particularly insulting for New York was that one of its citizens became the centerpiece of this obnoxious opera that carried his name. Leon Klinghoffer grew up in the Lower East Side of the city. Even his family was appalled by this ugly farce. As his daughters, Lisa and Ilsa, objected to the opera that *"rationalized, romanticized and legitimized the terrorist murder of our father."*

In response to an August 20 opinion piece written by Deborah Lipstadt on the rise of European anti-Semitic incidents, the Reverend Bruce Shipman, an Episcopal chaplain at Yale University wrote to the *New York Times* blaming Israel for the rising European anti-Semitism. This knee-jerk reaction of linking attacks on Jews to Israeli actions led to his resignation and an apology. *"Nothing done in Israel or Palestine justifies the disturbing rise in anti-Semitism in Europe or elsewhere."*

*

Correcting the rise of political anti-Semitism.

Anti-Semitism is politically motivated. In Germany, the Nazis targeted the Jews in part because they represented liberal democracy and emancipation, the antithesis of everything that an authoritative Nazi Germany stood for.

It was the same back in authoritative Catholic Spain that viewed the Jews as outside their theological control yet prospering in their society and led to the expulsions and inquisition of Spanish and later Portuguese Jews. It was as political in its motives as it was religious.

We saw it under authoritative soviet communism where Jews were the scapegoat, as they had been under the tsarist rule.

We see the politics being played out in the drive of intolerant Islamic domination of which the Palestinian problem is a part. Jews are constantly the target in Muslim and Arab worlds. Almost a million Jews were driven out of Arab countries in a regional wave of anti-Semitism that still festers despite the absence of Jews. Anti-Semitism is embedded in both the Hamas and Palestinian charters.

In every case, brutal regimes put a Jewish face as a target for their repression. They blamed Jews for all the ills of their societies and the world.

Politically they point to Jews not as having contributed to their society but instead inventing Jewish conspiracies and plots against a state or a religion. This is the trope of Jews plotting to control the world, and the purported global influence and power of Jews or Zionists -they are interchangeable - as predicted in the infamous *'Protocols of the Elders of Zion,'* a rabid anti-Semitic screed that, alongside *'Mein Kampf,'* is a best seller in much of the Arab world today.

It's important to see it as a political tool, a platform if you will, of political forces imposing themselves on the masses by bringing them to oppose the Jews as the perceived enemy, a ploy that brings them to power, or allows them to hold on to power.

We see attempts at this power play in Greece with the *'Golden Dawn'* party or with *'Jobbik'* in Hungary that use Jews as a platform on which to tread up the political ladder, dragging the uninformed and ignorant masses with them.

It's the organization of politics against the Jews. We are seeing that being played out today against Israel.

In the Europe of Theodor Herzl, the visionary of modern-day Zionism, there were Jews who saw this force being brought against them because they were successful cosmopolitans without a country of their own. Although they were successful insiders they were looked on as alien outsiders.

As mentioned earlier, this was true of the Spanish and Portuguese Jews. It was so for Russian Jews and especially for Jews in the Nazi era. It equally applied to the Jews of Arab lands.

So the urge developed for Jews to have a country of their own in their ancient homeland, to become a country like any other, to be considered normal in their own land. They thought this would solve all their problems. It didn't.

People like Herzl saw a Jewish state as saving liberalism. A Jew-less country's defects could not be blamed on non-existent Jews. If no Jews were there, so it was believed, they would have no one to blame. It would put an end to anti-Semitism. How wrong they were! They misunderstood the variables of anti-Semitism.

The Arabs saw the opportunity of using Jews as a political lightning rod to concentrate attention away from their own defects, divisions, internal unrest and poverty by drawing the grievances of their people away from their failed leadership onto an enemy that was perceived to be exploiting them and dishonoring their religion - the Jews.

Israel has misunderstood the nature of this Arab anti-Semitism. Leaders thought that if only Israel reached out in peace they would be welcomed, or at least be left alone. If only Israel won the wars waged against it by the losing Arab armies they would appreciate Israel's strength and determination and leave Israel alone in peace. When Israel established its permanency, it was assumed, the Arabs would become reasonable but, when it comes to the Jews, nobody and nothing is reasonable.

Today we have a world that plays down Palestinian anti-Jewish tendencies that obsessively pressures and threatens Israel to surrender hallowed Jewish land, essential to its vital security. They claim, by making the Jewish state do their bidding, peace will descend on earth. And, if Israel does not comply with their demands, well, it's those pesky Jews, don't you know!

What are Israel and its advocates to do about this phenomenon? The first thing to do is to stop playing the defendant. Once you accept the role you lose the incentive to play the role of the prosecutor. You place yourself in the dock of the accused. This is the Jewish experience through the ages. Jews have always been judged by others, never the other way round. Jews, through the ages, have always looked for acceptance from people and nations in which they lived. They rarely found sanctuary. More often they were judged and prosecuted for crimes uncommitted. Jews were always automatically put on the defensive. Sadly, Israel has played this role all too often.

What Israel should have done in 1947 when the United Nations Partition Plan was rejected by the Arab nations, and later with the 1948 declaration of Israel's independence, was to have demanded and prosecuted the Arab world to recognize Israel's legitimacy. How dare they countermand a United Nations resolution that recognizes the establishment of a Jewish state? As members of the United Nations they were, and are, bound to accept resolutions and the legitimacy of them. Even today, non-compliant nations must be brought to book. They must, finally, be stopped from their dangerous rebellion against recognizing the right of Jewish state of Israel to exist. This brand of anti-Semitism has set back world peace for decades. It has led to the death of thousands and the disaster that is today's Middle East.

Israel must demand that world bodies reform their political thinking and stop imposing a different double standard to Israel and instead judge others by the norms they apply only against the Jewish state.

European parliaments vote to recognize *'Palestine.'* In this we see cynical politicians cater to a rising constituency that will ensure their warm seats of power. We do not see right-minded politicians address the real context of the Israeli-Arab-Palestinian conflict.

If Europe were truly against the plague of anti-Semitism they would admit to the anti-Semitic characteristics of an Arab-Palestinian cause they avidly support. They ought to be too horrified to stand shoulder to shoulder with it. Instead, they turn a blind eye to it and, instead, put their collective political weight, not against the anti-Semitic Palestinians, but onto the Jew among nations – Israel. This is wrong. Israel, Jews, and right-minded people must demand that European parliaments rescind their ill-advised recognition of a Palestinian state until a Palestinian leadership drops its violent and anti-Semitic language and intent.

The Arab and Muslim world, including Palestinians, must reform themselves, cease their anti-Semitism, right the wrongs of centuries, and work for a better world. Only then can we have a chance of amicably solving issues such as the Arab-Palestinian-Israeli conflict.

*

The disproportionate concentration on Israel.

One of the worrying things that political anti-Semites have succeeded in doing has been to scare many European and American Jews into identifying themselves as Zionists and supporters of Israel.

This issue arose at a January 2015 annual meeting of the Women's International Zionist Organization (WIZO) in Tel Aviv.

This is particularly disturbing when pro-Israeli voices are silenced by intimidation on campuses throughout Britain and America. One effect of this void is that only the anti-Israel linked to pro-Palestinian propaganda is broadcast and, as a result, is picked up by the media and by politicians. A concentration on Israel that limits opposing voices and ignores far more burning world issues has a tendency to heap disproportionate language and attention on to the Jewish state.

Professor Irwin Cotler spoke about the preoccupation with Israel as having the effect of sanitizing other evils. This expression may give the impression that Israel is evil along with others, which would be totally and patently wrong. What Cotler was saying is that Israel is picked on, for whatever reason, for unhealthy and wholesale criticism and condemnation out of all proportion in comparison with massively gruesome slaughters, human rights abuses, and international crimes committed by dictatorial and undemocratic regimes that are allowed to get away with them because the limited time and concentration of bodies like the United Nations, European parliaments, and the European Court of Justice all take a jaundiced approach against Israel.

The terror attack on the offices of Charlie Hebdo brought to the fore the issue of the assault against a free press, but governments and, indeed, the world's media had little to say about the closing down of free speech and the arrest, imprisonment and murder of journalists in countries headed by Turkey but including Iran, China, Russia, Saudi Arabia, Jordan, Qatar, Egypt, Bahrain, Cameroon, Azerbaijan, Eritrea, Ethiopia, Syria, Somalia, Vietnam, Thailand, and the Palestinian Authority and Hamas.

Israel is a free and democratic country, but so many undemocratic countries are among those who regularly vote to condemn Israel for other offences while giving themselves a free pass.

Even in democratic European bodies, the awful oppressive and repressive records of countries are ignored, silent against the loud and constant sound of anti-Israel criticism and condemnation for comparatively minor misdemeanors that are exaggerated out of all proportion, and garbed in a supposed mantle of illegality to add weight to their proposition.

An example of this is the discourse that constantly reprises what Israel *"is doing"* to the Palestinians was expressed in a Jerusalem Post article written by David Weinberg which is featured in this book. Wrongly describing what Israel is *"doing to the Palestinians"* as *"genocide,"* *"crimes against humanity,"* and as a *"threat to world peace and security"* adds to the vilification against Israel and Zionism, promotes the campaigns for boycotts, divestments and sanctions against Israel, and feeds into the latent anti-Semitism of a not small part of a population who then feel justified and emboldened to take out their anger against the closest Jewish targets they can find. This book is replete with some of the examples of this phenomenon.

*

Imams and anti-Semitism.

Like all the other European Muslim Jew-killers, 22 year old Omar El-Hussein, Danish son of Muslim immigrants, who killed a film director, and a Jewish volunteer security guard outside a synagogue, in Copenhagen, was not deradicalized by an imam in the name of Islam.

This raises the question, how many imams condemn anti-Semitism in their mosque sermons? The answer is probably not many.

*

ADDITIONAL INSIGHTS INTO FIGHTING ANTI-SEMITISM.

Anti-Semitism on Campus.

In 2011, the Students for Justice in Palestine chapter at Northeastern University, which was suspended by the university administration this past year for its bigoted conduct toward Jewish students, decided to hijack a Holocaust remembrance event on campus in order to publicly protest the existence Israel.

Unfortunately, the memory of the Holocaust is too often abused by enemies of Israel or Jewish life – in the past two weeks swastika graffiti has appeared on the campuses of both Emory University and Yale University.

Woefully, the faceless nature of the swastika graffiti – the vandals have yet to be identified on either campus – place the incidents on the less extreme side of anti-Jewish activity this year. The negative experiences of too many students sympathetic to Israel's cause and purpose on many North American campuses extend well beyond spotting chalked or spray-painted swastikas on campus.

In August, a Jewish student of Temple University was punched in the face by a peer. I soon spoke to the victim, who phoned me from the hospital. He explained that when he approached the table of Students for Justice in Palestine (SJP) at a campus activities fair to correct inaccurate claims in their literature, tensions escalated to the point that one anti-Israel student blindsided him and smacked him across the face. When I spoke to two witnesses over the phone, they told me that the victim had been called a *"kike"* soon after being punched.

At Ohio University, in early September, the student body president took the *"ALS Ice Bucket Challenge,"* but instead of conducting the charity fund-raiser in a typical fashion, she dumped a bucket of fake blood on herself in support of alleged Palestinian suffering at the hands of the Israeli state.

In the video she made of her theatrics, she explained: *"As student senate president, I'm sending a message of student concern about the genocide in Gaza and the occupation of Palestine by the Israeli state"* before endorsing the anti-Semitic Boycott, Divestment and Sanctions campaign against Israel.

Just weeks later on the campus of Loyola University, SJP verbally assaulted Jewish students, hurling a variety of insults at them before creating a human wall to block their attempt to advertise a Birthright Israel trip.

One student told The College Fix, an online paper, that members of SJP approached the table and asked students, *"How does it feel to be an occupier?"* and *"How does it feel to be guilty of ethnic cleansing?"* The SJP chapter was later temporarily suspended.

Unrelenting vilification of Israel on college campuses is fueled partly by ignorance, but often simultaneously by an animus toward at least one leg of the *"Israeli trifecta":* The State of Israel, the Land of Israel and the Judeo-Christian values which shape Israeli society. The first group of ideologues spends the majority of its time taking issue with how it perceives certain policies of the State of Israel. Often these students are ignorant as to the reality on the ground and find it easy to side with the perceived Palestinian underdog as the story is told in the mainstream media.

The lens under which Israel's behavior is measured more closely resembles a proctoscope than a microscope.

But almost without fail, those American college students who spend the their time rallying against policies of the State of Israel spend just a little too much time surrounded by folks who take an issue with the Land of Israel. This second group of students attempts to erase any connection between the Jewish people and their homeland. And while members of this group likely deny harboring any overt hatred toward the Jewish people, they simply hate Israel with a fervor that they do not apply to other nations or issues.

And almost without fail those who claim to take issue simply with Israel as a modern nation-state spend too much time promoting and cheering individuals that deeply oppose the Judeo-Christian values for which the Jewish people and the State of Israel, and America, stand. The third group largely manifests through overt hatred and is the reason why Holocaust remembrance events are exploited to protest Israel. It is this toxic mix, with some overlap, that leaves groups such as Students for Justice in Palestine and J Street as the self-appointed guardians of human rights and Arab nationalistic narratives.

Concern for the plight of Arab women, and LGBTQ citizens of the Arab and Muslim world, do as much to stir fervor in Students for Justice in Palestine as water helps power an automobile.

It's a non-starter. They'd rather reprimand Israel and fuel their group's engine with pernicious rage toward the Jewish state – the Palestinian cause is relegated to nothing more than a figurative tool to ostracize Israel though noxious combination of hatred, intimidation and radicalism on campus.

On September 22, Palestinian Authority President Mahmoud Abbas, who is in the tenth year of his four-year term, addressed a crowd at Cooper Union in New York City. "*I have held in my own hand and seen the seeds of peace,*" he explained. "*The seeds of peace are the young Palestinians, Israelis and others all over the world who form peace groups on college campuses, like J Street and Students for Justice in Palestine, those are the seeds of peace.*" Abbas' remarks about campus organizations are notable because they are concurrent with his constant, deliberate encouragement of a Palestinian narrative that seeks to demonize and destroy Israel rather than unite and build a future Palestine.

The current forces aligned against Israel on campus fuel an atmosphere of hatred and disdain, which must be rejected immediately.

While groups such as Students for Justice in Palestine openly promote evil, the more ostensibly moderate must be challenged as well.

Evil is evil, as in the case of SJP. But it is also evil to actively work to elevate groups and people, under a guise of legitimacy, that promote a form of global collectivism that curiously enough leaves room for everyone and every state but the Jewish one. Groups such as J Street must be held to account for this behavior.

In his October 14 article in The Wall Street Journal, Bret Stephens wrote that "*nature abhors a vacuum, and so does power: American retreat means someone else – someone we don't like – is going to step in."* While Stephens warned of a geopolitical climate absent an active and functioning US foreign policy, the threat of a vacuum jockeyed by inimical voices looms large on college campuses. If we leave an opportunity for those with misguided and insidious ideologies to take over the narrative, manipulate the truth and dictate the tone of the atmosphere on campus, they will.

Those on campus interested in Israel's cause have a moral responsibility to speak out and demand the presence of a moral compass – insisting on the elevation of humanity and modernity over barbarism. Are we prepared to handle the repercussion of a generation of college students familiar with the concept of justice solely absent a rigid definition? We shouldn't test it.

Daniel Mael is a senior at Brandeis University, a reporter for TruthRevolt.org and a contributor to the Franklin Center for Government and Public Integrity.

MLK, tokenism and the rebound of Jew hatred.

In 1963, Dr. Martin Luther King penned an article in *The National Review* titled *"A Bold Design for a New South."* In the piece, Dr. King laments what he calls the *"tokenism"* of American society, specifically America's satisfaction with mere modicums of freedom – as opposed to absolute liberation.

He wrote that Americans *"have been persuaded to accept token victories as indicative of genuine and satisfactory progress."* Dr. King praises America's innate desire to pursue and maintain a free society from its birth in 1776, to the *"shedding of the evil of chattel slavery in 1863,"* to its fight against fascism in World War II.

Yet at the conclusion of the piece, Dr. King still objects to the current situation, saying, *"There segregation, the evil heritage of slavery, remains."*

Dr. King's message teaches us that we can only be satisfied when all human rights are obtained – not just a few.

The civil rights movement which Dr. King spearheaded illustrated that we must demonstrate until total emancipation is established and full liberation is realized.

This lesson is especially relevant today as terror spreads across Europe, North Africa and the Middle East, and as Jews flees Europe for Israel.

Just as in 1963 white Southerners were actively advocating for policies of discrimination and segregation against blacks, today there are many – both journalists and statesmen – who place blame on Jewish victims of oppression rather than those who do the oppressing. In doing so, they perpetuate the idea that Jews should be disenfranchised and marginalized.

• Rula Jebreal, for example, on a segment on CNN, implicitly suggested that it was the Jews' own fault that they were being persecuted in France and elsewhere. She stated that *"extremists"* – who target Jews because they are Jews – were on the rise because of Israel's alleged policies of *"segregation."* To wit, extremists are fighting against Jewish *"oppression"* by fighting for oppression of Jews a la Adolf Hitler.

• In a broadcast on MSNBC, reporter Ayman Mohyeldin suggested that attacks against Jews should be contextualized and that one should take into consideration Israel's immigration laws when discussing such matters.

• The BBC's Tim Wilcox suggested that anti-Semitism against French Jews was justified because of the state of Israel.

• CNN Anchor Ashley Banfield justified Palestinian lynching of Israeli civilians because many would grow up to defend their country and enroll in the Israel Defense Forces.

• In 2013, The New York Times published a piece that idealized attacks on Jews, calling attempted aggression against Jewish Israelis vis-a-vis rock throwing *"nonviolent peaceful resistance."* This is as senseless as suggesting that when Dr. King marched through the South Side of Chicago in 1966 and white protesters threw rocks at him, they were simply engaging in "nonviolent peaceful resistance" against a civil rights leader.

• In the United States, we provide material support in the form of hundreds of millions of dollars to the Palestinian Authority – a regime that calls almost daily for the lynching of Jews in the streets of Israel and which honors racists – like Leila Khaled – who have been successful in murdering Jews.

• We indirectly finance Hamas via funds that are sent to the United Nations Relief and Works Agency – funds which are supposed to go toward helping the residents of Gaza but which often end up in Hamas' coffers.

This collective lip service to the idea of *"Never Again"* is simply that: priggish conversation we engage in to make ourselves feel good. Yet we are content with mere *"tokens"* of freedom. We believe we are saying something of great substance when we condemn anti-Semitism with statements of *"Yes, that is horrible."* Yet, all too often we follow those statements with qualifiers of, *"but I understand why it happened."*

These *"yes, buts"* are the language of tokenism. Here a little, there a little. We are plaster saints who talk the talk without backing our words up with deeds:

• We claim to stand for Jewish self-determination but do so only in principle. We entertain and promote the racist notion that Jews should be banned from living in Judea and Samaria simply because they are Jews. We would never say that Blacks or Asians should be banned from living in a place merely because of their ethnic identity – and rightfully so. Yet we do not extend this same right to Jews.

• We appear at rallies and press conferences that express solidarity with Jews in France after others have just been slaughtered – while bashing Jews who secure themselves in order to prevent such a slaughter from happening in Israel.

- We lament when Jews are murdered in a supermarket near Paris, while finding justification for the prohibition of Jewish existence in Ramallah.

- In the selfsame breath, 1.5 million joined hands and avowed that they supported the Jewish community all while marching in lock step with Mahmoud Abbas – one of the primary government leaders today who perpetuates anti-Semitism.

- We claim to have sympathy for Israelis when rockets are launched against them, and yet become angry when Israelis dare to attack those who did the launching.

- We tweet out, *"Je Suis Juif,"* because it's trendy, but insist that we certainly are not Jews who want nothing more than the basic right to pray at their holy sites, including the Temple Mount.

As if actors in our own theater of the absurd, we preserve that which we claim to eschew.

These suggestions that victims of persecution should be held responsible for what is done to them or should be discriminated against because of who they are should elicit moral outrage from decent human beings everywhere. Yet such ideas are accepted as legitimate viewpoints. Today, if anyone suggested that black males deserved to be lynched because they were infringing upon the right of the white elite to oppress them, they would receive backlash and the opprobrium of their peers – and rightfully so.

But overt justification of Jew hatred continues to air on prime-time television with little-to-no protest – suggesting that we have yet to build a society that Dr. King envisioned: where prejudice against Jewish people is socially taboo.

Our mistaking of scraps of freedom for authentic emancipation yields consequences: Jews are told that they have rights but only when those rights come with limitations and reservations to our liking. If this pattern persists, there will be more incidents like those in France, and more Jews will be targeted and slaughtered simply because they are Jews. Our cowardice and artificial support for basic human rights for the Jewish people has led to a global social pandemic wherein Jews are attacked with impunity and anti-Semitism is routinely justified by journalists and state governments alike.

Altering the status quo requires reflection: We cannot escape this role we have played in enabling Jew hatred to spread around the globe.

This week we remember Dr. King's legacy and his dream of love and justice covering the breadth of the earth. Yet, until radical changes occur in our attitudes toward animosity against Jews, Dr. King's dream will remain a dream deferred.

Chloe Valdary is a consultant for the Committee for Accuracy in Middle East Reporting in America and a fellow at the Lawfare Project. She is the recipient of the 2015 David Bar Ilan Award for outstanding student leadership on campus on behalf of Israel. Chloe Valdary is also the author of 'Reclaim the Zionist Dream.'

UnChosen.

As a philo-Semite of some four decades and counting, when I read recently that Cameron Diaz and her beau Benji Madden had been married in a Jewish-themed ceremony, I must say I nearly choked on my latkes in sheer molten excitement. They had the whole works; the chuppah, the seven blessings, the crushed wineglass, the Yichud. Furthermore, the couple *"publicly identify as Jewish"* although they have no Jewish ancestors and are not known to have converted. Rachel Shukert, writing in *Tablet*, saw this as part of a trend towards philo-Semitism: *"For the first time in the history of America, Jewishness — and not just the bagels-and-lox part — is aspirational. There's a Seder in the White House, and rabbis gave the invocation at the conventions of both major political parties ... Ralph Lauren built an empire giving us all WASP anxiety; now the WASPs want to be Jews."*

That may be the case in the Land Of The Free, but over here in bitter old Europe it's not a good time to be a Jew. The new Islamism has combined with the old idiocy and given anti-Semitism a grotesquely fresh'n'funky hit of new blood, leading to the recent terror in France. Even in Germany, who you'd think would pay some sort of lip-service to playing nice, a survey by the Bertelsmann Foundation to gauge current German-Israeli relations ahead of World Holocaust Day found that 81 per cent of Germans say they want to put *"the history of the persecution of the Jews behind them."* I bet they do! But as it also showed that 48 per cent of Germans have a bad opinion of Israel while only 36 per cent have a good one, the few Jews left with roots in Germany may not be wishing to dust down their lederhosen and mosey back to the Old Country any time soon, indicating as this does a certain clod-hopping, thigh-smacking lack of sensitivity.

It's easy for an Englisher to look down on Germany and France, but here things have been getting worse for a long time. A Jewish friend told me that after visiting a synagogue in Barbados, she knew that somehow it was different from every London shul she had attended, but she couldn't work out why before it finally came to her in an awful flash – it was UNGUARDED. Europeans have been calling our capital *'Londonistan'* for years. When the black flag of ISIS was flown over a housing estate a few miles from Parliament last year, the slow sleepwalk towards a state of self-immolation seemed to become reality, leaving us wondering how we got into a situation where popular fast-food chains use halal-only meat, while the police ignore the mass gang rape and trafficking of non-Muslim girls by Muslim men for fear of disturbing *"community relations."*

And alongside this sucking up to Islam there has grown a more vicious attitude towards Jews in a classic move of the coward siding with the bully in a bid to avoid being the target of his wrath. Hence the survey this week by the Royal Institute of International Affairs that showed a surge in negative attitudes toward Israel since a previous study two years ago. According to the data, 35 per cent of Britons now say they *"feel especially unfavorable towards"* Israel compared to 17 per cent previously. This means that Israel is regarded more unfavorably by Britons than Iran while only North Korea is disliked more.

It doesn't help that this country has always had a strange cult of Jewish journalists who never seem happier than when whipping up hatred against Israel. After the recent events in Paris, they were out in full self-flogging force, such as Will Self, who happily tied himself in knots on the television news explaining why it was essential for fascists not to have their feelings hurt. (I suppose that when you're such a self-loathing half-wit that you *"formally resign"* from being a Jew, as Self has, sucking up to those who hate you most is the logical end-game.) Like Self, Laurie Penny is a Jew who seems almost parasexually obsessed with being punished by Islamofascism. (She once wore a hijab and gushed about how happy she felt it in, the entitled ass-hat.) Her opinion on the Paris atrocities: *"Racist trolling is not heroism. Je Ne Suis Pas Charlie."* On their rampage, the Islamofascists murdered, amongst others, a Muslim policeman, a French-Caribbean policewoman, an Algerian cartoonist and Jewish civilians. And she calls us racist! Isn't racism hating everyone who's not like you? Sums up Islamism perfectly.

The most charitable view of these clowns is that they suffer from *rationalist naivete*, the liberal error of believing that we are all rational actors. Whereas in fact – as with the Nazis – there are non-rational actors who cannot be reasoned with and whose ideas must be fought to the death. The uncharitable view is they are simply vile cowards. Never mind. As the Diaz wedding proved, the most interesting, intelligent and attractive people have long clamored to join the clan – you can afford to lose a few spineless runts.

Over the past decade I have lost jobs and friends for my allegiance, yet it was a small price to pay for the knowledge that I can never be numbered among the grim, grinning ghouls of Jew-hatred (who also sadly number a few Jews amongst them). If you are a Jew in Europe, best to abandon these clapped out old kingdoms to Islamofascism. You can go to Israel. And for the first time last year, more made Aliyah from

Western Europe than from the poorer countries. Never mind: Europe's loss will be Israel's gain.

And me, I can just retreat into my own little world, the one I inhabited as a redneck teenager before I ever met you. And dream of next year in Yerushalayim.

UNCHOSEN: MEMOIRS OF A PHILO-SEMITE by Julie Burchill is published by Unbound. Julie Birchall is a British novelist and writes for the Sunday Times and Guardian newspapers.

The New Anti-Semitism.

The resurgence of Jew-hatred in Britain should be a cause of concern for everybody. Instead, it has become the prejudice that dare not speak its name.

Last year, there were 375 anti-Jewish attacks in Britain-the second highest total since the figures were first collected and a 7 per cent increase on 2002. Jews are being attacked in the street; synagogues and cemeteries desecrated; schoolchildren bullied because they are Jews.

Of course, this is nowhere near as bad as it is in parts of Europe. However, what should concern us is that according to a new survey, while anti-Jewish attitudes are now going down again in almost every country, in Britain they have risen steeply during the past two years. This is surely because Europe is now alarmed enough to acknowledge the problem has arisen and try, however inadequately, to address it. Here, however, the very phenomenon is still denied.

Israel, of course, is the complicating factor in all this. When people think of anti-Semitism, they think of the Nazis. They believe they themselves think well of the Jews, as Jews. And they certainly don't take kindly to being told they are anti-Semites when as far as they're concerned, all they're doing is criticizing Israel. People like me, they say, are waving the shroud of the Holocaust to conceal the crimes of Israel's Prime Minister Ariel Sharon. And a number of Jews say the same thing, too.

But neither I nor anyone else says Israel shouldn't be criticized, even strongly. What I'm talking about goes far beyond legitimate criticism and turns instead into irrational and malevolent hatred. What we're seeing now is a new mutation of the virus of Jew-hatred. Whereas previously the aim was to eradicate the Jews, now it is to eradicate the Jewish state. Instead of Jews being demonized, the Jewish state is demonized. Israel, the one democracy in the Middle East, is now viewed with a loathing that is never applied to Arab dictatorships. Anti-Israelism and, in particular, anti-Sharonism are being used as a fig-leaf for hatred of the Jews. And this twisting of the narrative of Jewish victimhood into one of Israeli oppression has legitimized an eruption of explicit prejudice against Jews, which has resulted in a grotesque tacit alliance between progressives, the far-right and the Islamic jihad.

Presentation of Israel in public discourse is pathologically unbalanced, and morphs seamlessly into classic anti-Jewish stereotypes. I am talking here about a wholesale moral inversion, in which the very worst is automatically believed of people who normally tell the truth, while claims made by those who have told demonstrable lies are reported as proven fact; in which victims are treated as victimizers, and vice versa; in which respectable British people say openly that they sympathize with the mass murder of Jews by Palestinians because they are *'fighting for their freedom'*; and in which Israel is being systematically delegitimized and dehumanized.

Media coverage of Israel has become an unstoppable torrent of lies, distortions, libels, abandonment of objectivity for malice and hatred, and obsessional vilification and demonization. It ignores or downplays the fact that Israel conducts military operations only in self-defense. Israel's history is routinely denied or ignored, so its attempts to protect life are falsely represented as acts of murder. Doubtless, as with all military occupations it is committing some human rights abuses which should be condemned. But *all* its military actions are seen as human rights abuses, even where -- as in the notorious massacre-that-never-was in Jenin -- it suffered a relatively severe death toll because its tactics aimed to minimize the loss of innocent life. Intrinsic to this misrepresentation is the prejudice that the Jews do revenge and punishment. The result is that it seems the Jews alone are obliged not to defend themselves but to submit passively to mass murder.

Double standards are routinely applied. The killing of Sheikh Yassin was hysterically condemned - and described by the BBC as murder - while Britain actively seeks to kill Osama bin Laden and his lieutenants. Israel is damned for its behavior while silence is maintained over countries doing far worse. These double standards shape the language used. So Israel has *'death squads', 'killing fields'* and *'executioners'*, while Palestinian human bombs are routinely sanitized as *'gentle', 'religious'* and *'kind'*. Ariel Sharon has been turned into a war criminal on account of the massacre in Sabra and Shatila in 1982 by people who simply airbrush the actual killers, the Christian Phalangists, out of the reckoning altogether - along with another, larger massacre in Lebanon's camps a couple of years later, but in which Israel played no part and which is therefore not even discussed.

Impossible expectations are made of Israel that are not made of any other country. It is the target of systematic and egregious lies and smears. It is presented in the worst possible light by people eager to believe that all its actions are malign even where the facts clearly refute such assumptions. The attacks it fends off or suffers, which occur dozens of times a week, are downplayed or not reported at all. Instead, Palestinian attacks are presented as responses to Israel aggression even though, since the start of this conflict 100 years ago, it has always been the other way round.

Israel is presented as crushing the Palestinians under a jackboot, and the settlements are obsessively dwelt upon as the obstacle to peace. I don't approve of the settlements; and I also deplore the inevitable brutalization that has afflicted Israel and which marks any occupation. But the presentation of the issue ignores the fact that more than 95% of the disputed land was offered to the Palestinians in 2000 to form a state of their own, provoking only the response of the current war of mass civilian murder. It ignores the fact that the only reason for the harsh measures Israel takes is because the Palestinians are murdering its citizens. It ignores the fact that before this current war started, economic growth was fastest among the Palestinians in the territories, and their rate of infant mortality the lowest, of any Arab country.

Yet Israel is being singled out as a leper state, an enemy of humanity. It is blamed for the demise of the road map, ignoring the fact that the reason this collapsed was that the Palestinians refused to carry out the map's first requirement, to dismantle the infrastructure of terror, and indeed used the PA's own militias and even policemen to carry out that terror.

Instead, Israel is blamed as the cause of the global jihad, on the basis that if only it allowed a state of Palestine the jihadists would pack up. This ignores the fact that a state of Palestine has now been offered more than once, each time provoking the response of violence; it ignores the repeated statements by the Palestinians that their aim is to annihilate Israel; it ignores the stated aim of the jihadists that their aim is to Islamize the world; and it ignores the carnage occurring across the world among Christians, Buddhists, Muslims, Jews and others in pursuit of that agenda.

Instead, Israel is demonized as a Nazi or apartheid state and thus the source of the poison. Such comparisons are a monstrous libel. Israel's Arabs have full civil rights including membership of the Knesset and Supreme Court. The equivalent in Britain of the murders of Israelis over the past three years would amount to around 10,000 souls. If this had happened here, carried out by people backed by states pledged to eradicate Britain, we would be at war. To characterize Israel's attempts to defend itself in these circumstances as Nazism is obscene. It also legitimizes violence against Jews and prepares the intellectual ground for the destruction of Israel. People are now saying openly it was a mistake for Israel to have been created. Why is the Jewish state the only country in the world that people in Britain are now singling out for destruction and the ethnic cleansing of its population?

The main reason, I suggest, is widespread and profound ignorance. People in Britain tend not to know very much about *'abroad'*; and the media repeatedly fail to provide balanced facts and context. If people knew the facts about what is happening now and about Middle East history, their perspective would be rather different. Their ignorance has created a vacuum in which has flourished a propaganda narrative based on lies, which in turn has enabled shallowly buried prejudice to reassert itself.

This propaganda has been promulgated by the political left, which has appropriated the narrative of Palestinian oppression and malign Jewish power. It has done so because it believes the west is always the oppressor while the third world is always the oppressed. So even if the third world is perpetrating acts of murder against the west, it must have good cause because it is always *'the victim'* of the west. The left has also embraced post-modernism, which has produced a wholesale denial of objectivity and truth which allows in propaganda based on lies. It taps directly into the long and inglorious tradition of communist Jew-hatred. And finally, it needs a new cause to embrace after the fall of communism; with economics now out of the frame, it has turned its attack instead on race, culture and national identity - and Israel rings up all three on the fruit machine.

In appropriating the Palestinian narrative, the left has also implicitly condoned the explicit Jew-hatred on which it is based. That is why it is silent about the torrent of medieval anti-Semitism pouring out of the Arab media, which appropriates symbols and motifs from classic European anti-Semitism and from Nazi propaganda. Thus, Jews are represented as devils that drink the blood of gentile children and want to take over the world, and the early twentieth century forgery *'The Protocols of the Elders of Zion'* is serialized on Egyptian television.

And this demonization of the Jews in the cause of Palestinian suffering has also revived Jew-hatred in the church. Certainly, there are many Christians who are hostile neither to Israel nor the Jews. Indeed, some of the strongest supporters of Israel are evangelical Christian Zionists. And the Catholic Church has made strenuous efforts in recent years to remove the stain of anti-Jewish feeling from its doctrines.

Nevertheless, within the Protestant churches there is a serious problem. Church leaders, periodicals and aid agencies are viscerally hostile to Israel - and there is a doctrinal factor involved which goes beyond fashionable attitudes. Canon Andrew White, the Archbishop of

Canterbury's envoy in the Middle East, told me that Palestinian politics and Christian theology have become inextricably intertwined. A radical Palestinian theological revisionism, which was trying to de-legitimize the Jewish state through a reworking of Scripture, had revived a largely discredited replacement theology - the ancient doctrine that the Jews had forfeited God's love and with it all His promises to them, including the Land of Israel - through widespread contact between Palestinians and British Christians involved in humanitarian work in the disputed territories. This, he said, was having a huge impact. Christian pilgrimages only visited Christian sites in Palestinian areas, only spoke to Palestinians and spoke to virtually no Jewish Israelis.

The leader of one such pilgrimage talked to me of Zionists committing genocide against the Palestinians. The websites of Christian aid agencies represent Israel as a malevolent occupying power, with no reference to the fact that some of the refugee camps in which they work are factories for human bombs. I spoke to a bishop whose ideal was not a two-state solution but the destruction of the Jewish state -- and who implied that Israel would merit sympathy for its casualties only if it were powerless to defend itself. I spoke to a vicar who said Israel was fundamentally an apartheid state, that he hoped it would be *'brought to an end'* by the uprising of the people, that God's promises to the Jews had been inherited by Christianity and that the covenant between God and the Jews was conditional on their support for human rights.

The Palestinian canon Naim Ateek is revered in church circles in Britain. Yet his book, *'Justice and Only Justice'*, inverts history, defames the Jews and sanitizes Arab violence. Modern anti-Semitism gets precisely one paragraph; Zionism is portrayed not as the despairing response to the ineradicable anti-Semitism of the world, but as an aggressive colonial adventure. Courageous Jews are those who confess to *'moral suicide'* and who say that Judaism should survive without a state; real anti-Semitism says Ateek, is found within the Jewish community in its treatment of the Palestinians. He uses the Bible to de-legitimize the Jewish state by misrepresenting the Jews' relationship with God. Through tendentious history and the hijacking of scripture, Ateek vilifies the Jews as oppressors and war-makers and tells them, in effect, that their salvation lies in abandoning their state and scattering to the four winds.

He is not alone. The hugely influential Colin Chapman's book, *'Whose Promised Land?'* also uses theology to de-legitimize Israel. Although Chapman carefully condemns anti-Semitism and says the Christians have not superseded the Jews, he says nevertheless that the Jews' only salvation is through Christ. Christians now share the Jews' privileges; through Christ, the division between Jews and Christians broke down and they have therefore become as one *'new'* man. And this *'new man'* therefore doesn't warrant a Jewish state. Chapman de-legitimizes Israel quite explicitly on theological grounds in his conclusion: '*The coming of the kingdom of God through Jesus the messiah has transformed and reinterpreted all the promises and prophecies in the Old Testament.*' His conclusions that violence was always implicit in Zionism and that Jewish self-determination is somehow racist are grotesque slurs.

Church leaders vehemently deny they are prejudiced against Israel or that their attitudes are infused by a revival of replacement theology. But other Christians tell a different story. I have been told of sermons riddled with anti-Jewish feeling lightly masked as anti-Zionism. One church source said that what he was hearing from the person in the pew was *"a throwback to the visceral anti-Judaism of the middle ages."*

Someone wrote to me last week to say this: "*I am a Christian who has recently left an Anglican Church because of replacement theology. I find it both amazing and frightening that so many evangelical Christians are embracing these doctrines. It has shocked me to learn that so many Church leaders believe that the way to solve the crisis in Israel is to hand over land to a regime that will not rest until every Jew is in their grave.*"

Incredibly, this Melanie Phillips article was written back in 2004. Her message returned with force in 2014/5. - Barry Shaw.

Melanie Phillips is a journalist and public commentator. She is the publisher, editor-in-chief, and co-founder of emBooks. She is the author of many books including 'The World Turned Upside Down.'

RECOMMENDED READING.

The World Turned Upside Down   Melanie Phillips.

Reclaim the Zionist Dream   Chloe Valdary.

UnChosen   Julie Birchall

The War of a Million Cuts   Manfred Gerstenfeld.

The Aleppo Codex   Matti Friedman.

Israel Reclaiming the Narrative......Barry Shaw.

ACKNOWLEGEMENTS.

It is impossible to write a book like this without years of research.

Dipping into the wealth of knowledge and words inevitably leads a writer to mine the writing and minds of others. This has been the case in bringing this book to fruition.

The start of my day begins with breakfast and a daily read of the Jerusalem Post. My eye frequently spots a news item or comment that awakens the muse in me. It often alerted me to items worthy of research that helped my concentration in authoring this book.

Some people distain the social media. I feel that's unjust. I find The Times of Israel informative and it offered valuable material to the thrust of my thesis. These print and social media newspapers do brilliant work in offering their readers a wide spectrum of life, both Israeli and Jewish, as well as accurately portraying world events, often with unique information.

On the topic of anti-Semitism, I am impressed by the research done by Manfred Gerstenfeld and Robert Wistrich, and I have featured a small contribution from Manfred in this book.

I have the deepest respect for Professor Irwin Cotler. As well as being an international renowned jurist and champion for human rights and a campaigner against anti-Semitism, he is the most charming person.

Martin Sherman and I share precious time discussing aspects of the predicament that Israel finds itself, both internally and externally. We do not agree with each other of some issues, but we share a friendship and respect for each other. I have included some of Martin's writing in the book.

Melanie Phillips has been an outspoken fighter for justice and decency for Israel. She has courageously entered chambers where only the brave dare tread. Her articles and more recently her radio program on Voices for Israel are always full of clarity and truth, even if that truth is painful for some to hear.

Michael Dickson is an amazing advocate for Israel. As Israeli Director of StandWithUs he does outstanding work in educating young people about Israel and correcting the misinformation that often surrounds the Middle East conflict and Israel. Apart from that, he is an all-around nice guy.

Chloe Valdary is a rare and valued person. She is a Christian, black, outstanding advocate of pro-Israel activism on campus. Her voice and words merit audiences everywhere. She views the attacks on Israel from a unique perspective and challenges them with a profound intelligence that defeats Israel's detractors.

Julie Birchill comes from the world of British pop-culture to declare her undying love of the Jew. She loves their brains more than their bodies. *"Jews are smarter than the rest of the world, so suck it up gentile losers!"* I included her words because of her rare quirky perspective.

I have yet to meet Matti Friedman, an outstanding journalist who has stepped back from the mire of convenient reporting to appease an editor or to comply with convenient perceptions to courageously expose why the media is so biased against Israel. I look forward to brainstorming with him over a lunch or drinks.

Daniel Mael is an eloquent advocate for Israel in the snake pit of American campus life. It takes no small amount of gumption to confront the blatant Israel haters.

David Weinberg writes a perceptive column in the Jerusalem Post. He is the Director of Public Affairs at Bar-Ilan University's Begin-Sadat Center for Strategic Studies and also a sharp critic of Israel's detractors and of post-Zionist trends.

Anti-Semitism shows itself in multiple forms. I have attempted to concentrate on the cross fertilization of this virus in the discourse of the pro-Palestinian, anti-Israel, camp. I acknowledge that I have only given a random selection of locations and incidents where this Israel-hating Jew-hatred has expressed itself. The range is so global as to make it impossible to encompass the vastness of this disease into one readable book.

The final preparation of this book would not be possible without Spotlighting. I thank them for their creativity in designing the book cover. I wanted something stark and dramatic to highlight the subject matter. I think they succeeded.

Thanks also to Jack Cohen. I am hopeless when it comes to how to find and operate computer widgets, or whatever you call them, that I needed in editing this book. Jack helped guide me through the intricate wonders of the computer.

And thank you for picking up this book. I hope that you found it readable and informative.

314

Printed in Great
Britain
by Amazon